# Sovereignty in Exile

THE ETHNOGRAPHY OF POLITICAL VIOLENCE

Tobias Kelly, Series Editor

A complete list of books in the series
is available from the publisher.

# Sovereignty in Exile

## A Saharan Liberation Movement Governs

Alice Wilson

PENN

UNIVERSITY OF PENNSYLVANIA PRESS

PHILADELPHIA

Published by
University of Pennsylvania Press
Philadelphia, Pennsylvania 19104-4112
www.upenn.edu/pennpress

Printed in the United States of America
on acid-free paper

1 3 5 7 9 10 8 6 4 2

*Library of Congress Cataloging-in-Publication Data*
ISBN 978-0-8122-4849-4

*For my parents*

## CONTENTS

If you shrink from the labors of sovereignty,
do not claim any of its honors.

—Pericles

# Sovereignty in Exile

# Introduction: The Social Relations of Sovereignty

The heat of the day softened, and we began to stir from our midday slumbers. Thirsty for air, we emerged from the tent to resume the morning's abandoned labors. It was nearly the end of my month-long sojourn with a family of camel herders in the pasturelands that my hosts called, in the accent of the Hassaniya dialect of Arabic, the *badīah*.[1] Having traveled a few weeks previously from the refugee camps where my hosts usually resided, now that I was in the pasturelands, I understood those refugees who longed from the refugee camps for the calm of herding. Any sense of tranquility in the pasturelands was interwoven, though, with the thrill of being out of the harsh Algerian *ḥamādah* desert, where the refugee camps were located, and in Western Sahara itself, the territory on which the refugee community looked as its homeland.[2] Yet as I looked out onto unbroken steppeland as far as the eye could see, I could also understand those refugees who, finding themselves in the *badīah*, itched for the bustle of the refugee camps. In the pasturelands, one could only hope for the company of visitors if one heard the distant hum of a car. The first person to detect it would call out, "I can hear a car!" The growing rumbling would spread hope and excitement that it would deliver a guest.

But this late afternoon we were taken by surprise. Almost silently, a lone man and his camel came upon us. As my host sister, Khanātha, and her aunt prepared with glee to welcome him, they proudly taught me a new word for such a traveler arriving by camel, *bijāwī*.

When the visitor reached us, elaborate greetings broke out from all parties. As Khanātha prepared a drink of sweetened milk for our visitor, I observed the rider's face. It bore the marks of long years in the desert. He was of the generation known and praised in the refugee camps for having fought for Western Sahara's liberation movement against neighboring Morocco, which had partially annexed Western Sahara in 1975.

For his part, once he was settled in, our *bijāwī* set about feeding his beast of burden some dried lentils. Khanātha's cousin remarked to me, not without tenderness, that the camel was worn out. I followed her eyes across the scrawny hump and back to the camel's neck. As I expected, the camel was branded. I had seen colonial-era lists of each tribe's camel brand and could recognize a few. This brand left no doubt: it traced FP, for Frente Polisario, Western Sahara's national liberation movement. Based in the refugee camps in nearby Algeria, the Polisario Front (henceforth Polisario) had sought both to set up a state for Western Sahara and, while doing so, to ban tribes. As its camel brand symbolized, Polisario had literally taken the place of tribes. In a context where refugees constantly saw bags and boxes of rations branded with the name of the state that had sponsored them, Polisario's stamp on its camel also echoed the claim of a state power that could produce, own, and distribute its own resources. Afterward, I pondered that this camel, not only in its brand but also in its state of exhaustion and resilience, might be read as a potent symbol for the liberation movement itself.

This book explores sovereignty and state power through the case of a liberation movement that set out to make itself into a state. This state has a name: the Sahrawi Arab Democratic Republic (SADR). SADR was founded by Polisario in the wake of Spain, the former colonial power, finally abandoning the territory over which Polisario and Morocco have since been locked in a conflict that has come to be synonymous with stalemate. SADR (a partially recognized state) and Polisario (a liberation movement rather than a political party) are closely related, although the relationship between them is not straightforward and is the subject of debate among Sahrawis who may take different views as to which should be granted more importance (Es-Sweyih 2001: 86–87). But together Polisario and SADR form an unusual governing authority. Because their sometimes indistinguishable fusion is both similar to and different from conventional notions of "state" and "party-state," I shall refer to this governing authority by the term "state-movement"—unless either Polisario or SADR, as a distinct entity, is at stake. As the camel brand powerfully symbolizes, in seeking to generate state power, the state-movement envisaged that it had to take the place of a previous and alternative governing authority, tribes. Indeed, following the trend in various postcolonial states and liberation movements in Africa and the Middle East of seeing tribes as undesirable—to the extent that they were judged divisive of national identity, imbued with hierarchies that threatened egalitarian aspirations, and liable to manipulation by colonial authorities—the state-movement initially conceived of itself as banning tribes altogether.[3]

Nevertheless, this book examines how the relationship between the unmaking of tribes and the making of state power took a more complex form, which I explore through the metaphor of a palimpsest. Initially, there were *aspirations* on the part of the state-movement to ban tribes (Part I). These aspirations can be understood as creating a palimpsest, premised in the first instance on a process of "writing over" the social relations of tribes so as to obscure them from view. Over time, however, *compromises* arose whereby the social relations of tribes were taken up by the state-movement as fertile resources for making state power (Part II). That is to say, the social relations of tribes came to reappear in the palimpsest in invited or tolerated ways. Yet there were also *dilemmas* where tribes reemerged in ways that both officers of the state-movement and lay refugees found disconcerting (Part III). These can be understood as unruly or uninvited reappearances of the social relations of tribes in the palimpsest. These aspirations, compromises, and dilemmas have shaped political and economic life for Sahrawi refugees. Given the inextricability of political and economic relations, this book's examination of the remaking of sovereignty among Sahrawi refugees brings an ethnographic lens to a range of fields spanning the political and the economic: the creation of administrative categories, legal reforms, aid distribution, marriage practices, local markets, and contested elections.

What makes this palimpsest especially compelling is the fact that it plays out in extraordinary circumstances—those of a liberation movement seeking to build revolutionary state power in exile. As such, the Sahrawi refugee case opens up wider questions about the nature of state power and sovereignty, the constraints and possibilities of exile, and the vicissitudes of revolution. In order both to frame the ethnographic analysis that will follow and to foreground some of the broader debates to which the case of Western Sahara speaks, this Introduction outlines the book's approach to sovereignty, state power, and exile. In the Conclusion, looking back on the intervening ethnographic chapters, I reflect on revolution as the forging of a moral contract.

## The Social Relations of Sovereignty

Many Sahrawis, in the refugee camps and beyond, might find it odd to pursue an inquiry into sovereignty through the case of the state-movement. Refugees often expressed convictions— also relayed in political slogans, for example, "A full struggle to impose sovereignty and independence"—that sovereignty (*al-siyādah*) was denied to Sahrawis, curtailed by Morocco's partial annexation of Western Sahara. At best, the desired sovereignty would only be within reach in those parts of Western Sahara under Polisario's control (see Figure 1).

While Sahrawis seemingly had a clear notion of what the sovereignty that they desired might entail, for scholars, sovereignty is an increasingly contested concept. Perhaps the most persistent perception of sovereignty (which would be shared by many Sahrawis) is that of a supreme form of governing authority concentrated in the hands of a state that rules over a defined territory. This notion is heavily indebted to the ideas of Max Weber (1965). Nevertheless, such a conceptualization has come to be seen as a "fiction" (Brown

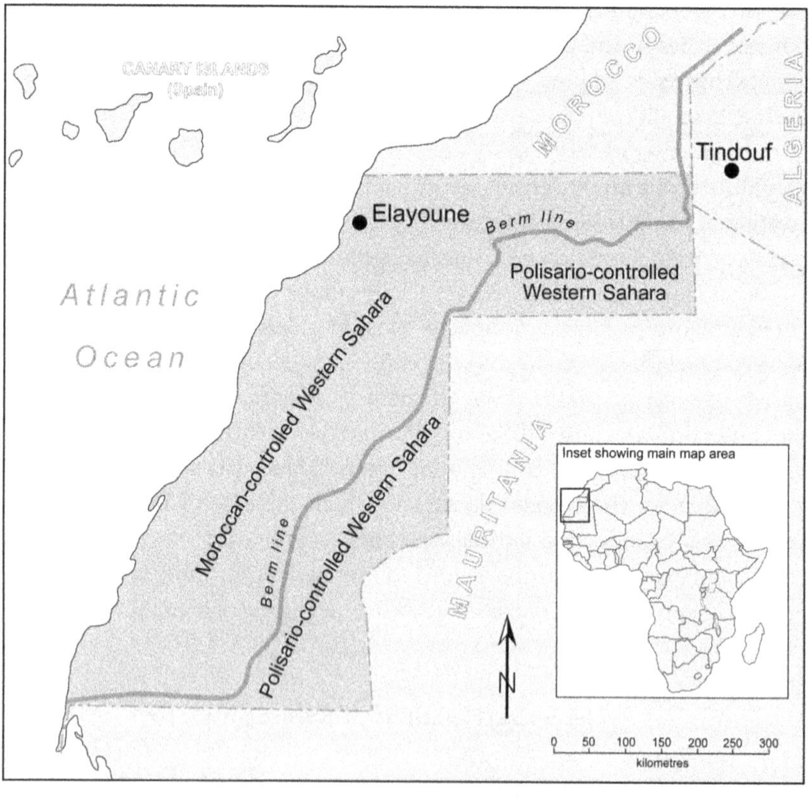


Figure 1. Western Sahara.

2010). It has been pointed out that, in practice, the claims of state power to enjoy inviolable sovereignty over domestic affairs and in relations with other states are routinely violated (Krasner 1999). The meaning of sovereignty has been shown to have developed and changed across time and space (e.g., Hansen and Stepputat 2005; Ong 2006; Benton 2009; Chalfin 2010; Kalmo and Skinner 2010b). This casts doubt on whether one meaning for sovereignty can be helpfully applied to different times and places (Kalmo and Skinner 2010a).

Given such varieties of sovereignty, it may be futile to seek "a single agreed-upon concept of sovereignty for which one could offer a clear definition" (Kalmo and Skinner 2010a: 5). It may, however, still be helpful to propose an analytical framework through which to approach—but not necessarily to define—sovereignty. This book explores sovereignty through a framework of social relations.

Anthropologists are already familiar with exploring state power as a set of social relations (see e.g., Verdery 2003; Chalfin 2010; Navaro-Yashin 2012). In a strikingly explicit approach to state power as social relations, David Sneath (2007) adapts the work of Neera Chandhoke to explore a "state relation" of social relations between governing authorities and governed persons. He uses this framework to analyze premodern, aristocrat-ruled polities in the steppelands of Inner Asia as non-territorially-based forms of a state relation (rather than examples of "kinship society" as is claimed in some academic and popular discourses). For Sneath (10), such a notion of a "state relation" between governing authorities and governed constituencies has the advantage of further calling into question the alleged importance of territoriality for state power and sovereignty.

It is not merely state power that can helpfully be reassessed from a social relations perspective, though. As Brenda Chalfin (2010: 42) points out, in many of the studies where state power is approached as a set of social relations, it is more broadly sovereignty that can be understood as a social relation. My suggestion here is that sovereignty be approached in terms of social relations, with these social relations converging on particular "projects of sovereignty." State power would be one such project of sovereignty.

To approach sovereignty as social relations opens up several fruitful analytical possibilities. First, it is suggestive of how the social relations of state power may be one kind of project of sovereignty—but that the social relations of sovereignty might take other non-state-centered ethnographic forms. In the Sahrawi case, I argue that, historically, tribes at particular historical moments have also been projects of sovereignty. Second, sensitivity to the social relations of projects of sovereignty facilitates the ethnographic tracing of how the social relations of one project of sovereignty may be reconfigured in the making of another project of sovereignty. As concerns the state-movement, I trace how the social relations of one project of sovereignty (tribes) are at times recycled in the making of the social relations of another project of sovereignty (state power): for instance, in the ways the state-movement claims and distributes resources, settles disputes, presents itself as democratic, and manages social inequalities. Third, a social relations approach to sovereignty, especially in a case of displacement such as for Sahrawi refugees, invites us to rethink the place of territory for sovereignty.

As we saw, territory has been taken to be fundamental in classic, if now questioned, definitions of the (presumed) sovereignty of state power.[4] Yet, from an anthropological perspective, territory is problematic as a general criterion for state power or sovereignty. For instance, sovereignty over people has, in particular historical contexts, been considered more relevant than, or as relevant as, sovereignty over territory (e.g., Lovejoy 1983; Hansen and Stepputat 2005; Sneath 2007; Comaroff and Comaroff 2009).

Territory (that of Western Sahara) is of course vital to sovereignty in the form to which the state-movement aspires. In practice, the state-movement has access to about a quarter of this territory already, the Polisario-controlled parts of Western Sahara (see Figure 1).[5] But, in terms of the everyday social relations of the state-movement, the desired territory is distant and mostly (or entirely) inaccessible. The refugees' lives, homes, everyday encounters with each other and with their principal political institutions focus on the refugee camps, as the following chapters describe. The refugees' displacement from their claimed territory, and the resources to be found there, might thus seem to reiterate a case for foregrounding not sovereignty over territory but sovereignty over people—here as played out in the relationship between the state-movement and the refugees whom it governs.

The ensuing ethnography indeed highlights how the distancing of territory in the case of the state-movement does not mean an absence of the social relations of sovereignty. Yet, if territory is distant or inaccessible here, one of the means through which the social relations of the state-movement as a project of sovereignty are constituted is through the manipulation of other, mobile resources. These include refugees' labor, which the state-movement seeks to claim, and rations, which the state-movement distributes to refugees (Chapter 4).

The importance of the circulation of resources between people in constituting the social relations of the state-movement invites us to consider how sovereignty over people and resources (whether in territorial or other forms) may be *related*. In her interpretation of sovereignty as a process of "make-believe," combining acts of both imagining and making, brought to the fore in the case of the legally ambiguous Turkish Republic of Northern Cyprus, Yael Navaro-Yashin (2012: 43) has explored sovereignty as "an enactment of agency (back and forth) between people and things in and on a given territory." In the circumstances of Sahrawi refugees' displacement, where exile prevents daily engagements in and on the territory that remains very much desired, it is helpful to reconsider the relationship between sovereignty, people, territory, and things in the light of anthropological approaches to property. From an anthropological perspective, property is understood as a social relation between persons with regard to things (rather than as a relation between persons and things).[6] When sovereignty is approached in terms of social relations, it can be conceptualized along analogous lines: sovereignty would represent social relations between persons—governing authorities and governed persons—in relation to "things," that is, resources not necessarily in territorial form. In other words, territory would be a common, but not essential, form of resources in reference to which the social relations of sovereignty play out.

The approach taken in this book, prompted by the ethnographic context of Sahrawi refugees, is thus to conceptualize sovereignty as social relations between governing authorities and governed constituencies played out in relation to resources, not necessarily in territorial form. A social relations approach to sovereignty allows us to make such connections between extraordinary and ordinary projects of sovereignty.

## Decentering State Power from Projects of Sovereignty

A social relations approach to sovereignty envisages state power as one particular project of sovereignty and is open to the ways the social relations of one project of sovereignty may be recycled in the making of another. This approach lends itself to questioning whether apparent characteristics of sovereignty that have sometimes been assumed to be exclusive to state power may pertain to a broader range of "projects of sovereignty," not limited in form to state power. These questions are put to an ethnographic test in the case of the state-movement, where I suggest that the social relations of tribes are at times recycled to make the social relations of state power.

There have been ample calls to undermine the apparently exclusive claims of state power to sovereignty—not least in the exposition of the "fiction" (Brown 2010) and "hypocrisy" (Krasner 1999) of the ideal of sovereignty. On a practical level, when sovereignty is interpreted as the power to decide over the right to life, anthropological studies have suggested that, while state power clings to this power, it cannot claim it exclusively but operates alongside other nonstate actors such as vigilantes, gangs, and nonstate governing authorities (Hansen and Stepputat 2005). The disparate entities that exert a claim over the right to life have been seen as matrices of "overlapping sovereignties" (e.g., Comaroff and Comaroff 2009).

In the Middle East and North Africa (MENA), another means of calling into question the relationship between state power and sovereignty has been the reconceptualization of tribes—a contested term (see Chapter 1)—as "domains of sovereignty" (Weir 2007). The influence of such arguments on the analysis here is clear. If such arguments have been made especially for cases when tribes administer laws to the people associated with a given territory, they are nevertheless part of a critical reassessment of the relationship between state power and the alleged "nonstate" (see Chapter 1).

The notion that sovereignty should take the form of a state power that enjoys supreme authority over a fixed territory has been criticized, then. Yet this notion has survived intact as a particular *form* of sovereignty, the exclusive claims (in theory) of state power to which are sometimes explicitly, sometimes implicitly, left unchallenged. Only to a limited extent have mafia gangs or tribes been deemed alternative sovereign powers or domains of sovereignty. Mafia gangs may decide in de facto terms on the right to life. Tribes may enforce their own rules for their own members in their own territories. But in both cases such "alternative" sovereign powers have been assumed not to enjoy other forms of sovereign power, claims to the enjoyment of which have been left to state power. Thus, the Weberian understanding that the sovereignty of state power entails a monopoly on legitimate coercion within a defined territory (Weber 1965) is assumed to be an exclusive claim made by and of state power (whether realized in practice or not). Such a claim is assumed not to be applicable to, say, mafia gangs or tribes. Likewise, the Schmittian notion that sovereignty can be defined as a monopoly on deciding on the state of exception (Schmitt 1985) is readily assumed to be a claim made specifically of and by state power (see Chapter 3).

*Sovereignty in Exile* challenges these assumptions, and in so doing further decenters state power from discussions of sovereignty. I look specifically at how two monopolies associated with state power may not, on closer examination, be exclusive to it but may also pertain to projects of sovereignty in other forms. As regards a claimed monopoly over legitimate coercion, I examine the state-movement's recourse to such a monopoly in order to legitimate the appropriation of resources (in the form of refugees' labor) (Chapter 4). As regards a claimed monopoly on the state of exception, I assess how the state-movement asserted the right to decide when laws hold and when they did not; I observe this through its banning of tribal laws and its introduction of its own state laws (Chapter 3). In both areas, I nevertheless show ethnographically how the state-movement recycled the social relations of tribes (*qabā'il*, s. *qabīlah*). I argue that, if the state-movement drew on the social relations of tribes in making the social relations of state power in these areas, this is because, at specific previous historical moments, tribes in Western Sahara had been engaged in analogous activities. Politically dominant tribes appropriated resources (tribute) under the threat of legitimate coercion (raiding). These tribes also decided when laws held by introducing their own tribal laws (*a'rāf*), which overrode Islamic punishments for crimes. The state-movement could recycle the social relations of tribes in these areas as it sought to establish itself as a state power with a monopoly over legitimate coercion for the appropriation of resources and a monopoly over the state of exception. I thus suggest how claims associated with the sovereignty of state power may not be exclusive to sovereignty in that form. Rather, they may also pertain to other "projects of sovereignty," such as tribes at specific historical moments in the territory now known as Western Sahara.

My argument builds on ongoing scholarly debate (see Chapter 1) about how tribes in specific historical circumstances in MENA may share compatibilities with state power. I make two contributions to this debate. First, I suggest ways that, in specific historical contexts, tribes may also have enjoyed forms of sovereignty that have often been presumed to be exclusive to state power, such as an exclusive claim to legitimate coercion deployed for the appropriation of resources and an exclusive claim to deciding on the state of exception. Second, I show ethnographically the specific ways in which one project of sovereignty—here, tribes—can be remade into another—such as state power.

## Governance-in-Exile

A third framework taken up in this book concerns the role of exile. In one sense, exile is a backdrop for transformations experienced by Sahrawis that could, in theory, have taken place outside exile. In another sense, however, exile serves as an incubator for transformations that perhaps, outside exile, might have struggled to take off.

Anthropological studies of refugeehood have stressed the intensifying qualities of exile, especially when exiles live in refugee camps. Whether confronting depoliticization and disempowerment (e.g., Harrell-Bond 1986), or hyper-politicization as nationalists or a political opposition (e.g., Malkki 1995a; Frésia 2009), refugees' experiences can be profoundly intensified as a result of being in exile in camps. In the case of the state-movement, its agendas for political and economic reform were indeed intensified by the fact that they took place in exile. Dispossession through displacement in a desert proved—ironically—a highly fertile environment for pursuing social egalitarianism and ruptures with a tribal past. Refugees' (initial) dependence on the state-movement for the provision of their material wants allowed the state-movement, at least at first, to erase certain erstwhile distinctions between tribes by providing the same goods for all refugees, such as the same marriage prestations for all (Chapter 5). The need in exile to call on everyone for labor to build and staff institutions from scratch could become a vehicle for breaking up or disguising clusters of those related through tribes (Chapter 2).

Yet the case of the state-movement—like other long-term governing authorities in exile, such as Tibetans in India (e.g., McConnell 2016) and Palestinians in Lebanon in the 1970s (e.g., Peteet 2005)—does not only illustrate the potency of exile as a prism of intensification for social change. The state-movement and other similar cases also point to how we need a more expanded concept than that of government-in-exile. The latter narrowly implies an elite government, displaced from territory and population (McConnell 2009). For the state-movement and cases such as Palestinians and Tibetans, though, it is crucial that *both* a civilian population *and* their governing authority are displaced. These circumstances provide an opportunity to practice state power in a very literal form: what Jacob Mundy (2007) has called "performing" nationhood and "pre-figuring" the state and what Fiona McConnell (2016) calls "rehearsing" the state. This book advocates an expanded notion of not just a government-in-exile but "governance-in-exile," or the practice of state power by a displaced government on a displaced population under its control.

"Governance-in-exile" as a broader notion than that of government-in-exile underscores, as Michel Agier (2011) and others have stressed, some of the limitations of thinking of refugees in terms of "bare life." According to Giorgio Agamben (1998), "bare life" is life that can be killed with impunity. Such bare life is routinely produced, Agamben suggests, in spaces of exception, such as camps—concentration camps, detention camps, camps for holding asylum seekers or unwanted migrants, and refugee camps. In a sense, Sahrawis—both refugees and indeed Sahrawis living under Moroccan annexation—can be approached in terms of "bare life." Since the 1960s, Sahrawis have been declared (by the UN, and later by the International Court of Justice) to have a right to self-determination. Yet they have not been allowed to take this right up. While allowed to remain alive, in exile or under annexation, Sahrawis can nevertheless be understood as bare life in the sense that their rights have been shown to be repeatedly violable, with impunity.

It is nonetheless problematic to reduce Sahrawis, and others whose rights are routinely denied, to bare life. In practice, on the ground one finds more ambiguous situations than a stark division between citizens in the polis and those, such as refugees in camps, who are excluded from the polis as bare life. Sahrawi exiles are engaged in an innovated citizenship in the refugee camps, where they vote, take part in governance themselves, and hold officers to account (see Chapter 7). Sahrawi refugees, then, belong to a polis of some kind. By approaching the state-movement as not merely a government-in-exile but as an instance of governance-in-exile, I underscore how a context that could be seen as a site for the production of bare life can at the same time accommodate the practice of state power by a displaced government on a displaced population under its control.

## Situating an Exception

The aims of this book include engaging with ideas about sovereignty, state power, and exile, as I have discussed in this Introduction, and about revolution, as I take up in the Conclusion. The aims do not extend to making an argument about whether the state-movement is a "state." An interesting debate could undoubtedly be held on this question. A case could be made for how the state-movement fits the four qualities of sovereignty that, according to Krasner (1999), are claimed by, and regularly violated in, the practice of state sovereignty. For instance, it could be said that the state-movement enjoys some degree of "international legal sovereignty" as understood by Krasner (3). The SADR has recognition from other states and signs agreements in the international sphere in its capacity as a member of the African Union. The state-movement also has a degree of what Krasner calls "Westphalian sovereignty" (4) to the extent that it claims non-interference in the refugee camps. For instance, it holds off the UN High Commissioner for Refugees (UNHCR) from carrying out a survey in the camps (see Chapter 5) and asserts that Algerian police officers and military forces (and civilians) should not enter the camps without permission. It also operates a degree of "domestic sovereignty," (4) in setting and applying its own laws, as well as a degree of "interdependence sovereignty," (4) vetting its borders for people and things. From Krasner's argument that sovereignty, inherently and consistently violated, amounts to hypocrisy, it would follow that any practical shortcoming of the state-movement in living up to an ideal of sovereignty would not distinguish it from other forms of state power.

To ask how a certain notion of sovereign state power applies—or does not apply—in this instance carries a risk, however. Existing parameters for probing state power and sovereignty may be reinforced, rather than questioned. Instead, my purpose here is to study the state-movement to examine fresh perspectives, namely, the relations between different projects of sovereignty, and how the social relations of one project of sovereignty may be remade into those of another.

The aims of this book cannot be reduced to the study and explanation of an anomalous form of government. Undoubtedly, for those interested in the Western Sahara conflict, this ethnographic study—the first to draw on such extensive fieldwork—of the relationship between governed subjects and governing authorities in the Sahrawi refugee camps may be of interest for its own sake. Social scientific studies of Western Sahara have focused on themes such as the politics and international relations of the conflict (e.g., Zunes and Mundy 2010; Roussellier and Boukhars 2014), the development of Sahrawi nationalism (e.g., San Martín 2010), and the gendered politics of Sahrawi nationalist representations (Fiddian-Qasmiyah 2014). *Sovereignty in Exile* is distinctive in drawing on long-term ethnographic fieldwork so as to present an intimate portrait of governance, daily life in exile, and revolutionary change in the refugee camps. The book thus helps place Western Sahara on a figurative map of national liberation movements (e.g., Halliday 1974; Lan 1985; Sāyigh 1997; Takriti 2013), revolutions (e.g., Davis 1987; Dunham 1999; West and Raman 2009; Hegland 2013; Holbraad 2014), and anomalous forms of government representing territories of unresolved status (e.g., Feldman 2008, Navaro-Yashin 2012; McConnell 2016). Nevertheless, as Ilana Feldman (2008) and Yael Navaro-Yashin (2012) have shown in their studies of Gaza and Northern Cyprus, respectively, a study of an exceptional governing authority is not only relevant for understanding exceptions but is of greatest interest for shedding light on the "norm" (Schmitt 1985; Agamben 1998). Here, then, I study an exceptional case to illuminate state power and sovereignty in the ways suggested above.

In the remainder of this Introduction, I introduce the hassanophone context and then the Western Sahara conflict. Western Sahara is typically little known in nonspecialist circles; for readers unfamiliar with the conflict, I address its entrenchment and how this dispute has shaped the Sahrawi population. I then describe the research environment in the refugee camps and present an overview of the book.

## From Arabization to Colonization

The conflict over Western Sahara is a recent chapter in an ongoing history of an awkward relationship between state power and the northwest Sahara. The region is home to "the Moors," Bedouin who speak the Hassaniya dialect of Arabic. Over the thirteenth to sixteenth centuries CE, Arab tribes who had previously migrated from southern Arabia across North Africa moved into the northwest Sahara. There, they mixed with Berbers and black Africans. The Arabs brought their language (which in this region came to take the form of the Hassaniya dialect), kinship structures and, in some cases, patronyms (Norris 1986).

The hassanophone region—and, within it, present-day Western Sahara in its own right—can be understood as a "residual category" (Davis 1987), an area identifiable by the fact that it does not "fit" within surrounding regions. Prior to European colonialism, the steppelands inhabited by Hassanophones were beyond the reach of bordering imperial powers, such as the Moroccan sultanate, the empire of Mali, and the Songhay empire. The region was not internally homogeneous. For instance, from the late eighteenth century, the north of present-day Mauritania saw the development of emirates (see Bonte 2008). But arguably it is still helpful to think of the hassanophone zone as a region, where the inhabitants shared more with each other than they did with their non-Hassanophone neighbors (de Chassey 1984).

Notably, Hassanophones had no single name for themselves, equivalent to "the Moors." They conceptualized two principal kinds of internal division and stratification. On the one hand, Hassanophones belonged to tribes (*qabā'il*, s. *qabīlah*), political associations to which members could be born or recruited via pacts and whose members shared rights and responsibilities with regard to each other. Both tribe and *qabīlah* are controversial terms in anthropology (see Chapter 1). On the other hand, Hassanophones belonged to status groups ranging from military and religious elites to tributaries, artisans, slaves, and freed slaves (see Chapter 1).

There was no local nomenclature to encompass a collective entity or "people" comprising all members of different tribes and status groups. Nobles and tributaries together were *bīḍān* ("white"). Artisans, slaves, and freed slaves were technically excluded from the category *bīḍān*. A distinction was made, though, between hassanophone "blacks," *sūdān*, and blacks from outside the hassanophone region, *kwār* (Taine-Cheikh 1989). Some commentators adopt *bīḍān* as a general term for Hassanophones (e.g., Caratini 1989b; Gimeno 2007). Nevertheless, to do so is to reproduce implicitly the domination of the *bīḍān* status groups over status groups originally excluded from the term. I use "Hassanophone" here as a general term for speakers of the Hassaniya dialect who, today, are found in southern Morocco, disputed Western Sahara, Mauritania, southwest Algeria, and parts of Niger and Mali.

In the territory now known as Western Sahara, the northwestern coastal region, along with southern Morocco, enjoyed a climate that, while arid, was suitable for raising sheep and goats and for some agriculture. Farther south, as rainfall levels dropped, livelihoods focused more intensively on the raising of sheep, goats and camels, according to the suitability of pasturelands. Rainfall permitting, occasional agriculture was also practiced (Caro Baroja 1955). As in other economies of mobile pastoralism, animal husbandry was accompanied by related activities such as trading, raiding, and extorting or paying tribute. The hierarchical relations between status groups were reflected in raiding and tribute practices: military elites raided, and their clients, *znāgah*, paid tribute.

By the nineteenth century, three groups came to prominence in what would later become Western Sahara. Dominant in southern Morocco and the northwestern part of present-day Western Sahara were the Tekna, usually referred to as a confederation of tribes. Their trading networks spread to Senegal (Lydon 2009). In the northeastern part of what became Western Sahara, as well as the southeast and adjoining northern Mauritania, the Rgaybāt tribe grew in population (especially thanks to the co-optation of members through pacts and marriage strategies, as discussed in Chapter 5) and in territorial dominance (Caratini 1989a). In southwest Western Sahara and adjoining areas of Mauritania, the Awlād Delīm tribe and its allies were dominant (López Bargados 2003).

There being no central political authority in what would become Western Sahara, there was considerable rivalry between these tribes (or, in the case of the Tekna, between a confederation and neighboring tribes), especially between the Rgaybāt and the Awlād Delīm (see López Bargados 2003). In the wake of the scramble for Africa, when Spain claimed the territory inland from a former coastal colonial fort, a new rival, European colonialism, would make its mark on the territory. Over the course of several decades after the Berlin Conference in 1884, when Spain was awarded the territory, the borders of Spanish Sahara gradually formed (see San Martín 2010). The Spanish presence was initially limited to the coast, however, until Spain's "pacification" of the tribes in 1934. Even thereafter, though, resistance to colonialism continued. In 1958, Spanish and French forces combined forces in "Opération Ecouvillon" to stamp out an armed uprising in the territory (Hodges 1983: 78–79). In the aftermath, many families from Spanish Sahara fled, some of them settling in southern Morocco (see Gómez Martín 2011).

Spain would not begin seriously to exploit the resources of its colony until the 1950s, when it turned its attention especially to phosphate and fishing resources. By this time, the local population—still for the most part mobile pastoralists—may have numbered some 13,500 (Mercer 1976: 127). Nevertheless, it has been notoriously difficult to gather past and present population figures for Western Sahara. With colonialism, the local tribes began to be seen—and eventually to see themselves—as the population of a named territory. Already in 1953, Ángel Domenech Lafuente (1953) refers to the "saharaui" population of the territory. In the context of the current conflict over Western Sahara, "Sahrawi" remains a controversial term (see Zunes and Mundy 2010: 92–3, 110–11). It has a literal meaning in standard Arabic of "belonging to the desert." Pro-Moroccan discourse often contests that "Sahrawi" can describe a national identity. The Moroccan constitution of 2011 avoids the term and refers to the "saharo-hassanie" component of Moroccan identity. Most Hassanophones from tribes who have a historical presence in present-day Western Sahara, however, use "Sahrawi" as a description of their perceived national and ethnic identity. I follow them in using that term here.

As Spain increased its exploitation of Spanish Sahara, its impact on the local population also intensified. From the 1950s, more and more Sahrawis began to settle in urban spaces established by the Spanish. Previously, the only significant site of sedentarization had been Smara, established by the religious and political leader Shaykh Malʿainīn in 1869. Razed by the French in 1913, Smara had then lain in ruins. Colonial geographer Ángel Flores Morales captures the transitional moment at which Sahrawis began to turn to sedentarization. In an early account of the Spanish Sahara (Flores Morales 1946), he does not mention an indigenous settled civilian population in any of the towns in Spanish Sahara (Elayoune, Smara, Villa Cisneros [later Dakhla]) or the military bases mentioned (La Guera, Bir Ganduz, Tishla, Zug, Guelta de Zemmour). He describes Elayoune as "destined" to be a political, military, and commercial hub (105). Flores Morales' map of travel routes across the territory shows camel tracks rather than roads (158).

In his updated and abbreviated publication of several years later (Flores Morales 1954), the situation has changed. Elayoune has now "become" the political, military and commercial hub of the colony (7). The beginning of an indigenous urbanized population is described, which forms a fascinating crossover of nomadic encampment (*frīg*) and "neighborhood": "There are settlements which are dependent on the military bases, where the indigenous people have adopted sedentary life and live in tents which together form a 'frīg' or neighborhood" (7). In some cases, Sahrawis have begun living in houses—a practice unmentioned for Sahrawis in Spanish Sahara in Flores Morales' earlier, longer study. In the later publication, the camel tracks have gone from the map of the territory.

What such maps could not show was how Spanish colonialism was affecting tribes. As Pablo San Martín (2010: 44) describes, there has been a "myth" of Spanish colonialism in Spanish Sahara as a muted affair whose engagement with the local population was marked by neglect or even benevolence. This myth glosses over a number of deeply significant effects. After the "pacification" of the tribes, only Sahrawis serving in the Spanish colonial force, the Tropas Nómadas (nomadic troops) were allowed to bear arms. Former client tribes taunted erstwhile tribute collectors that they were "all *znāgah* now" (Caro Baroja 1955: 33). Some client tribes, such as the Awlād Tidrārīn who had become clients of the Awlād Delīm prior to colonialism, once freed from the constraints of tribute paying, prospered under colonialism. Nomadic encampments began to appear that were composed of a mix of tribes (Molina Campuzano 1954: 8).

In contrast to a diminishing importance of tribes and status groups in certain contexts was the colonial reconstitution of tribes in particular forms. Tribal leaders, *shuyūkh*, were imbued with new powers by the colonial authorities, such as the representation of their tribes in the parliamentary forum Spain created for the colony, the Djemaa.[7] In some cases, *shuyūkh* were created where they had not existed before (Caro Baroja 1955: 44). For San Martín (2010: 45), Spain took up tribal leaders as the colonialist and orientalist version of Francoist assumptions that notables could speak on behalf of others. He also suggests that local discontent with the newly powerful *shuyūkh* helped fuel a shift from tribal loyalties to incipient nationalism (45)—reflected, for instance, in the refusal of some young Sahrawis to name their tribe in a 1973 study (47).

By the 1970s, Spanish Sahara was serving Spain well. The territory had one of the higher levels of income per capita in Africa (see San Martín 2010: 54). But decolonization was in the air.

## A Neglected Conflict

From 1964, the UN included Spanish Sahara in its list of non-self-governing territories. Spain was initially reluctant to leave but faced pressure not only from the UN but also internally from incipient Sahrawi nationalism. The latter was stoked by various factors: new experiences of Sahrawis living and working together in urban contexts, the experience of colonial rule under Spanish institutions, Sahrawis' access through the radio to information about UN resolutions, and young students' contact with nationalist ideologies in universities abroad (see Hodges 1983: 151–53).[8] Following in the heels of an early nationalist movement, headed by Muhammad Bassiri and repressed by Spain in 1970, in 1973 a group of young Sahrawis founded the Front for the Liberation of Saguia al-Hamra and Wadi Dhahab (the northern and southern geographical regions of Spanish Sahara respectively). The front was generally known, though, by its Spanish acronym, Polisario. It waged a campaign of armed resistance to the Spanish presence and advocated independence.

Facing external and internal pressure, Spain began to plan for decolonization via a referendum on self-determination. It conducted a census to register voters in 1974 (Sahara Español Gobierno General de la Provincia 1975). The extent to which this census could accurately take into account a population marked by legacies of, and ongoing, mobile pastoralism and members of which had dispersed in the wake of Opération Ecouvillon was to become a later point of controversy in efforts to ascertain who counted as a member of the "people of Western Sahara" and would be eligible to vote in a referendum. A UN visit to the territory in May 1975 found overwhelming popular support for Polisario and independence (Hodges 1983: 198–99).

As it seemed increasingly likely that Spain would leave the colony, neighbors Morocco and Mauritania put forward claims to the territory. While Mauritania's claims were based on "cultural affinity" between the two territories, Morocco claimed to have enjoyed sovereignty over (parts of) the territory prior to Spanish colonialism. Indeed, claims to a "Greater Morocco" (including Spanish Sahara, Mauritania, and parts of Algeria and Mali) had been forwarded by Morocco's Istiqlal party since 1956 (Hodges 1983: 85–99). At a time when the Moroccan monarchy had recently suffered two attempted coups from the military and needed to boost popular support, there were clear political advantages to the monarchy's bid to expand the national territory and to deploy the army far from Rabat. Both Morocco's and Mauritania's claims were presented to the International Court of Justice (ICJ). Its advisory finding on October 16, 1975, (see Chapter 1) did not find in favor of either claim, however, and reiterated the right of the people of Western Sahara to self-determination.[9]

Morocco nevertheless interpreted the details of the finding—that some tribes at discrete points in time had sworn oaths of religious allegiance to the Moroccan sultan that, according to the ICJ, did not amount to territorial sovereignty—as confirmation of its claims. It organized a massive civilian "retaking" of the Sahara in the form of a Green March of thousands of Moroccan civilians, who crossed a few miles into Spanish Sahara on November 6, 1975 (Hodges 1983: 220–23). While these civilians quickly crossed the border back into Morocco on November 10, the Green March was effective in securing popular attachment among Moroccans to the "Moroccan Sahara" and in further pressuring Spain and other international actors toward Morocco. Faced with Francisco Franco's approaching death, Spain signed the Madrid Accords with Morocco and Mauritania on November 14. In these Accords, Spain agreed to hand over the territory to Morocco and Mauritania. The details of the Accords—including significant economic concessions to Spain on the part of Morocco and Mauritania—were initially kept secret.

The UN General Assembly disagreed as to how to respond to the Madrid Accords, to the point of passing two different resolutions on the same day. One ignored and one "noted" the Accords—but both still called for the accommodation of the right to self-determination of the people of the territory (Hodges 1983: 235–36). Behind the scenes, the United States privately acquiesced that the Sahara should be given to Morocco (Mundy 2006b). In the days following the Accords, Moroccan and Mauritanian troops began to annex the territory (see Hodges 1983: 223–24). The last Spanish officers left Spanish Sahara on February 26, 1975. In response, Polisario founded the Sahrawi Arab Democratic Republic on February 27, 1975.

In the wake of the joint annexation, Polisario launched into fighting a war against both Morocco and Mauritania. Mauritania withdrew in 1979 and recognized the SADR in 1984. From the early 1980s, Morocco built a series of military walls designed to keep Polisario's Sahrawi Popular Liberation Army (SPLA) away from the main water, urban, and mineral resources. The resulting wall, often known as the "berm," divides Western Sahara between a westerly portion under Morocco control and an easterly portion under Polisario control (see Figure 1).

With neither Morocco nor Polisario able to win the war outright, the UN brokered a cease-fire in 1991 and set up its Mission for the Referendum in Western Sahara (MINURSO).[10] As MINURSO set out to register voters for a referendum in the 1990s, potential voters needed to "prove" membership in a Sahrawi tribe to qualify to vote. In this context, tribes came to be mentioned publicly again in the refugee camps, where previously their mention had been banned. Both Morocco and Polisario put forward more voters than were accepted by MINURSO; Morocco in particular was criticized for its techniques of bringing in extra alleged voters to the territory and using intimidation to try to sway the results of the verification processes (Ziai 1995). The verification process led to a potential electorate of 86,386 voters, out of a total of 244,643 applications (Zunes and Mundy 2010: 192). The majority of applicants hailed from Morocco (99,225) or from Moroccan-controlled Western Sahara (83,971). As Zunes and Mundy (2010: 192–93) point out, together these applicants amounted to "more than double the 72,370 names on MINURSO's updated version of the 1974 Spanish census, and more than four times the number of applications sponsored by Polisario from the refugee camps (42,337)." Five percent of applicants from Morocco and just under half those from Moroccan-controlled Western Sahara were accepted as voters. Morocco went on to present over 40,000 appeals against the verification results (Zunes and Mundy 2010: 212).

A referendum vote, however, has not been held to date. In 2004, the latest of a series of UN plans floundered when it became clear that Morocco would not allow a vote that included independence as an option—even when Polisario agreed that Moroccan settlers who had been in the territory since 1999, and who were believed to outnumber Sahrawis, could also vote. Polisario would not agree to a vote that did not include independence. Faced with this stalemate, the UN Security Council refused to impose a solution. Political stalemate has held ever since. Even rapprochement between Morocco and Algeria in the wake of the Arab Spring left stalemate intact and Western Sahara off the agenda (Zoubir 2012). Zunes and Mundy (2010: 216–17) surmise that, if the UN went to such effort to register voters but has not pressured to hold a vote, the reason may be that the UN fears being unable to impose the result of a vote, should the result be independence. Zunes and Mundy's analogy that, since the cease-fire, the struggle between Morocco and Polisario continues on virtual battlefronts—the corridors of the UN, voter registration figures, international reputation for "good governance"—seems apt.

The stalemate in Western Sahara reflects a clash between political realities and declared rights. Morocco enjoys strong international political support from key allies, especially France and the United States. The impact of pressure from Morocco and its allies can be observed in specific decisions of UN bodies: to alter a report that was critical of Morocco (What's in Blue 2012); to refrain from publishing the report on Western Sahara by the UN High Commissioner on Human Rights; and to exclude human rights monitoring from the MINURSO mandate, despite calls for human rights monitoring in the Commissioner's (leaked) report, and in NGO reports (e.g., Amnesty International 2011; Human Rights Watch 2012, 2014).[11] The Moroccan monarchy continues to enjoy popular support in Morocco for the unifying national cause of the "Moroccan Sahara." Fear of the costs of losing this popular support has been explored as one of the reasons for Morocco's continuing partial annexation, even though the economic costs of the annexation are plausibly greater than the economic benefits gained from Morocco's exploitation of phosphate and fishing resources in Western Sahara (Von Hippel 1996).[12]

Morocco's legal position is not as robust as its political position, however. No country other than Mauritania, 1975–1979 (when it was a joint annexing power), has officially recognized Moroccan claims to Western Sahara. The UN still considers Spain to be the de jure administering power in Western Sahara and Morocco to be only its de facto administering power.

For its part, Polisario enjoys political and material support from allies, especially Algeria, Morocco's rival for hegemony in the Maghreb. But Polisario also enjoys a strong legal position. What is now called Western Sahara has been recognized by the UN as a non-self-governing territory since 1964. Polisario has also been recognized as the representative of the Sahrawi people by the UN since 1979. Thus far, Polisario's strong legal position has kept Western Sahara on the UN Security Council agenda.

Meanwhile, the stalemate has resulted in a divided territory and a divided population. Annexed Western Sahara is ruled by Morocco as part of Morocco. With an estimated 100,000 Moroccan military personnel (Arieff 2012), the annexed territory is a highly militarized space. While some Sahrawis work closely with and benefit from Moroccan rule, many others have been organizing a wave of protests against Moroccan rule that, since 2005, they have been calling their "Intifada" (Mundy 2006a). Possibly the largest demonstration to date by annexed Sahrawis took place in October–November 2010. Despite prefiguring by a few weeks the Arab Spring uprisings that would sweep across North Africa and the Middle East, these protests received little international attention outside specialist circles (see Wilson 2013).

Separated from annexed Sahrawis by the berm and just over the border in Algeria are the refugees. Hailing from both towns and pasturelands, refugees fleeing the annexation of Western Sahara began from 1976 to settle in refugee camps formed near the Algerian military base and town, Tindouf. The latter is located in southwest Algeria some 50 km from the border with Western Sahara. Algeria delegated authority over the refugee camps and the territory between them to Polisario.[13] The governing authority whose rule the refugees experience on a daily basis is, therefore, not Algeria but the state-movement. Although Polisario remains an armed movement and maintains an army, the SPLA, which is stationed in bases in the Polisario-controlled areas of Western Sahara, the camps are run as an overtly civilian space. There are no weapons on display there; indeed, the state-movement forbids weapons to be carried in the camps. Nevertheless, there is arguably a "mentality of militarization" in the camps. The SPLA enjoys enormous popularity among refugees, its very mention usually triggering ululation from women within earshot.

The size of the Sahrawi refugee population has long been disputed. It is not unusual for the size of an exiled population to be controversial (e.g., Harrell-Bond, Voutira, and Leopold 1992; Gale 2007). In the Sahrawi case, the size of the refugee population is perceived to be important in determining not only the provision of aid but also the likely outcome of an eventual vote on self-determination. While the state-movement conducts its own census (see Chapter 4), it does not let the UNHCR conduct a census of its own. As a result, questions surround estimates of the population in the camps. The UNHCR estimated 129,863 refugees between 1998 and 2000 (Zunes and Mundy 2010: 128). Satellite images were used by the World Food Program in 2005 to estimate 100,000 refugees (Zunes and Mundy 2010: 128).

As is the case with other refugee populations, such as Mauritanian refugees in Senegal and Somali refugees in Kenya, Sahrawi refugees live in camps located in a region with whose local population refugees share a language (here, Hassaniya), in some cases political ties through tribes, and in other cases kinship. There are no public figures estimating the balance among the population in the camps of refugees and "local" Sahrawis based in or near Tindouf since before the conflict. It is also the case that those who came to the camps hailed not only from Western Sahara but also from southern Morocco and Mauritania. (In some cases, as the UN voter registration suggested, not all those in the camps hailed from "Sahrawi tribes.") New arrivals to the camps continued in the 2000s and may plausibly continue as long as the camps exist. As I explore in Chapter 2, by design on the part of the state-movement, the physical layout (neighborhoods) and administrative structure (places of work) of the camps were originally meant to mix up refugees, rather than congregate clusters of refugees by tribe, status group, or place of residence prior to exile.

Before the refugee population took shape, at its second Popular General Congress in 1974, Polisario had espoused policies such as the abolition of slavery, the emancipation of women, and the prohibition of tribes (Hodges 1983: 163–64). When it began to govern a civilian population in exile, the state-movement had the opportunity to enact these policies, leading what it called its revolution (*thawrah*). The notion that the refugee community is conducting a revolution has persisted through the long years of exile. For instance, during my fieldwork I heard both refugees and officers of the state-movement make reference to being engaged in a "revolution" aiming at "[the] liberation [of persons]" (*taḥrīr al-insān*). Over the years, the nature of revolutionary initiatives has inevitably altered. In what I shall call the early revolutionary period (from 1975 to the 1991 cease-fire), the state-movement was heavily influenced by the revolutionary model of Muammar Gaddafi's Libya. The Libyan style of popular committees was adopted (see Chapter 2). In this period, the state-movement also exerted tight internal political controls, including the repression of perceived political opponents. In 1988, there was a political crisis when refugees' protests against abuses of power on the part of the state-movement were themselves repressed. This crisis set in motion a process that has been described as the "Sahrawi perestroika" (Shelley 2004: 179). The period after the 1991 cease-fire, what I shall call the late revolutionary period, saw multiple political and economic transformations in the camps and within the state-movement that mirrored international transitions: from war to cease-fire; from economic dependence on rations to a flourishing movement of people and goods in, from, and through the camps; from unchecked governing powers to increasing internal reform to check the power of the state-movement and increasing demands for such checks from the refugees. As Parts II, III, and the Conclusion explore, the late revolutionary period brought new challenges for revolutionary ideals of social egalitarianism, as well as new means of voicing continuing popular appetite for the pursuit of revolutionary aspirations.

The state-movement has developed, and has reformed over time, its own structures of governance. These include a Parliament (Chapters 2 and 7), law codes, law courts, and prisons (Chapter 3). Despite the unusual status of the state-movement as regards international norms of state power, I argue that there is not an absence of state power in the camps. Rather, there is a surfeit of state power, from rations distributions to elections, SADR driving licenses, and SADR marriage licenses for refugees going abroad. During the time I lived with Sahrawi refugees in various locations in and beyond the camps, the social relations of this governing authority became my object of study.

## Research in and Beyond the Sahrawi Refugee Camps

In February 2006, I made my first trip to the Sahrawi refugee camps. A few weeks earlier, I had contacted the Polisario office in London to discuss the possibility of conducting research in the camps. Two Polisario representatives had invited me to join a small group from the UK who would be visiting the camps for the official celebrations of the anniversary of the SADR's foundation on February 27. Polisario provided me with a letter of invitation, on the grounds of which the Algerian Consulate in London granted me a visa to enter Algeria. With this visa, I flew to Algiers, headed to the domestic terminal, and whiled away the hours until the flight for Tindouf, typically scheduled at around 11 p.m. On that first visit, on arrival at Tindouf, some 1,450 km from Algiers, as I proceeded to hand in my Algerian landing card to the Algerian officer, I was uncertain as to what to put as my address. He added for me "RASD," the French acronym for SADR.

Over the course of two years of fieldwork with Sahrawi refugees, January 2007-January 2009, and follow-up trips in 2011, 2012, and 2014, this routine of how to access the camps would become familiar. Because Algeria did not offer more than ninety days on one visa, after a maximum of ninety days in the camps in any one trip, I had to return to London to start again from the beginning. One development, however, was that the state-movement began issuing its own landing cards in Tindouf, with the result that visitors to the camps filled out two landing cards, one for Algeria and one for the state-movement.

The formalities of landing cards completed, along with other foreigners arriving in Tindouf to visit the camps, I was picked up by the state-movement in a robust 4x4 vehicle that would take us to the camps. On the way, while still following a tarmac road, we passed through a "checkpoint" at which the car crossed from one side, manned by Algerian officers, to the other, manned by officers of the state-movement. After a short time and as the tarmac ran out, we reached the camps, known to the refugees as "the tented place" (*al-mukhayyam*). On that first trip, along with other members of the group who had traveled from the UK, I was billeted with local families in different locations. When I returned in January 2007 for fieldwork, I began living with one of these families.

By the time of my first visit to the camps, they looked very different from the pictures of the early revolutionary period. Then, the "tented place" was literally composed mostly of row upon row of cloth tents, provided as shelter for the refugees. Most of the refugees had arrived in exile without significant possessions (Hodges 1983: 233), including (where relevant) the goat-hair tent used in mobile pastoralist settings. In the early revolutionary period, the few buildings made of more durable materials were administrative buildings, schools, and health care centers.

Over the course of the early years of exile, a layout for the camps was developed. A settlement known as Rabouni, which had originally included residential areas, became a specialist center for government buildings and ministries. From 1976, three separate large-scale residential provinces, *wilāyāt* (s. *wilāyah*) were developed, each named after a major city in Western Sahara: Elayoune, Smara, and Dakhla. A fourth, Auserd, was added in 1985. Each *wilāyah* was in turn divided into districts (*dawāir*, s. *dairah*, as locally pronounced), and each *dairah* into four neighborhoods. The original name for a neighborhood, *ḥayy*, was still preferred in daily usage after the official name was changed to *baladīyah* in 1995. Between Rabouni and Smara, there was a residential school offering training courses for women, named February 27 (after the founding day of SADR). Over time, the four *wilāyāt* and February 27 came to host the most significant civilian populations. February 27 was made into a *wilāyah* in 2012 and renamed Boujdour.

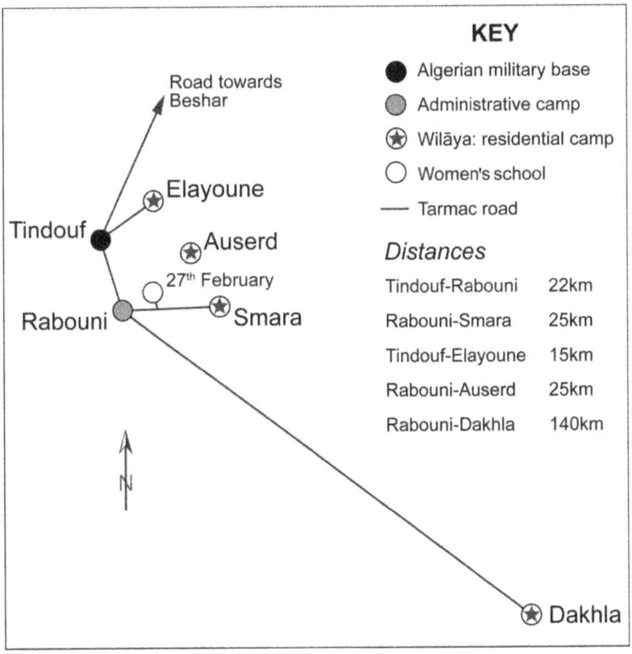


Figure 2. Sketch map of the Sahrawi refugee camps, c. 2011.

Since it was known as February 27 during most of my fieldwork, I use the earlier name here.

Despite the constraints of exile, the state-movement followed other liberation movements in placing great emphasis on welfare provisions to its citizens. Each *dairah* had a primary health care center and nursery, and, early on, local primary schools were set up. Each *wilāyah* had a small hospital, and Rabouni's hospital had a team of Cuban doctors who catered for some operations. When unable to provide services within the refugee camps, the state-movement benefited from the help of "friendly countries" (Algeria, Libya, Cuba, and others) to give refugees access, for free, to further services. Complex health needs were addressed in Tindouf, in other Algerian cities, or in Spain. By the late 2000s, there were limited secondary school places in the camps, and other students continued their education in Algeria (or, under Gaddafi, in Libya). Generations of Sahrawi refugee students received university education abroad (for free) in a range of "friendly" countries—although not all of these graduates have remained in the camps (see Chapter 7).

By the late 2000s, in residential areas, cloth tents were outnumbered by zinc-roofed rectangular rooms made of mud-brick or, in some cases, concrete (see Wilson 2012). Following the economic opening up of the camps after the cease-fire of 1991, the late revolutionary period saw each *wilāyah* also acquire marketplaces (see Chapter 6). Private trade had been conspicuously absent in the early revolutionary period, when there was only one shop per *dairah*, run by the state-movement and with very limited wares. Indeed, the refugees in the early revolutionary period had had little access to money at all. In the late revolutionary period, however, refugees had increasingly diverse incomes (see Chapter 6). These included not only rations but also resources from aid programs, remittances, trade, and pensions from Spain for former colonial employees. The regular currency in use in the camps was the Algerian dinar—although refugees counted coins and notes in multiples of twenty times the currency's face value.

With commerce flourishing in the camps, material shortages were less acute in the 2000s as compared to the 1980s. But water shortages were, for most of 2007 and 2008, chronic. Water trucks' delivery schedule for filling families' individual metal tanks was irregular. Only February 27 and Rabouni had mains electricity (albeit at times intermittently). The rest of the camps relied on solar panels, with which families charged car batteries and from which they ran light bulbs, radios, and television sets linked to satellite

Figure 3. View of Smara camp, 2011 (photo by Alice Wilson).

dishes. The latest Al Jazeera news bulletins—or soap opera storylines—were regularly available in refugee homes.

The refugee camps—though geographically remote and located in the harsh *ḥamādah* desert, infamous for its extreme temperatures in both winter and summer—were "connected," rather than isolated spaces. This was not only because refugees were avid consumers of international news. By the 2000s, members of the refugee community took advantage of the greater freedom of movement since the cease-fire to go physically back and forth between destinations ranging from Tindouf, other Algerian cities, Spain, France, Italy, and Mauritania to Morocco and Moroccan-controlled Western Sahara—in the latter case with complicated political ramifications (see Chapter 7).[14] Some were involved in intra-Saharan trade with Mauritania, Mali, and Algeria.[15] Most often, individual household members rather than a whole household would travel from the camps, and many migrants made return journeys back to the camps. The latter can be thought of as an anemone. Those who leave are often drawn back, either physically by making visits, or economically and emotionally by sending remittances. As one senior male interlocutor put it, "[People] have to go back [to the camps] to recharge their batteries." The camps also continue to attract newcomers such as Sahrawis from the Moroccan-controlled areas and persons from neighboring countries attracted to the promise of rations.

Over the course of my fieldwork, I lived with four families. Their stories indicate a degree of the diversity of backgrounds and interests among refugees—to whom I refer by pseudonym here.[16] Sumaya, in her late forties or early fifties in 2007, lived in February 27 camp. She served actively on committees of the state-movement and had been a Polisario activist from her youth. She enjoyed a degree of material comfort at home, thanks to the remittances sent by her husband, Fadili, from Spain. He had residential papers that permitted him to work in Spain, and, between periods of work, he would visit the camps. Thanks to his earnings, by 2011 they had rebuilt their home in the coveted style of concrete rooms connected by roofed passageways, allowing circulation between living spaces without exposure to the sun.

Once I had found a Hassaniya teacher, I moved closer to his home on the other side of February 27. There I lived with Khadīja, who was probably in her late fifties. Khadīja was born and raised in a nomadic encampment (*frīg*, pl. *firgān*) but moved after her marriage to live in Elayoune, the capital of Spanish Sahara. By the time she, her husband, and, by then, four children became refugees, Khadīja had been enjoying life in the city—with mains electricity, running water, a fridge, and a washing machine—for several years. Khadīja recalled long hours of work for the state-movement in the early revolutionary period. By the late 2000s, though, she focused her energies on running a small store from her home and a rudimentary "Turkish" bath (*ḥammām*) that operated in the winter months.

Having found, during visits away from February 27 to the *wilāyāt*, that each offered different atmospheres, in late 2008 I moved to live with Zaynabu and her family in Smara. Of a similar generation to Khadīja, Zaynabu had also been born in a *frīg*, in the northern part of Western Sahara. On marrying, she had moved to her husband's *frīg*. She, her husband, and their three children came into exile from the pasturelands. After bearing her husband three more children in exile, Zaynabu was widowed. She went on to remarry a fellow refugee, Brahim, and to bear him two children. In parallel, Brahim was still married to the wife with whom, prior to exile, he had shared a home in the city of Smara, Western Sahara. Brahim and his elder son were herding in the pasturelands, again in the northern part of Western Sahara, when the war broke out. As a result, Brahim's family was separated. Those in the city fell under Moroccan control, and those who were in the pasturelands became refugees. In 2008 Zaynabu and her family ran a small store from their home, and her eldest son ran a store at the marketplace. One married daughter and a daughter-in-law worked (for what amounted to symbolic wages) for the state-movement in administrative roles. A son-in-law who lived next door to Zaynabu combined service in the SPLA with running a taxi when he was home in the camps.

I lived finally in Auserd with Māghalāha. With her young family of one child, she had left the pasturelands in northern Mauritania around 1980 to join the refugee camps, where four more children were born to her and her husband. Māghalāha frequently volunteered to take part in events for the state-movement, such as the Sahrawi Cultural Festival. The family relied on the income of two adult, then unmarried sons. The elder worked for the state-movement in the Ministry of Information in Rabouni, and the younger worked locally in Auserd building mud-brick and concrete rooms.

Having studied classical Arabic for two years prior to my fieldwork, with the help of host families and my Hassaniya teacher, in a few months I became fluent in Hassaniya. This became the main language of my research (although some government employees with whom I shared fluency in one of Spanish, French, or English spoke to me in their preferred of these languages). In most of my formal interviews, interviewees preferred not to be recorded, so I made handwritten notes in a mixture of English and Arabic. Outside formal interviews, when I was joining in family activities, I rarely used a recorder. I later wrote up my notes in notebooks, recalling where I could exact words used and at other times paraphrasing in English what had been said. As a result, there may be fewer direct citations from interlocutors in this study than found in other ethnographies.

Often, the first words I would hear in the day would be admonitions from a parent or an older sibling to other family members to get up and pray. My host sisters and I would begin to stir from our blankets on the floor of the mud-brick room or tent where we had bedded down for the night. (In the hot summer months, we would simply sleep outside). Morning tasks awaited able-bodied adults and older children—loading water cans and transporting water to the kitchen and latrine, lighting up charcoal on which to make tea, moving solar panels into position to catch the best light, plugging in phones to solar-charged car batteries, going to buy missing items for breakfast, getting children ready for school. Most family members would gather for at least one or two, if not all three, of the rounds of tea that composed a Sahrawi tea "session." I might ask which family member could walk with me to an interview, or I might be expecting to spend the day with the family, joining in household tasks, social visits, or rations collections. Wherever the day took each person, if not everyone had returned for lunch around 2 or 3 p.m., the family would expect to find themselves once again together after sunset for the evening tea. In those camps without electricity, television did not usually accompany this evening gathering. The evening tea, over which we whiled away the hours until a light dinner sometime after ten, was the time for exchanging news, stories, phone calls, and, for some families, tuning in to the SADR radio news broadcast. In the colder months, as we sat or lay on the floor in a circle around the tent or room, we wrapped ourselves in the blankets from which, after dinner, we would once again lay out our simple beds.

Moving host families, as I did, is not conventional in fieldwork. Nevertheless, I found that keeping in touch with the various host families as I moved between them, usually by public taxi, meant that I was able to compare different experiences of everyday family life, as well as special occasions. In addition, I joined two "pseudo" families. The first was the group of Sahrawi university students based in Damascus, where I spent four months in the summer of 2007. Having escaped the heat of the *ḥamādah* desert (an escape to which many refugees aspired, and some achieved by going to Mauritania, the pasturelands, or Spain), I continued language training in standard Arabic in daytime courses, and I practiced Hassaniya at night with the students. They gathered nightly in the Polisario representative's office in Damascus—an apartment that, in their gatherings, was treated very much as a tent.

Back in the camps, I joined in the pseudo-family life of the Ministry of Information, where I taught English once or twice a week. Many of the workers regularly stayed overnight, to avoid the costs of the shared taxis that ran between camps and to meet early or late radio shifts. The female broadcasters became another host family to me.

I was also able to arrange a trip to the pasturelands in April-May 2008, where I stayed in a nomadic encampment (*frīg*) with members of Māghalāha's family—and met the *bijāwī* and his intriguing camel. I draw on all these different sites within and beyond the camps to analyze relations between Sahrawi refugees and their experiences of governance within the state-movement.

The Western Sahara conflict has impeded research access for anthropologists seeking to conduct long-term fieldwork in the refugee camps. While there are many ethnographic studies of Hassanophones, mostly in Mauritania (e.g., Villasante de Beauvais 1998; Fortier 2000; Tauzin 2001; Boulay 2003; Bonte 2008; but see also Popenoe 2004), for a long time the most important ethnographic studies of Sahrawis were historical (Caro Baroja 1955; Caratini 1989b). Sophie Caratini's (2003) later essays draw on short research trips to the camps in the 1990s. There had been no anthropologist working for long-term fieldwork (of a year or more) in the camps between their formation in 1976 and my arrival in 2007 for two years of fieldwork. The ethnography of the camps, including long-term fieldwork projects and multisited fieldwork, is, however, growing (e.g. Gimeno 2007; Corbet 2008; Farah 2010; Deubel 2012; Isidoros 2015; Tavakoli 2015; Irwin forthcoming; Solana forthcoming).

One challenge during fieldwork was the potential unwillingness of refugees to discuss controversial topics—such as the political crisis of 1988 but also, in some cases, tribes. As Māghlāha's son, Mal'ainīn, once told me with a reproving sigh when I had asked for clarification about the tribe to which a colleague belonged, "people don't like tribalism." Such caution applied to conversations among refugees who chose to remain within the bounds of political correctness, as well as to conversations with an anthropologist. Sometimes euphemisms were employed such as "the big family" for tribe and "the people who make things" for artisans (traditionally a stigmatized group). Some interlocutors were unwilling to broach sensitive topics at all with me. For example, I never learned to which tribe Sumaya belonged. On the whole, though, such persistent reticence was less common than interlocutors' openness to sharing with me their stories, observations, frustrations, and aspirations.

Questions of governance in the Moroccan-controlled areas of Western Sahara are not addressed directly here. In a brief research trip to Moroccan-controlled Western Sahara in 2012, I stayed with Brahim's first wife and with the siblings and half-siblings of Zaynabu's children and stepson in the camps. Relatives of another host family from the camps told me on the phone, however, that they were "too afraid" to remain in the city and left at the time of my visit. Because of the political challenges of living conditions—and, by extension, research conditions—in the annexed areas, the focus of this research has remained the refugee camps.

To write of a conflict zone is inherently controversial and likely to attract criticism from all interested parties. I hope through this study to explore useful ways of rethinking the categories of sovereignty, state power, exile, and revolution and to offer insights into lives about which many assumptions have been made, the lives in question often remaining little known and much misunderstood.

## Overview of the Book

The three Parts of *Sovereignty in Exile* trace the layers of a dynamic palimpsest whereby the relations of one project of sovereignty, initially obscured by those of another, come to show through in invited and uninvited ways. Part I examines the "Aspirations" to overwrite the social relations of tribes with those of state power. Chapter 1, "Hindsight Visions," sets the stage by examining the debated relationship between tribe and state power in MENA. I situate within these debates my interpretation of tribes in Western Sahara as a "sphere of consented solidarity" and, at specific historical moments in what became Western Sahara, a project of sovereignty in their own right.

Chapter 2, "Revolutionary Foundations," turns attention to the ethnographic analysis of the camps. The chapter addresses how the state-movement set out initially to displace tribes by "overwriting" them. The state-movement introduced new kinds of segmentation in the form of new administrative categories and structures. It also created a public domain, comprising schools and hospitals. This public domain both constituted a tangible manifestation of state power and replaced institutions in which formerly the social relations of tribes were reproduced. Yet, in specific instances, such as public meetings meant to allow the refugees direct participation in governance, these meetings were presented as continuing the tradition of former tribal councils. The latter were celebrated as evidence that Sahrawis were "democratic before democracy." I approach such claims as a moment of a "trompe-l'oeil" effect in the palimpsest, where a particular *representation* of an underlying past (which may or may not have existed) is foregrounded.

Part II, "Compromises," addresses how the displacement of tribes has been modified over time, in favor of the state-movement sometimes seeking to use the social relations of tribes as a tool for governance. I explore this through three arenas of the social relations of sovereignty.

Chapters 3 and 4 examine how areas of the social relations of sovereignty often attributed specifically to state power may not be exclusive to it. Chapter 3, "Unpopular Law," considers how the state-movement sought to establish a monopoly on the state of exception, that is, deciding when laws do or do not hold. In doing so, it set out to displace tribes from that very role by seeking to eliminate tribal laws, *a'rāf.* In the early revolutionary period, this elimination was staged through Popular Justice Committees. Nevertheless, the late revolutionary professionalization of justice challenged the "detribalization" of judicial administration. Through the partial "retribalization" of judicial administration, I reflect on the relationship between law and sovereignty.

Chapter 4, "Tax Evasion," explores the unusual fiscal circumstances of the state-movement as a means through which to reconsider taxation as a trope of state power. I explore the work of governmentality that underlies the distribution of rations in the camps and the appropriation of refugees' labor on the part of the state-movement. I show how the state-movement reworks forms of appropriation and redistribution, previously associated with tribes, to pursue an "innovated taxation" in the camps. This innovated taxation suggests the broader importance of both appropriation *and* redistribution in North African and Euro-American notions of state power and sovereignty.

Chapter 5, "Managing Inequalities," examines the organization, legitimization and reproduction of social (in)equalities as an aspect of the social relations of sovereignty. I assess the management of (in)equalities in the case of Sahrawi refugees by examining how marriage practices, such as prestations and wedding celebrations, changed in the camps. Prestations and celebrations were standardized by the state-movement in the 1980s, with strong implications for staging social egalitarianism between refugees. But, in the late revolutionary period, the emergence of expensive weddings and prestations led to what I explore as a crisis of governance for the state-movement. My analysis calls into question refugees' views that "traditional" marriage ceremonies had "returned." Yet I suggest how the underlying meaning of "Arab marriage," as observed by generations of anthropologists working in MENA, had, perhaps, "returned."

Part III, "Dilemmas," considers apparent resurgences of tribes that are unruly irruptions in the palimpsest and arouse consternation for both refugees and state-movement leaders alike. Chapter 6, "Troubling Markets," addresses widely shared concerns in the camps that tribal loyalties might be exacerbating the potential for the marketizing economy in the camps to increase socioeconomic inequalities between refugees.

Chapter 7, "Party-Less Democrats," examines how both refugees and their leaders share concerns that tribal loyalties may influence the casting of votes in elections. Efforts on the part of the state-movement to pluralize electoral choices, so as to allay this possibility, indicate how a lack of multiple political parties and the presence of tribes may not preclude steps toward democratization. I explore how the imperfect reforms in the camps illuminate a broader phenomenon of "democratic casualties," whereby attempts to preserve and extend some forms of democratic participation may jeopardize others.

Finally, the Conclusion, "Revolution as Moral Contract," draws on the preceding chapters to suggest how a process of revolution as a moral contract has proved an enduring basis for Sahrawi refugees to continue their revolution through changing circumstances.

# PART I

## Aspirations

CHAPTER 1

# Hindsight Visions: Tribe and State Power as Projects of Sovereignty

I am not a tribesman. I am the Prime Minister.
—Recep Tayyip Erdoğan, January 30, 2009 (BBC 2009)

In February 2012, while in Auserd camp, I spent an evening with Māghalāha's neighbors. We settled in for tea in the tent, warmed by the glowing charcoal on which the teapot rested. Tumanna, mother of two daughters, the eldest of whom was at primary school, oversaw both tea and her daughter's homework. After some time, when her daughter had practiced her reading aloud, she put the textbook to one side. I asked her whether I could look too, and, when she consented, I began to flick through the pages of her history text book for the Sahrawi Arab Democratic Republic. From page to page, SADR pupils learned not only of the rise and fall of Islamic empires but also of how Arab tribes had come from southern Arabia to conquer the northwest Sahara, how the resulting Saharan tribes had fought wars among each other and kept at bay the neighboring Moroccan sultanate, and how these tribes had resisted European colonial powers. The front cover of the textbook, on which the name and flag of SADR were displayed, supplied an implicit coda to the recounted centuries of conflict between tribes and would-be state powers. The age of tribal internal divisions and tribes' rejection of state power, this front cover seemed to suggest, was the history that lay behind the founding of the SADR, which had replaced tribes and yet had continued the tradition of resistance to foreign state power.

Sahrawi refugees are far from alone in conceiving of the history of northwest Saharan Africa in terms of conflicts between state power and tribes. The notion of conflict between areas under state control and areas allegedly under the control of tribes that resist state power—spaces known respectively in the context of the Moroccan sultanate as *bilād al-makhzan* (land of state control) and *bilād al-sībah* (land of dissidence)—is an enduring theme in historical (and some contemporary) appraisals of the region and the Middle East and North Africa (MENA) more broadly. The aims of this chapter are twofold. I discuss critically the relationship between tribes and state power in MENA in order to examine how understandings of that relationship have informed the development of Western Sahara as a case of decolonization and disputed sovereignty. I then address how tribe, *qabīlah*, can be understood specifically in the context of Western Sahara.

It is notoriously difficult to define "tribe." Students of tribes have been warned that "it is impossible to find an analytic terminology that both takes account of indigenous categories and applies widely enough to be useful for comparison and classification" (Tapper 1990: 49–50). Nevertheless, this conceptual difficulty has by no means prevented, and has even fueled, intense debate about the relationship between "tribe"—whatever "tribe" may mean—and state power. For the purposes of taking up a comparative debate that has assumed the existence of "tribes," albeit as a problematic category, in the first part of this chapter, I use "tribe" as a provisional and imperfect working term. In the second part of the chapter, I explore meanings for tribe, *qabīlah*, in the specific context of the territory that has become present-day Western Sahara. Taking inspiration from the revisionist trend that calls into question alleged opposition between tribe and state power, I examine the *qabīlah* in Western Sahara as a "sphere of consented solidarity" that in specific historical moments (such as the eve of Spanish colonialism) may constitute a project of sovereignty in its own right. I argue against an implied tendency of seeing zones of claimed yet ineffective state power (*sībah*), or zones that have lacked even claimed yet ineffective state power, as zones of "lack." Rather, I suggest that such zones can be alternative projects of sovereignty to state power.

## A Vision of Tribe Versus State Power

The notion of opposition between tribes and state power is related to other supposed and long-standing antonyms, such as desert/sown, mobile/sedentary, "primitive society"/state, kinship/contract. While by no means particular to MENA, these related oppositions flourish there in specific forms. These include *badw/ḥaḍārah*, a contrast between fierce, brave, and rough nomads versus civilized city dwellers, and *sībah/makhzan*, which contrasts zones of ineffective state control (*sībah*) with zones of effective state control (*makhzan*). Such oppositions have been called into question for social anthropology as a discipline (e.g., Kuper 1988). In particular, these oppositions have been questioned with regard to regions that contain hinterlands that historically have been remote from state power, such as MENA, Inner Asia, and highland southeast Asia (Tapper 1983; Khoury and Kostiner 1990; Sneath 2007; Scott 2009). Before turning in detail to some criticisms of these supposed antonyms, it is helpful to recall how influential the notion of opposition between tribes and state power has been for MENA, and more specifically for Western Sahara as a decolonization case.

The political significance in North Africa, and the Middle East more broadly, of the opposition between tribes and state power was highlighted by the fourteenth-century North African scholar and historian Ibn Khaldūn (1958). For Ibn Khaldūn, tribes and state power were, in a sense, opposed. Tribes who lived in the desert held the political advantage of *'aṣabīyah*, solidarity, which made them fearless in battle. Emboldened by *'aṣabīyah*, periodically tribes would sweep in, attack, and conquer a center of state power, setting up their own dynasty to replace that which had been defeated. Nevertheless, once turned city dwellers, tribes lost the advantage of *'aṣabīyah*, and, over time, thus became vulnerable to defeat by *'aṣabīyah*-driven newcomers. Such Ibn Khaldūnian cycles, Ernest Gellner (1990) has suggested, lasted well into the nineteenth century—in cases such as 'Abd alQadir in Algeria, the Sanusiyya in Cyrenaica, the Mahdiyya in Sudan—and only came to an end with the new military and administrative technologies that favored state power. Yet the idea of zones of state control versus zones of failed or no state control has proved tenacious as regards the Middle East and North Africa. A recent incarnation of the trope is the "ungoverned spaces" in which Euro-American governments fear that terrorism breeds.

The notion of tribes opposing state power has shaped understandings of present-day Western Sahara. Saharan northwest Africa has its own nineteenth century "Ibn Khaldūnian moment" in the figure of Shaykh Mal'ainīn. Born in the Hodh region of present-day Mauritania c. 1830–1831, Shaykh Mal'ainīn became a religious leader and staunch opponent of European incursion into the territory inhabited by Hassanophones, *ṭrāb* (land) *al-bīḍān* (as it was known to them). In his resistance against European colonialism, Shaykh Mal'ainīn met initially with the help of the Moroccan Sultan Moulay Abdelaziz (reigned 1894–1908), with whose help he built his holy city Smara in present-day Western Sahara. In 1905, Shaykh Mal'ainīn swore allegiance to the sultan. But as the sultanate increasingly fell under the power of the French, and with Sultan Moulay Hafid (reigned 1908–1912) submitting to French requests to cut off military aid to Shaykh Mal'ainīn, the latter turned against the sultan. Shaykh Mal'ainīn revoked his oath and made a bid for sultanship himself. He died following defeat by the French army in 1910.[1]

The idea that, historically, the tribes of present-day Western Sahara were a force of opposition against the Moroccan sultanate also lies at the crux of the Western Sahara dispute and its classification as a decolonization case. The pro-self-determination position, upheld in UN Security Council resolutions and espoused by Polisario and its supporters, rests on the idea that, prior to European colonialism, present-day Western Sahara was ruled by tribes who did not submit to be ruled by the Moroccan sultanate. Such a position was also upheld in the Advisory Opinion of the International Court of Justice (ICJ 1975). The court found that, first, Western Sahara was not *terra nullius* prior to European colonialism and that, second, the Moroccan sultanate, while enjoying religious authority over some tribes in the north at discrete times, had not had territorial sovereignty over present-day Western Sahara such as would obviate the right of the people of Western Sahara to self-determination. These findings sufficiently endorsed the notion that tribes, and not the Moroccan sultanate, had ruled Western Sahara for the territory to be confirmed as a decolonization case.

## Revisions of Tribe and State Power

Increasingly, scholars have both emphasized that opposition is not the only form of relationship between tribes and state power and problematized the very notion of opposition between them. Three strands of such criticism are particularly relevant to Western Sahara.

### Tribes Creating States

A first challenge to supposed antagonism between tribe and state is apparent from Ibn Khaldūn's theory, and concerns how tribes can create dynasties of state power. Tribes' political advantage for achieving this, according to Ibn Khaldūn, was the strong loyalty, *'aṣabīyah*, that tribe members felt toward each other. With hindsight, it can be added that, in the pre-gunpowder world, tribes in steppelands suited to raising camels (in MENA) and/or horses (in Inner Asia) also possessed a more tangible political advantage, namely, the production of a powerful military weapon, the warrior's steed.[2]

Saharan northwest Africa is one of several regions where the paradigm of tribes mobilizing into a political force to take over and found state power is persuasive. In the eleventh century, Lamtuna Berber tribes from the northwest Sahara founded the Almoravid empire with Marrakesh as their capital. This empire stretched from the northwest Sahara across North Africa to Al-Andalus. Centuries later, if Shaykh Mal'ainīn also represented an Ibn Khaldūnian moment, then notably he too set his sights on state power and the sultanate itself.

## States Creating Tribes

A second challenge to alleged opposition between tribes and state power questions whether tribes have existed independently of states. Rather, it has been suggested, tribes and state power have coexisted, with tribes not only creating state power but also vice versa. For Tapper (1990: 51), "tribes and states have created and maintained each other in a single system, though one of inherent instability." At its most extreme, this position takes the skeptical form that tribes are (always) the creation of state power, for instance, to facilitate the rule of state power over peoples or regions whose governance would otherwise prove problematic (e.g., Fried 1975; Sneath 2007). From such a perspective, the question is not one of tribes standing in contrast to state power, but rather how the notion of such a contrast has been brought into being, principally by ideas held about what state power is or ought to be: "The concept of the tribal is generated by its relationship to the state" (Sneath 2007: 16). A less extreme position acknowledging the role of state power in creating tribes considers how tribal order may be generated not only bottom up but also top down (Caton 1990: 102).

The reconsideration of the interdependence between tribe and state power has provoked renewed reflection on the North African trope of *makhzan* and *sībah*. Edmund Burke (1972) describes how, in the early twentieth century, French colonial authorities sought to rigidify a distinction between *makhzan* as a zone of state control on the part of the Moroccan sultanate and *sībah* as a zone outside state control by the sultanate. In parallel, other dichotomies were hardened, such as that between Arab and Berber. These exaggerated distinctions became, Burke suggests, a "Moroccan Vulgate." In hardening these distinctions, the French created a premise for their colonial incursion, namely, to extend the control of state power into the *sībah* areas of dubious or ineffective state control. Burke stresses, however, that earlier French scholars' studies of the Moroccan sultanate and its notions of *makhzan* and *sībah* had not conveyed such a rigid picture. Rather, scholars such as Edmond Doutté and Eugène Aubin had argued for a more nuanced relationship between the two zones, whereby the *makhzan* had influence on both *makhzan* and *sībah* (Burke 1972: 178–79).

As scholars rethought the relationship between tribes and state power, they returned to the neglected earlier nuances of the influence of the *makhzan* on the *sībah*. In his reading of Robert Montagne's account of how the cleavage of a tribe into two halves is more noticeable in *sībah* tribes that in those of the *makhzan*, Pierre Bonte (2008: 148) suggests seeing such cleavages as a sign of the influence of the *makhzan* on the *sībah*. Such cleavages, Bonte observes, played to the *makhzan*'s interests in preventing the emergence of a political power in the periphery that could threaten central state power. Tapper (1990: 70) concurs that tribes that, because of their high degree of segmentarity (cleaving into subsections, each balanced against other such subsections), have been seen as the most likely candidates for being independent of states are "those in a position—and with the motivation—to maximize their segmentarity, practically and ideologically, in opposition to either a real state or the idea of a state."

The view that state power can create and influence tribes, even if denied by tribes, is important in several ways to Western Sahara. The Spanish colonial administration, preferring, like its colonial peers elsewhere, to deal with an indigenous political leader to facilitate control, imbued the figure of the *shaykh* or tribal leader with greater powers than those with which the role had previously been accorded (San Martín 2010: 40–46). This expansion included the creation of new *shuyūkh*; interlocutors complained to Caro Baroja (1955: 44) that the colonial authorities had created *shuyūkh* for tributary tribes, where previously the position had been the preserve of tribute-collecting tribes. As regards Western Sahara's classification as a decolonization case, Moroccan claims to the territory, as presented to the ICJ, have drawn on the idea that present-day Western Sahara fell within the sultan's realm even when the ties between the sultan and tribes in Western Sahara did not correspond to what the ICJ could recognize as territorial sovereignty. Morocco argued that the precolonial Moroccan state was unique. Even when the sultan lacked temporal authority over an area and its people, as was especially the case in *bilād al-sībah* (into which Morocco claimed Western Sahara fell), the sultanate claimed still to have enjoyed and enacted the authority to appoint officials, collect taxes, and receive oaths of allegiance (Joffé 1986). The ICJ, however, found that "oaths of fealty were personal and not indicative of sovereign control" and that, "despite the accepted uniqueness of the Moroccan state at the moment of Spanish colonial occupation, religious ties did not constitute sovereignty" (Joffé 1986: 24). The ICJ finding was a blow to the international legitimacy of Morocco's claims, yet it did not deter Morocco from insisting on its claims and acting on them to annex part of the territory. From Morocco's point of view, the findings of the ICJ confirmed its claims, these claims merely corresponding to a different conception of sovereignty from the territorial control on which international relations, and decolonization, rested.

Morocco's claims to the ICJ drew heavily on its interpretation of the unique nature of the Moroccan sultanate. It has, nevertheless, been called into question whether present-day Western Sahara can be understood through the lens of Morocco's *bilād al-sībah*. Pablo San Martín (2010: 24) stresses that in Spanish Africanist colonial documentation "the southern borders of the sultanate of Morocco were never situated south of the Draa, that is, in the northern part of the Tarfaya strip, as a systematic analysis of the works published between 1880 and 1934 unmistakably shows." Present-day Western Sahara, he suggests, would thus fall historically outside *bilād al-sībah*, lying between it and the emirates of northern present-day Mauritania (2010: 74). He describes that Hassanophones recognized the specificity of this area by calling it *khaṭṭ al-khawf* (the line of fear), a distinctive area within the territory inhabited by Hassanophones, *ṭrāb al-bīḍān*. The question whether present-day Western Sahara falls within or beyond the historical bounds of *bilād al-sībah* is at the heart of the legal construction of the case for self-determination in Western Sahara (see Abu-Mershid and Farrar 2014).

## Rivals for Compatible Goals

Alongside the observations that tribes create state power and that state power creates tribes, a third criticism suggests that tribes and state power are rivals because they are devoted to compatible vocations and interests: to organize political authority for the purposes of governing, to resolve internal disputes, to engage in relations with other political units, to appropriate and distribute resources according to legitimized ideologies about the relationship between members, and to offer protection for people and resources as well as asylum for in-migrants.

Endorsements of the notion of compatible interests between tribes and state power vary in their breadth. For some commentators, the common interests of tribes and state power most apply in the context of a rapacious brand of state power. As Philip Salzman (2016), drawing on Gellner, explains, tribes and state power were long-standing rivals because, as long as state power focused primarily on the appropriation of resources from its governed population rather than provision for subjects' welfare (in other words, when state power was run by Gellner's "thugs"), its closest competitor for the appropriation of resources was none other than the tribes who preferred to appropriate resources for themselves. Potential compatibility between tribes and state power has also been qualified on the grounds of perceived outstanding differences between the social and political relations that each can accommodate. For Tapper (1990: 70), "The essence of [the tribe] is indeed kinship and egalitarian democracy (the basis of a segmentary lineage system), whereas that of [the state] is territoriality (the basis of communities, rivalries and alliances) and central authority (the basis of patronage network)." Salzman (2016) likewise stresses a contrast: that tribal society rests on the dispersion of access to the means of coercion (arms) among a group of adult males not under the authority of a central leader and a limited extent of occupational specialization among tribe members. In contrast, for Salzman state power centralizes the means of coercion in the hands of a specialized group beyond the access of most members of the political community and accommodates greater potential for occupational specialization among members, with accompanying inequality and stratification.

The alleged distinctions between tribes and state power are not always taken to be so clear-cut, however. In her study of sedentary agricultural tribes in Rāziḥ, north Yemen, based on fieldwork in the 1970s to 1990s, Shelagh Weir (2007: 4) approaches tribes there as "mini sovereignty domains." Tribes have defined territories with borders; internal administrative systems; socially and occupationally stratified populations comprising natives, immigrants, defectors, and asylum seekers; and permanent offices of leadership. The distinctions that she points out between tribes and state power, namely, that tribes are part of the state in Yemen and that, in the case Weir addresses, tribes are "tiny 'face-to-face' polities with simple aims and administrations" (308)—seem to be differences of scale more than differences of kind. Earlier, Weir poses the question of whether, though not borne out for Rāziḥ, the notion of egalitarian social relations facilitated by segmentation—such as those to which Tapper (1990) and Salzman (2014) allude in arguing for distinctions between tribes and state power—may still be useful as an ideal type for comparative purposes elsewhere, such as for mobile pastoralists (Weir 2007: 5).

David Sneath (2007: 121–56) takes up exactly this question in his reinterpretation of "tribal societies" in Inner Asia, in which he discusses the Middle East—a region that has been iconic for this theme. For Sneath, the existence of an egalitarian, segmentary tribe does not live up to ethnographic scrutiny. Rather, tribes that were, according to the segmentary model, meant to be egalitarian and antihierarchical (and, for some commentators, kinship-based) proved on close analysis to be composed of stratified, hierarchical social relations with competing elites, such as Talal Asad (1970) showed for the Kababish Arabs in Sudan.

Such skepticism as to the empirical existence of egalitarian tribes calls into question the grounds on which distinctions between tribes and state power have been suggested. Sneath argues for the idea of the "state relation" (see Introduction), which he defines as the existence of "political authorities, systems of rules or arbitration, and the distinction between governing and governed persons" (Sneath 2007: 10). As he understands it, this "state relation" was not exclusive to a model of centralized state power over a defined territory but, in the premodern world, could exist in polities governed through dispersed forms of power often located in genealogically based hereditary elites. Such a perspective shakes the grounds for claiming strong distinctions between tribes and state power.

In approaching present-day Western Sahara, I wish both to draw upon and to expand upon the notion that tribes and state power can be understood as compatible. Anthropologists from Edward Evans-Pritchard onward have explored how zones that lack state power are not necessarily regions of disorder; I explore here how they might be zones of other social relations of sovereignty. I see both state power and tribes—in certain historical circumstances such as the eve of colonialism in Western Sahara—as two of the projects of sovereignty operating historically in northwest Africa. Most easily recognized as a project of sovereignty in the region has been state power in the form of a centralized authority seeking to govern, tax, and conscript the population of a fixed territory. In the case of the Moroccan sultanate, this was the *makhzan* ruling *bilād al-makhzan*. The Ottoman empire operated such a center of state power in coastal Algeria, too. Zones of claimed but disputed and ineffective state control, such as the *bilād al-sībah* of the Moroccan sultanate, came to be presented by the eve of French colonialism, Burke (1972) has shown, as if they were zones of the absence of state power. Yet earlier readings (Edmond Doutté, Eugène Aubin) of how the *makhzan* may have shaped the *sībah* in particular ways have now been reasserted (Bonte 2008: 148). This suggests how *bilād al-sībah* was not so much a zone of lack but, rather, in my terms, a zone of different kinds of social relations of sovereignty. Likewise, present-day Western Sahara, which the ICJ placed neither in *bilād al-sībah* nor in present-day Mauritania's emirates, is considered here as a zone of a different set of social relations of sovereignty, not a zone of lack. To examine that project of sovereignty, I turn to the meanings in the context of Western Sahara of the contested term *qabīlah*.

## Tribe: A Polysemous Term

*Qabīlah* is one of a number of terms in use in the Middle East and North Africa commonly translated as "tribe." The meaning of *qabīlah* has come to be highly contested, especially, as we have seen, in its relationship to state power. The difficulties in defining the term are only compounded by the fact that tribes across the Middle East and North Africa are "diverse polities" (Weir 2007: 1). Thus there is considerable skepticism that a single term can be useful for comparative analysis (see Tapper 1990). Acknowledging these difficulties, Shelagh Weir (2007: 2) nevertheless argues that it is still useful to retain tribe as a "portmanteau term . . . for territorial polities whose members share a common allegiance, which exist in a matrix of similar polities with which they have relations, and which have always been potentially or actually formally subordinate to some kind of 'state'."

*Qabīlah* or local equivalents, however, must be understood as dynamic terms. The meanings attributed to *qabīlah* not only vary geographically but also evolve over time in a given setting. Thus historians and anthropologists have illuminated historical junctures during which actors changed the meaning of *qabīlah* or an equivalent term (Shryock 1997; Casciarri 2006;

Lecocq 2010). Yet as Weir goes on to analyze for Rāziḥ, Yemen, even beyond geographical and historical distinctions in the meanings of *qabīlah*, the term may be used with multiple meanings within a particular ethnographic setting. Thus, in Rāziḥ, *qabīlah*, as well as terms for its component parts such as *bayt*, are, in fact, used polysemously. On the one hand, *qabīlah* is "applied to a hierarchy of sociologically distinct, nested structures which . . . constitute some kind of politico-legal grouping or alliance larger than a descent-based clan" (Weir 2007: 78); yet, when Rāziḥis "want to stress or exaggerate the solidarity or status of other structures," they sometimes refer to them too by the same term, *qabīlah*. Such polysemy is by no means exceptional to Rāziḥis (Weir 2007: 78). Polysemy in the use of *qabīlah* for multiple "levels" within tribal structures has been observed in Cyrenaica (Albergoni 2000). Lecocq (2010: 11) describes a similar polysemy in the use of *tewsit* for multiple political entities and administrative units among the Touareg. Perhaps such polysemy has been more widely the case than has been suggested in accounts of anthropologists, colonial administrators, or indigenous actors keen to present a clear "explanation" of tribes and their structures.

The diversity and dynamism in the meanings of *qabīlah* underscore the importance of specifying the ethnographic context to which any discussion of *qabīlah* relations applies. My examination of (some of the) meanings of *qabīlah* for Western Sahara on the eve of Spanish colonialism is intended as specific to this ethnographic context. (Unless otherwise specified, further discussion of the term *qabīlah* in this book should be taken to refer to the *qabīlah* in its ethnographic manifestations in the territory that has become Western Sahara.) *Qabīlah* relations in *ṭrāb al-bīḍān*, the territory inhabited by Hassanophones, may have shared similarities, but they also clearly varied (for instance, emirates developed in northern present-day Mauritania from the late eighteenth century). Thus, the present discussion does not attempt to discuss *qabīlah* relations across *ṭrāb al-bīḍān*, but limits itself to the area of present-day Western Sahara. I seek to recognize a diversity of meanings even within this context and point out similarities and differences with other related or analogous contexts in the northwest Sahara and MENA more broadly. I analyze social relations that I take to be constitutive of a *qabīlah*, such as rights and responsibilities, the management of resources, and social and political stratification. I then address more specific details such as the nomenclature and scale of *qabā'il* in Western Sahara, although the discussion offered here necessarily falls short of a historical analysis such as can be found elsewhere (Norris 1986; Caratini 1989a; López Bargados 2003; Lydon 2009). To the large corpus of analyses of the social relations of tribes in the Sahara, North Africa and Middle East, the present analysis offers two contributions. First, I perceive the *qabīlah* as a "sphere of consented solidarity," the terms of consent varying to include coercion. I seek to capture through the notion of (ambiguous) consented solidarity the conflicting dynamics of inclusive participation, as well as stratification and exploitation. Second, drawing on these conflicting dynamics I understand "*qabīlah* relations" as social relations comprising dual dynamics, both solidarity to a named *qabīlah* and a stratified hierarchy of status groups.

Perhaps the most uncontroversial quality of a *qabīlah* in Western Sahara (and elsewhere) is that it has a name.[3] Members feel a strong sense of solidarity, which entails collective responsibility for offenses committed by or against a member of the group. In the precolonial setting, membership in a *qabīlah* in Western Sahara granted access to resources in the form of pasturelands associated with a named *qabīlah* and priority access to water resources in those pasturelands. Prior to colonial "pacification," persons wishing to traverse or graze in pasturelands associated with another *qabīlah* had to undertake an act of submission, the sacrifice of an animal, or else risk attack.[4] Membership in a *qabīlah* may be preferably expressed in a discourse of kinship and agnatic descent from a shared ancestor. In fact, however, historically persons might either be born into a *qabīlah* or recruited into membership through political means such as a pact, *'aṣabah*, also entailing the sacrifice of an animal (Caro Baroja 1955: 18–22). In some cases, as we shall see, there is no claim among *qabīlah* members to shared descent from a common ancestor.[5]

The extent to which solidarity and corporate responsibility among members of tribes can go all the way back to a claimed, often eponymous, common ancestor, is one of the points of controversy for scholars of tribes in MENA. According to the model of segmentation made famous for anthropologists by Evans-Pritchard (1940), whereby a tribe is subdivided into nested sections and subsections, solidarity is activated at the highest segmentary level exclusive of common ancestry with the offending party. An Arab proverb captures this principle: "I against my brother, my brother and I against my cousin, my cousin and I against strangers." Nevertheless, anthropologists have called into question the helpfulness of this model. As Emrys Peters (1967) showed, disputes among the Bedouin in Cyrenaica were not in practice resolved according to the principles of segmentation.

In what became Western Sahara, a *qabīlah* was subdivided into sections and subsections. The terms for this given by Caro Baroja (1955: 14, 16) are *fakhdh* and *ahl*. As is the case for tribes elsewhere, the extent to which in the territory which became Western Sahara the principle of segmentation informed the way disputes were conceptualized and played out in practice must be problematized. According to David Hart (1998), among the Rgaybāt, the *qabīlah* that rose to dominance in northern Western Sahara from the seventeenth to the nineteenth centuries (see Caratini 1989a), such strong emphasis was placed on solidarity among all Rgaybāt (who numbered several thousands) that conflicts, such as over livestock raiding or compensation for offenses, did not take place between sections and subsections.

Another polemical question in the analysis of tribes in MENA is that of relations of stratification and (in)dependence, both within tribes, between tribes, and between tribes and state power. As noted, interpretations about the relationship between *qabā'il* and the Moroccan sultanate on the eve of Spanish colonialism have been crucial to the very constitution of Western Sahara as a decolonization case. It is also important to take into account stratification within a *qabīlah* and between *qabā'il*. In the Sahara, control over resources has long been mediated through control over people. Any member of a *qabīlah*, and indeed any *qabīlah*, can be situated within hierarchical relations that take the form of status groups. The existence of these hierarchical status groups contravenes the notion of tribes as egalitarian, and their existence has sometimes been underrecognized. For instance, Gellner (1990: 110) suggests that the hierarchical status groups of the Touareg, Saharan neighbors of the Sahrawis, are "atypical," although they are "also occasionally encountered elsewhere, though in less extreme form." Stratified status groups, such as slaves, butchers, and artisans, have nonetheless been observed widely in MENA, not only across the Sahara but also beyond (see e.g., Patai 1962; Lancaster 1981; Weir 2007).

The status groups of Hassanophones are typically represented along the following lines. Of highest and noblest status were warrior and religious elites. The warrior status group was known by several names: *ḥassan*, named after the Beni Hassan arabophone tribes who invaded Saharan northwest Africa from the thirteenth to the sixteenth centuries; and *ahl al-madfaʿ* (the people of the gun). Until colonial "pacification," tribes of the warrior status warred against each other and were known for camel raiding and slave raiding beyond *ṭrāb al-bīḍān*. Religious elites were known as *ahl al-kitāb* (the people of the book) or *shurafā'* (descendants of the prophet).[6] In the local accounts of the Arab conquest of Saharan northwest Africa, warrior elites were claimed to be descended from the Arab invaders and religious elites from the existing Berber elites. As elsewhere in North Africa (Gellner and Micaud 1973), in the northwest Sahara, clear-cut distinctions between "Arabs" and "Berbers" must be questioned, however (Bonte 2008: 197–238). Tribes might change status from "Arab" to "Berber" or vice versa over time. After warrior and religious elites came their tributaries, known locally through the term *znāgah*. Following them were artisan specialists, *muʿallimīn*, and griots, *igawen*, who were more common in present-day Mauritania but were not unknown in what would become Western Sahara.[7] Artisans could affiliate (and change affiliation) to patron tribes. Freed slaves, *ḥarāṭīn*, and, below them, slaves, *ʿabīd*, have been conceptually portrayed in some accounts as occupying the lowest status groups (e.g. Caro Baroja 1955: 50–51). Nevertheless, a Hassaniya proverb suggests that *muʿallimīn* were regarded as of lower status than even slaves (Caro Baroja 1955: 47). Strict marriage rules prohibited women from marrying into a status group lower than their own and prohibited *muʿallimīn* and *igawen* men or women from marrying outside their status group. (The revolutionary reworkings of these prohibitions are considered in Chapter 5). These prohibitions reinforce the notion of a hassanophone "social pyramid" with clear distinctions between status groups.

Nevertheless, it is problematic to match the notion of such an ordered hierarchy with named *qabā'il*. There could be no such thing as a *qabīlah* of artisans, for instance. Rather, any particular family of *muʿallimīn* was attached to a strong *qabīlah*—and might switch allegiances if circumstances made this necessary or desirable. Thus, it may be more helpful to think of *qabīlah* relations as situating persons within a series of hierarchies and oppositions: free/unfree, strong/weak, lineage/non-lineage (Lecocq 2010: 7). Some *qabā'il* were strong and free, and their members kept lineages to provide the basis of their claims to be considered so. Such a *qabīlah* could attract protégés of the lower ranks of status groups: *znāgah*, *muʿallimīn*, freed slaves, and slaves. Protégés could benefit from access to the pasturelands of their protectors for their livestock and could call upon their protectors for taking up collective responsibility if one of their numbers was killed or committed a crime. The benefits of protection came at a price. In precolonial times, it was forbidden for protégés to bear arms. As Caro Baroja notes (1955: 33), in the 1950s, those formerly of *znāgah* status taunted their erstwhile protectors that "everyone was *znāgah* now," for Spain had forbidden indigenous inhabitants of the Spanish Sahara from bearing arms.[8] Before colonialism, *znāgah*, who were weak, dependent *qabā'il*, also paid tribute in livestock to their protectors. Tribute could take various forms (Caro Baroja 1955: 34–41). One form of tribute was *ḥurmah*, a payment made annually directly from the tent of a client to the tent of a patron. Another was *ghāfar*, paid from the head of *qabīlah* or section thereof to the head of another.[9]

Stratification and exploitation within a *qabīlah* exist in tension with discourses of egalitarianism among members of a named *qabīlah*. One manifestation of egalitarian discourse is the notion of collective responsibility: that each male adult is equally responsible for providing/claiming compensation when one of his number is the victim/perpetrator of an offense. An egalitarian discourse also manifests itself in the structures of political decision making, another polemical theme in analyses of tribes in MENA. Some commentators have emphasized the apparent lack or weakness of political hierarchy for tribes or sections thereof to support the notion of egalitarian social relations. From such a perspective, the tribal leader, in arabophone contexts commonly known as *shaykh*, has been seen a leader who is "first among equals" and has no greater power than the extent of his powers of persuasion (e.g., Lancaster 1981; Leinhardt 2001). Other accounts, however, have placed greater emphasis on the role of hereditary elites in governing tribes (e.g., Asad 1970).

As regards present-day Western Sahara, on the one hand, the *shaykh* has been seen as a figure enjoying a certain kind of political prestige above that of his peers. For Caratini (2003: 197), this arose from his belonging to a particular genealogical group, his reputation for wisdom, and his network of alliances and protection. For Caro Baroja's (1955: 24) interlocutors, there were no set characteristics of a *shaykh*, and the criteria varied over time, although it was important that he was both "rich" and "old." On the other hand, any authority enjoyed by a *shaykh* in the precolonial context coexisted with that of collective bodies for decision making.

According to Caro Baroja (1955: 23–24), a *qabīlah* or section had a council, *jamā'ah*, in which its most notable, wise, and respected members gathered to take decisions for governing. He explains that compensation offered by the family of the perpetrator of a crime was put for consideration to the *jamā'ah* (18); laws for the *qabīlah* were decided by the *jamā'ah* (44); the *jamā'ah* could also form the basis for selecting an executive council empowered to make a treaty (24). Alongside the *jamā'ah* was another institution of collective decision making, called *ait arba'īn*. The name is composed of the

Berber word *ait*, for "family" or "house" (often used in the name of a tribe), and the number forty, *arba'īn* (in Arabic). The term *ait arba'īn* is not exclusive to Hassanophones, councils going by that name also being found in berberophone southern Morocco (Hart 1998). Among Hassanophones, the *ait arba'īn* has been understood as a consultative and decision-making body at a higher level than the *jamā'ah* of a *qabīlah*. Some accounts present the *ait arba'īn* as a tribal (Hodges 1983: 14) or intertribal (Pazzanita 2006: 13) council that met in times of serious difficulty, such as undertaking hostility against other *qabā'il*. By asking older Sahrawis whom I met and those Saharawi who professed to being knowledgeable in the history of the Saharawi people about the *ait arba'īn*, I gathered a number of other interpretations. In one account, the *ait arba'īn* was held whenever a pool of rainwater (known as a *ḍiyah*) collected, and, at the meeting, it was decided how the water was to be kept clean from soiling. Anyone who infringed that agreement would be punished.[10] In another account, the *ait arba'īn* only applied to the Tekna *qabā'il*.[11] In a third account, I was told that there had been a finite number of *ait arba'īn* meetings in the history of the Western Sahara tribes, one among the Tekna, another among the Rgaybāt, and another among the Awlād Delīm.[12]

If available accounts of *jamā'ah* and *ait arba'īn* are inconclusive about their scope, scale, and purpose, there are indications of Sahrawis' attitudes toward them. In the 1950s, Rgaybāt interlocutors took pride in their convictions that decisions were taken at such councils (Caro Baroja 1955: 23). Pride in the perceived democratic ethos of a perceived heritage of *jamā'ah* and *ait arba'īn* had become a nationalized discourse among Sahrawi refugees in the late 2000s (see Chapter 2). Nevertheless, to the extent that these institutions can be understood as "democratic," this can only be in the limited sense of a "gentilicial democracy" (Bourdieu 1962). The field of participation was only extended to a narrow category of senior adult males. Women, and weak or dependent males, such as those recently accepted as new members of a *qabīlah* following a pact, would have been excluded (Caro Baroja 1955: 23). Caro Baroja's interlocutors' complaints that a *shaykh* should only exist for strong tribes raises the question of whether councils were specific to strong tribes. One of the institutions that was locally taken to represent the allegedly egalitarian ethos of the *qabīlah* rested, then, both on structures of participation and exclusion.

In present-day Western Sahara, members of a *qabīlah* are endowed with shared and asymmetrical rights and responsibilities with regard to persons and resources. Drawing on this tension between participation and exclusion, I interpret a *qabīlah* in Western Sahara as "a sphere of consented solidarity." This "sphere" is inherently flexible, its contours liable to vary by situation. When a *qabīlah* assumes its most powerful manifestation, the sphere includes, for a strong *qabīlah*, various protégés and attached groups: tributaries (who may constitute a weak *qabīlah*), *mu'allimīn*, freed slaves, and slaves. Protégés could claim protection and access to resources by virtue of their inclusion in the most expansive manifestation of the sphere of solidarity. Yet protection could be withdrawn from them, and such protégés could be excluded from participation in the political institutions of decision making of an inner, narrower "sphere."

The extension of, and submission to, protection raises the question of consent; the importance of consent for understanding the workings of a *qabīlah* is perhaps suggested in the term *qabīlah* itself. The Arabic root of *qabīlah*, *q-b-l*, has the meanings of "assent, consent."[13] But I use the term here drawing on the ambiguities of consent: for "consent" may be coerced. Certainly, coercion—in the form of the risk of violence—underpinned protégés' consent to the terms of their "protection." The question of consent, central to political life and governance, also points to how the *qabīlah* is a space of governance. The members of any *qabīlah*, whatever its position with regard to other *qabā'il*, are governed and subject to a set of rules. In practice the rules are generated and imposed by those with the most advantageous position with respect to the asymmetrical distribution of rights and responsibilities.

"Solidarity" is in reference to the solidarity, *'aṣabīyah*, that is meant to bind and motivate members of a *qabīlah*. But I employ it with the proviso that solidarity subject to consent is conditional and fragile, vulnerable to breaking up into crisis or lack of solidarity. Indeed, the *qabā'il* of Western Sahara (Caratini 1989b) and those of the hassanophone zone more generally (Bonte 2008), as well as farther afield, are hives of internal competition (even if theoretical models have led to the ethnographic neglect of such dynamics of competition).

It is when a *qabīlah* takes its most powerful manifestation as a sphere of consented solidarity, enjoining shared and asymmetrical rights and responsibilities with regard to persons and resources, that, in specific historical moments, I suggest that it can be understood as a project of sovereignty. I understand the social relations of that project of sovereignty as comprising two potentially conflicting thrusts: on the one hand, loyalty and solidarity among *qabīlah* members and, on the other, stratified hierarchical social relations.

## *Qabā'il* in Western Sahara

Any representation of *qabā'il* in Western Sahara leads quickly to the question of polysemy in the meaning(s) or *qabīlah* and its constituent parts. Many Sahrawis have come to see their tribes as falling, by the eve of Spanish colonialism, into three significant groups: the Tekna, straddling southern Morocco and the northeast part of present-day Western Sahara; the Rgaybāt, spanning from northwest present-day Western Sahara to inner northern present-day Mauritania; and the Awlād Delīm, dominant in southwest present-day Western Sahara and coastal Mauritania. Yet the Tekna, having no claimed common ancestor, are not locally considered technically a *qabīlah*, but as a collection of *qabā'il*. There being no local "segmentarian" term to describe the Tekna as a whole, commentators have sometimes referred to them as a "confederation" (e.g., Lydon 2009). The Rgaybāt, whose members claim descent from an alleged common ancestor, Sid Ahmed al-Rgaybi, are technically a *qabīlah*, and referred to as such (e.g., Caratini 1989a). Their sections and population are on such a large scale that the Rgaybāt have also been considered by some commentators as a "confederation" (e.g., San Martín 2010; Zunes and Mundy 2010). The importance of supra-*qabīlah* alliances was also recognized by Caro Baroja (1955: 21), who writes of "'confederations' of *cabilas* [*sic*]." The recourse of commentators on present-day Western Sahara to the notion of confederation is all the more remarkable because no Hassaniya equivalent is used by Sahrawis.

In parallel with the tendency to promote the Rgaybāt as a whole to a "confederation," there is also a tendency to refer to their sections through the term *qabīlah*. Thus, in his list of *qabā'il* for Western Sahara, Hodges (1982) refers to the two main divisions among Rgaybāt, Rgaybāt al-Sharg (of the east) and Rgaybāt al-Sahel (of the west) as a *qabīlah* (see Appendix 2). In the late 2000s, Sahrawi refugees also referred to the "sections" of Rgaybāt as *qabā'il*. (When questioned directly on their use of *qabīlah* as regards the Rgaybāt, some refugees expressed awareness that, in referring to the sections of Rgaybāt as *qabā'il*, they diverged from Sahrawis in Moroccan-controlled Western Sahara, who were reported to use *qabīlah* for Rgaybāt, and not sections thereof.) In addition to variety in the use of *qabīlah*, there is also variety in the use of terms for "sections" and "subsections." Whereas for Hodges (1982: 342–45), the order from larger to smaller sections is *qabīlah*, *ahl*, and then lastly *fakhdh*, for Caro Baroja (1955: 14, 16), the order is *qabīlah*, *fakhdh*, and *ahl*. Recognizing that other terms are also used, such as *'arsh*, Caro Baroja admits that he is unable to suggest the range of persons to which this term applies (16). I address the legacies of segmentation for the state-movement in Chapter 2.

One possible source of local pressure for *qabīlah* to be used for different "levels" of segments is the variation in population size of each *qabīlah*. While questions regarding accuracy surround population figures for those who have come to call themselves Sahrawis, the figures collected by the Spanish colonial administration indicate the range of size of *qabā'il* (Table 1). The breakdown of voters per tribe in October 1966 gives a more detailed picture of the potential variation in population figures between tribes (Table 2). The final Spanish census of 1974 offers a further perspective on the population breakdown (Table 3).

The scale of a *qabīlah* with a presence in Western Sahara varied considerably, then. This variation cannot only be attributed to a majority of the members of a *qabīlah* living outside Spanish Sahara. A tribe such as the descendants of Shaykh Mal'ainīn (429 male voters in 1966), whose founder had

Table 1. Tents per Tribe in Western Sahara, Spanish Figures for 1954 (Mercer 1976: 127)

| *Tribe (original spelling)* | *Number of tents* |
| --- | --- |
| Rgaybat | 2,500 |
| Delim | 650 |
| Izarguiyen | 500 |
| Tidrarin | 500 |
| Arousien | 350 |
| Yagut | 350 |
| Masa Ali | 350 |
| Ma el Ainin | 200 |
| Lahsen | 200 |
| Sba | 100 |
| Usa | 100 |
| Others | 500 |
| Total | 6,300 |

Table 2. Male voters per tribe in Western Sahara, Spanish Figures for 1966 (Mercer 1976: 127)

| *Tribe [original spelling given]* | *Male voters* |
|---|---|
| Rgaybat Sahel (8 fractions) | 4,900 |
| Rgaybat Laguacem (9 fractions) | 3,286 |
| Awlad Delim (5 fractions) | 1,964 |
| Izarguien | 1,444 |
| Tidrarin | 1,101 |
| Arousien | 515 |
| Yagut | 139 |
| Musa Ali | 213 |
| Ma el Ainin | 429 |
| Lahsen | 709 |
| Sba | 56 |
| Berik Allah | 311 |
| Taubalet | 106 |
| Meyat | 102 |
| Filala | 95 |
| Aita | 93 |
| Foicat | 81 |
| Skarna | 49 |
| Miscellaneous | 840 |

died only at the beginning of the twentieth century, was much smaller in scale than older tribes.

The polysemy of *qabīlah* in Western Sahara extends to variations in political status, best understood in relation to the status groups: warriors, religious elites, tributaries, artisans, freed slaves, and slaves. The place of a whole *qabīlah*, and individual members, within the oppositions of strong/weak was not fixed. A *qabīlah* could change status from having been strong and independent to weak and protected. This befell the large *qabīlah* Awlād Tidrārīn, who, in the nineteenth century, became tributaries of the Awlād Delīm. They only "recovered" from that status in the changed circumstances of Spanish colonialism, when the distinction between strong and weak was undermined by the colonial state. Persons and families could also change *qabīlah* according to the political vicissitudes of seeking and needing protection. One elderly man in the refugee camps recalled a story illustrating this point. He explained to me why a mutual friend, who was from an artisan family, belonged to a Tekna *qabīlah*, whereas his ancestors had belonged to what was referred to in

Table 3. Summary of Spanish Census of 1974 (Solà-Martín 2007: 52–53)

| *Tribe (original spelling)* | *Total* |
|---|---|
| Erguibat Charg | 20,276 |
| Erguibat Sahel | 18,247 |
| Izarguien | 7,984 |
| Ait Lahsen | 3,540 |
| Arosien | 2,858 |
| Ulad Delim | 5,383 |
| Ulad Tidrarin | 4,842 |
| Chorfa | 4,632 |
| Northern tribes | 3,374 |
| Coastal and southern tribes | 2,362 |

the camps as a Rgaybāt *qabīlah*. Some generations ago, our mutual friend's ancestor had killed a man. His Rgaybāt protectors at the time had refused to offer to pay on his behalf the blood money, *dīyah*, the payment of which would avoid the threat of the offended party's retaliation. The ancestor was left with no choice but to flee with his family to another *qabīlah*, seeking their protection. Thus he came to "belong" to a new *qabīlah* (among the Tekna).

If, as we saw in the case of "everyone becoming *znāgah*," Spanish colonialism had already begun to undermine differences between status groups, then the flexibility within *qabīlah* relations was further eroded by the administrative course of the Western Sahara conflict. The focus of the UN Mission for a Referendum in Western Sahara, MINURSO, in the 1990s was on registering voters (for an eventual referendum on self-determination) on the grounds of proven membership in a tribe that had been present in Spanish Sahara. Each person wishing to vote had to "prove" membership in a tribe, be recognized as a member by a *shaykh*, and thus be inscribed in the voter register. In the moment of would-be decolonization, a colonial style survey assumed and created rigid identities, putting an end to the previous flexibility and ambiguity in *qabīlah* membership.

## Tribe and State as Projects of Sovereignty

Drawing on the growing interest of anthropologists in the points of compatibility between state power and tribes at certain historical junctures, I have argued here that state power is not the exclusive form of a project of sovereignty. I explored how *qabīlah*, a dynamic term not only between ethnographic contexts but also within a particular context, could be understood in the context of present-day Western Sahara as a sphere of consented solidarity where the terms of consent could vary to include coercion. I stressed the hierarchy and stratification as well as the solidarity encompassed in *qabīlah* relations. In specific historical circumstances, such as on the eve of colonialism, I understand the *qabīlah* in Western Sahara as a project of sovereignty and *qabīlah* relations as social relations of sovereignty. Through political institutions such as the *jamāʿah*, *ait arbaʿīn*, and *shaykh*, a politically dominant *qabīlah* governed, resolved disputes, and appropriated and distributed resources. That *qabīlah* relations were implicated in these activities leads me to argue in this book that *qabīlah* relations were recycled in the state-movement's efforts to create the social relations of another project of sovereignty, state power. Yet the *qabīlah* was also, initially for the state-movement, a rival to its state power. The state-movement was initially determined to overwrite and obscure *qabīlah* relations, as the following chapter explores.

CHAPTER 2

# Revolutionary Foundations: Unmaking Tribes and Making State Power

> We cannot help but believe . . . that the lines of tribe shall soon dissolve.
>
> —Barack Obama, Inaugural Address, 2009

Fanna was one of the few women who worked at a market stall in one of the markets that, by the late 2000s, existed in every district of the Sahrawi refugee camps (see Chapter 6). She and her husband took turns to run a shop in one of the Auserd markets, in which they sold clothes and shoes (brought in from Mauritania or elsewhere in Algeria) and offered sewing repairs. Both of them were adept in using the hand-powered sewing machine in the shop—the kind of machine to which many a household wished to have access for sewing tent sections, clothing, and other items. In 2008 I wanted some cloth bags to be sewn. Initially I had only seen Fanna's husband at the sewing machine. When I approached him to see if he was interested in making up the bags for me, he directed me to continue the discussions with Fanna, informing me when I could return to find her at the shop. After I met Fanna, she soon set about running up bag after bag. Over my visits to the shop to drop off cloth and collect bags, she patiently shared her story in response to my questions. Probably in her late thirties at the time, she talked calmly of her hard work over the years for the state-movement and, more recently, in the shop. Reflecting on how she owed her education and more to the state-movement, she summed up her feelings: "The state was my father." In a context marked by patrilineality and patriarchy, a father represents his offspring's access to material and social resources, including, for Sahrawis, social identity as part of a *qabīlah*. Fanna's words suggested that her father and the *qabīlah* he represented had been replaced in these roles by the state-movement.

This chapter explores the state-movement's aspirations to replace the *qabīlah*. The previous chapter situated the social relations of the *qabīlah* in what became Western Sahara within debates about sovereignty in northwest Africa. I suggested that the social relations of the *qabīlah* in Western Sahara, rather than constituting a "lack" of sovereignty, served at specific times as a project of sovereignty in their own right. Here I consider how the state-movement sought to wield a double-edged sword: it aimed simultaneously, sometimes literally through the same policies, at unmaking the social relations of the *qabīlah* and making the social relations of the state-movement. In other words, the unmaking of tribes and the making of state power were intimately related and could be mutually reinforcing.

Throughout this book, I interpret the coordinated unmaking of tribes and making of state power among Sahrawi refugees as a palimpsest. On the one hand, that which had gone before was to be made unseeable and unknowable. An effective means of achieving this was to produce "the new" to be superimposed in the place of "the old." In this chapter I trace the superimposition of new forms of segmentation and new institutions that constituted a tangible public domain. On the other hand, in parallel—and in contrast—to such "overwriting to obscure," at times that which had gone before was intended to be seeable and knowable within the context of the new. This leads to a "trompe-l'oeil" effect, whereby partial overwriting incorporates an intended impression of an underlying element. This effect can be observed in the state-movement's seeking to substitute its own institutions of participation and representation for those associated with the *qabīlah*, while at the same time making claims to "continue" and "expand" the latter's alleged democratic legacies.

Over the course of tracing these two techniques of palimpsest (overwriting and trompe-l'oeil), the chapter acquaints the unfamiliar reader with the layout of the camps and the institutional make-up of the state-movement. For readers already familiar with the liberation movement of Western Sahara, the discussion draws attention, as has hitherto rarely been the case, to how the state-movement's structures unmake the social relations of tribes, even as they make the social relations of state power.

## Overwriting Segmentation: Tents

Tribes in the Middle East and North Africa (MENA) are (in)famously associated with segmentation. As discussed in the previous chapter, in the prerevolutionary *qabīlah* of Western Sahara, as may be the case for other patrilineal settings in MENA, membership in a *qabīlah* places each person in a series of nested structures. For those who came to call themselves Sahrawis, these structures situated ego within an *ahl* (family), *'arsh* (branch), and *qabīlah* (tribe) (these were the terms preferred by refugees). Since—among other characteristics judged as unfavorable for a liberation movement (see Introduction)—*qabīlah* relations entailed hierarchical dynamics, one of the revolutionary goals adopted by the state-movement was to abolish tribes. In order to help achieve this, in the early revolutionary period (from 1975 to 1991), the state-movement sought to overwrite the forms of affiliation associated with the *qabīlah* and to situate persons within alternative systems of segmentation.

The most visible alternative system of segmentation pertained to the physical layout of tents in the camps, *mukhayyamāt* (in exile), as compared to tents' layout in encampments, *firgān* (in pasturelands). A visitor to the camps in the 1980s would have seen row upon row of cloth tents of the kind provided by aid agencies as emergency, temporary (in theory) shelter. This scene contrasted sharply with the image of a nomadic encampment, known among Hassanophones as a *frīg* (pl. *firgān*).

In classical Arabic, *farīq*—from which *frīg* is likely derived—means "team." Yet among the meanings of the classical root *f-r-q* is "separate, disperse." The *frīg* can indeed be understood as a part that has been separated out from a larger unit: the *qabīlah* or a section thereof. A *frīg* was composed of several goat-hair tents, *khiyām* (s. *khaymah*).[1] The heads of tent households within the same *frīg* would usually belong to the same section of the same *qabīlah*.[2] A *frīg* would follow the same migratory schedule as nearby *firgān*. Members of coordinated *firgān* belonged to the same *qabīlah* or section thereof; that is, they belonged to the same "sphere of consented solidarity" (Chapter 1) that offered protection. Some tents would house persons taking on the role, within that *qabīlah*, of protectors and others the protected. There might be attached families from a different *qabīlah* in name, but they would be part of a *frīg*, or a group of *firgān*, on the grounds of their attachment to the *qabīlah* of their protectors. In the decades preceding exile, it was reported by Molina Campuzano (1954: 8) that, following Spain's "pacification" of the tribes in 1934, the phenomenon had emerged of "heterogeneous" *firgān* that housed persons from different *qabā'il*. The fact that Molina Campuzano drew attention to this as new reinforces the fact that, until then, a *frīg* was associated with the identity of a particular *qabīlah*. By the 1950s, a *frīg* was typically composed of three to fifteen tents; a *frīg* of up to forty tents had become rare by that time, and the reports from earlier times of up to two hundred tents for defensive purposes virtually unknown (Caro Baroja 1955: 258).

Caro Baroja's sketch maps of the layout of *firgān* visited in the early 1950s show how the positioning of tents within the *frīg* reflected potentially hierarchical social relations and socioeconomic distinction. A *frīg* typically took the form of what he terms a "broken" row of tents (Caro Baroja 1955: 258). His sketches show how the tent of a *shaykh* might take the central position in that row, and the tents of slaves would be situated behind the tents of their owners (205, 220). Enough space was left in the layout of the *frīg* for the animals owned by a particular tent to be gathered near and behind them, without becoming mixed up with the animals of other tents (258). Finally, each *frīg* would typically be built out of sight of any other. The prerevolutionary nomadic encampment made manifest the social and economic hierarchy among members of the *frīg*. At the same time, it set itself up as a separate unit, albeit in a relationship of neighborhood with nearby *firgān*.

Caratini (2003) describes how the layout of the refugee camps as she knew them in the mid-1990s presented a sharp contrast with a *frīg*. She suggests that the refugee camps' row upon row of, for the most part, identical cloth tents, albeit interspersed by then with simple mud-brick rooms, represented an image of social equality (Caratini 2003: 33–34). Refugees recalled to me how it was strictly forbidden in the early revolutionary period for a tent to be set up out of place with respect to its row. If this discipline was so strictly enforced, this perhaps reflected the extent to which the layout of the camps, as has been noted for other refugee camps (Malkki 1995b; Agier 2002), functioned as a technique of power for producing certain kinds of subjectivities among the refugees. In the Sahrawi case, the layout of the tents within the camps helped produce a notion of social egalitarianism in which transgressive elements, such as the idea that the positioning of one's tent compared to others' could express one's hierarchical relationship within a *qabīlah* or one's distinctive socioeconomic circumstances, were fully or virtually excluded.

Caratini (2003: 33) points out that the camps' layout did not break completely with the resonances of *frīg* layout, but in fact subtly combined the two forms of encampment layout that could express lack of hierarchy and hierarchy, respectively. The first encampment layout, expressing hierarchy, was square, of the kind described by Caro Baroja (1955). Front, back, left, and right could be distinguished and deployed to express social order. The second encampment layout, expressing lack of hierarchy, was circular and defensive. No distinctions could be made other than for the middle of the circle. Caratini (2003: 33) points out that the overall layout of a Sahrawi refugee camp placed square districts, *dawāir* (sing. *dairah*), in a circle around the administrative buildings at the center of the province (*wilāyah*). She further explains that the combination of square and circle harked back to images that expressed both a society infused with hierarchy and lack of hierarchy (33). Appropriately, the suggestion of hierarchy favored the state-movement, whose administrative buildings for governance and health care were located at the center of each province (*wilāyah*) and, therefore, at the "front" of each constituent square *dairah* in that province.

I came to observe how daily habits, movements, and gestures embodied the placing of administrative buildings at the "front" of a residential unit and toward which refugees quite literally turned. Like other members of their neighborhood, Māghalāha and her daughters made frequent visits to their *dairah*'s administrative center, for receiving health care, dropping off a child at the nursery, collecting rations, doing routine paperwork, and attending extraordinary events such as a school's end-of-term prize giving. If an announcement were being made from a *dairah* loudspeaker, those gathered at home would urge each other to hush and subtly tilt toward the *dairah*, straining to hear the news. Social and spatial orientation designated the administrative buildings as the "front" of each neighborhood and a center of gravity.

To Caratini's insightful analysis of the layout of the camps, I would add the suggestion that the physical (and therefore visible) layout of the camps amounted to an alternative system of segmentation. The camps situated persons within the social relations of the state-movement, effectively overwriting the segmentation that previously situated persons within the social relations of the *qabīlah*. Formerly, each person lived in a tent that pertained to a *frīg*, associated with an *'arsh* and a *qabīlah*. The nomenclature of the tent and *frīg*, which I observed in the camps and in the pasturelands, could reflect that segmentation. In the pasturelands, a tent would be called by the *ahl* of the head of household, and a *frīg* referred to as the *khiyām* (tents) of a particular *qabīlah*. The layout of the camps changed the way that an individual tent fitted into the nested identities associated with a *qabīlah*.

From the early revolutionary period, while each person still belonged to a tent (*khaymah*), each tent pertained to a neighborhood (*ḥayy*), each neighborhood to a district (*dairah*), and each district to a province (*wilāyah*), the latter being the administrative form concurrent with a refugee camp. These administrative terms (not including *khaymah* / tent) are also those of the Algerian state's administration; Caratini (2003: 33) suggests that the Sahrawi refugees' administrative terms were taken from Algeria. The result of the incorporation of the *khaymah* into a nested administrative system of the state-movement is that residential patterns reflected and, quite literally, manifested not *qabīlah* identity but the very makeup of the state-movement. The *frīg*, previously identifiable with a particular *qabīlah*, effectively disappeared in the *ḥayy* and the *dairah*.

Several tents belonging to the same extended family might well be gathered together in the refugee camps. For instance, in 2008 Māghalāha lived in a row hosting her mother and three married sisters. Likewise, Zaynabu in Smara camp lived in a row of tents alongside her two eldest married daughters, her mother, and the niece who had grown up with Zaynabu's mother and had married Zaynabu's son. (Residential clustering around married daughters was new in exile—see Chapter 5.) If daughters had married husbands from their own tribes, the new residential pattern might result in several tents in close proximity housing families from the same tribe. Indeed, a particular area might be widely known by locals in that *wilāyah* for hosting "lots of tents" from a certain tribe. Yet any resemblance to a *frīg* was disguised to the point of virtual invisibility. Both Māghalāha and Zaynabu also had immediate neighbors who hailed from different tribes. Any cluster of tents that housed families from the same tribe was engulfed in the wider administrative structure. Physical gaps between residential clusters did not mark the limits of a tribe's residence but those of the administrative units of the state-movement.

The disappearance or "camouflaging" of residential units that reflected the social relations of the *qabīlah* is neatly illustrated by a comparison of a staged event in the Saharawi refugee camps with an analogous event in the

Naama region of Algeria (Ben Hounet 2009: 356). Naama's formerly mobile pastoralist population was by the 2000s predominantly seminomadic or sedentary. In the case of a yearly fair where the tribes of Naama come together in temporary encampments, they arrange up to four hundred tents in tribal groups. The fair, therefore, literally maps out the local tribes, section by section.

In the case of the Saharawi Cultural Festival, which I observed in December 2008, each *ḥayy* from each *dairah* set up tents at the festival site. The overall resulting layout was that the festival site constituted a microcosm of the refugee camps as a whole. In layout, the festival mapped the national community not by *qabīlah* but by administrative section. Māghlāha had joined a group of women from her neighborhood to inhabit a goat-hair tent for the festival, which she and her colleagues had decorated with "traditional" objects. The first time that I went to visit her at the festival, there was no way for me to orientate myself through the array of festival tents other than by asking where the tents of a particular administrative unit were, working my way through the units until I found "our" neighborhood. As would have been the case in the early revolutionary period, when it was actively forbidden to inquire about someone's *qabīlah*, at the festival, knowing someone's place in the administrative system was the way of knowing to which immediate social world he or she belonged.

## Overwriting Segmentation: "New" Branches

The relocation of the *khaymah* within the administrative structures of the state-movement was paralleled by less visible forms of alternative segmentation of at least two kinds: "the administrative organization" (*al-tanẓīm al-idārī*) and "the political organization" (*al-tanẓīm al-siyāsī*).

Until the mid-1990s, each adult woman in the camps was assigned to a Popular Committee, through which she was incorporated into the state-movement's administrative organization. The Popular Committees, along with congresses (see below) were inspired by Muammar Gaddafi's Popular Revolution in Libya.

Launched in 1973, Libya's Popular Revolution encouraged direct participation in Popular Committees to run institutions, and rejected the principle of representation in government (see Fathaly and Palmer 1980; Vandewalle 1995). In Libya, popular assemblies, called Basic People's Congresses, chose representatives for Basic People's Committees, with the latter, in turn, directing their concerns to a national General People's Congress. When people's participation in this popular revolution disappointed Gaddafi, in 1977 he added Revolutionary Committees, composed of specially selected Gaddafi loyalists.[3] Ostensibly meant to mobilize citizens for revolutionary participation, Revolutionary Committees infiltrated Popular Committees as well as other institutions, placing persons under surveillance. Libya adopted the slogan "committees are everywhere" (*al-lijān fī kulli makān*)—potentially more in reference to the Revolutionary, rather than the Basic People's Committees (Mattes 1995: 95).

In its administrative organization, the state-movement set out to emulate the Libyan Basic People's (rather than the Revolutionary) Committees. Sahrawi refugees' Popular Committees ran public services, ranging from health and education to dispute resolution and rations. Yaḥḍi, an older male refugee who had previously worked in the Justice Committee (see Chapter 3), recalled the prominence of Popular Committees at the time and laughed as, citing the Libyan slogan, he said, "We were like Libya: 'committees are everywhere'."

The number of Popular Committees underwent reform over the course of the early revolutionary period. From at least the mid-1980s and to the mid-1990s, there were five Popular Committees, covering the following areas:

1. The Red Crescent (responsible for distributing rations) (*al-hilāl*).
2. Health care (*al-ṣiḥḥah*).
3. Education (dealing with nurseries and primary schools) (*al-taʿlīm*).
4. Production (textiles and weaving) (*al-ṣināʿah*).
5. Social Affairs and Justice (*al-shuʾūn al-ijtimāʿīyah*).[4]

Each team of Popular Committee workers would be under the guidance of the neighborhood-level head of that Popular Committee, known colloquially as "the owner" (*ṣāḥib*/*ṣāḥibah*) of that sector. She, in turn, would report in to the *dairah*-level head of that sector, who would report in to the head of the province, the *wālī*. The incorporation of persons into the administrative organization broke down the associations of the prerevolutionary division of labor with *qabīlah* relations. Formerly, there was a tendency for particular status groups to engage in certain kinds of work and a tendency of persons linked through *qabīlah* relations to work together through coordinated labor pooling, known as *twīzah* (see Chapter 4). Through conscription into Popular Committees for women, or the army for men, however, refugees worked together not because they were fellow members of a *qabīlah* or a status group but because they were fellow members of the state-movement. Indeed, after visiting the camps in the 1990s, Caratini (2003: 40) remarks that refugees looked back on the early revolutionary labor pooling as controversial precisely because of its social mixing.

In addition to incorporation into the administrative organization, each adult refugee was assigned to a group for political orientation as part of the political organization. In residential areas, these groups were known as cells. Ten adult women would be assigned to an eleventh woman who was head of the cell, a position known as *ʿarīfah*. Significantly, the adult women living together in one *khaymah* would not be recruited to the same cell, thus decreasing the likelihood that the cell would reproduce kin groups. Sahrawi refugee cells thereby potentially contrasted with Palestinian committees in the West Bank, in which, Iris Jean-Klein (2003) suggests, politically active women continued to operate within a sphere of social relations close to those of their kinship ties and network. In the army and ministries, men would also be assigned to small groups for political orientation. Women's cells and men's groups would in turn report to higher-ranking officers in the field of political orientation. In the case of the all-female cells in the *wilāyāt*, the political organization, like the administrative organization, culminated in the figure of the *wālī*.

The camps' administrative and political organizations have often been described (e.g., Lippert 1992; Bäschlin 2004). Rarely, though, has the principle of double incorporation been analyzed for its effects. Through these forms of incorporation, every adult person in the camps was drawn into the state-movement and subject to its demands, in both administrative fields (work that must be done for the liberation effort) and in political terms (through cells and groups of political orientation). The comprehensiveness of this pull for dual incorporation was not lost on the refugees, however. Yaḥḍi told me a joke that used to circulate in the 1980s, one that Māghalāha and other older refugees later recognized as I told them what he had said:

> The head of the political organization in a *dairah* and the head of the administrative organization in the same *dairah* had a falling out. The administrative head asked everybody who was in the administrative organization to come over to his side and sit with him. All the

> women who were gathered got up and went over to join him. The political head then asked everybody who was in the political organization to come over to his side and sit with him. All the women there got up again, this time to move over to sit with him.

What I wish to highlight from the joke is that each person was expected to cultivate both aspects of her membership in the political community: as an administrative worker and as a politicized subject. The joke also suggests that, even if an account of the refugee camps from the 1980s suggests that joining a committee was not compulsory (Lippert 1985: 9), in practice participation was universal.

The name in the camps for the network of units of political orientation (also used to designate the headquarters for political orientation in the administrative headquarters, Rabouni) was *furūʿ*, "branches." The term was previously part of the terminology of segmentation (even though Caro Baroja (1955: 16) was unable to define its remit). Its parallel use underscores how the state-movement's political organization—and its twin, the administrative organization—served as alternative forms of segmentation.

Similarly, the term *tābiʿ* ("following"), from the verb *t-b-ʿ* (follow), was used for political affiliation in both the state-movement and among tribes. Refugees used *tābiʿ* to designate to which part of the state-movement's political organization a person was affiliated, for instance, to explain where someone voted (see below). When ʿAbdi, Māghalāha's son aged in his early twenties, was describing to me how, in the pasturelands, a certain *qabīlah*, previously the tributary of a strong *qabīlah*, still tended to graze with the erstwhile recipients of their tribute, he used the same idiom. Members of the weak *qabīlah* had in past times been affiliated as tributaries to ("*tābiʿ*") the stronger *qabīlah*. The relations of affiliation to the state-movement were understood as alternatives and, in a sense, equivalent, to the relations of incorporation into a *qabīlah*'s sphere of consented solidarity (see Chapter 1).

The replacement of tribal incorporation with administrative incorporation has been observed as a technique of statehood across Arab states (Ayubi 1995: 125). For the state-movement, it offered advantages beyond the usual encouragement of popular loyalty toward state power. The social relations of the *qabīlah* were infused with hierarchies of status and prestige usually acquired at birth. In contrast, in the structures of the state-movement, there should in theory be no hierarchy between the different residential areas, committees, and branches of political orientation. The administrative forms of incorporation, thus, served the state-movement's ambitions to promote social egalitarianism between citizens.

## Transforming Households and Making State Power Tangible

At the same time as the *frīg* was physically engulfed by the layout of the camps, the activities and social relations of households were transformed in exile.

Anthropologists have long been interested in how households—understood as the basic unit of production, consumption, distribution, and investment (Guyer and Peters 1987)—grant insight into social processes and reproduction taking place beyond the confines of the household itself (Yanagisako 1979; Harris 1981). For Henrietta Moore (1994), the household, like other social institutions such as banks, schools, and the army, is concerned with the production of persons with particular kinds of "social identities," appropriate for the wider context of social relations. Moore's point can perhaps be usefully approached through the prism of Katherine Verdery's (1996) reflections on the production of social dispositions. Verdery explains that in socialist states the secret information services produced "paper," that is, files of information about the people ruled by the regime in question. But these were only the immediate products of that system: "the ultimate product was political subjects and subject dispositions useful to the regime" (Verdery 1996: 24). We might say that households produce immediate products, persons, and ultimate products, persons with particular kinds of dispositions. Or (see Pine 2002), particular politico-economic systems produce immediate products of certain kinds of households, which, in turn, produce ultimate products of persons with dispositions useful to that politico-economic system.

The prerevolutionary *khaymah* produced an ultimate product of persons with social dispositions suitable to membership in a *qabīlah*. This happened in a number of ways beyond the effect of segmentation whereby, in belonging to a *khaymah* in a *frīg*, a person claimed and was claimed by a *qabīlah*. Persons with social dispositions suited to the social relations of the *qabīlah* were also produced, almost literally, in the teaching of genealogies and status relations to young members. A more subtle means of producing such dispositions was through socialization in work relations and education. From around age seven, a hassanophone child learned the occupations particular to their status group (see Chapter 1), whether as a religious specialist, animal herder, artisan, or domestic slave (de Chassey 1976: 122). The layout of the *khaymah* was also a space through which status hierarchies could be learned. Slaves were not allowed beyond the threshold of their owners' tents (Caratini 1989b: 85). During my fieldwork, a shy teenager hanging around at the entrance of a tent was laughingly teased by a woman seated inside (who was already a mother at the outbreak of the revolution and could therefore recall well the time of slaves) with the words, "What are you doing, hanging around in the doorway like a slave?"

The social and economic changes brought about by the revolution and exile shook to the core the previous tendency of the *khaymah* to produce persons with social dispositions suited to the *qabīlah*. Not only was the *frīg* layout dismantled, but economic and social activities were literally transferred out of the tent and relocated in the structures of the state-movement.

In the prerevolutionary mobile pastoralist context, each *frīg* had tended to rely on the labor and resources of its own members for production and consumption, alongside stylized reciprocity between *firgān*. The *frīg* thus resembled Marshall Sahlins's (1972) notion of the domestic mode of production (DMP)—although Caroline Humphrey's (2002: 164–74) important qualifications of the DMP, such as that each unit saw itself as spiritually and socially incomplete (here, as part of a *qabīlah*), would also apply. Among Hassanophones, labor pooling took the form of *twīzah*, the sharing of sex-segregated tasks—such as tent sewing for women and shearing for men—between members of different *firgān*.

In the early revolutionary period, however, persons and households relied for their physical survival on humanitarian donations (see Chapter 5). These were initially provided by Algeria and then later by the international community. Yet this aid was always distributed through the structures of the state-movement itself, with the effect that the immediate experience of the refugees was of dependence on the state-movement. The labor to deliver rations and the labor to produce goods locally (such as floor mats for tents or clothing) were also coordinated by the state-movement through the Popular Committees. Labor mobilized through Popular Committees replaced the stylized reciprocity between *firgān* characteristic of the prerevolutionary setting.

Alongside households' new relations of dependence on the state-movement and labor pooling, the Popular Committees, and other personnel of the state-movement, literally extracted many of the activities formerly staged in the *frīg* and redeployed them in a new, public domain that was accessible to all refugee citizens. Randa Farah comments:

> The Polisario assumed and transformed many of the functions of the traditional bedouin camp (the *freeg*), which comprised the basic socioeconomic unit in Sahrawi society. The *freeg* consisted of a few *khiyam* or tents (families) who moved together and cooperated in providing food, shelter, education, and healthcare for their individual members. By taking on these functions, the Polisario generated a discourse of "progress" that discouraged tribal affiliations and reinforced a sense of national belonging through shared practices. (Farah 2008: 82–83)

Interlocutors often liked to recall for me, with pride (and nostalgia), "the good old days" when not only the iconic areas of education, health, food, and shelter but also the very nuts and bolts of everyday domestic labor had been shifted into a public domain. By the 1980s, herds of up to three or four hundred sheep and goats had developed in the camps (Firebrace and Harding 1987: 34).[5] There were cooperatives with herds, as well as animals with individual owners (Lippert 1985: 13). In the accounts I collected in the late 2000s, interlocutors recalled of the early revolutionary period that those refugees who had acquired some animals could not keep them in individual pens. Rather, there was "one pen" for everyone, and "one time" for opening and closing it, with individual family pens not allowed. This is in sharp contrast to a typical image of the camps in the late 2000s, where women and children would be seen going back and forth to feed their sheep and goats kept in some of the hundreds of family-run animal pens.

The shortage of firewood, gas fuel, and even cooking equipment meant that in the early revolutionary period individual households did not cook their own meals. "There was one gas ring for the whole row of tents, and one woman cooked for everyone," one woman, who had grown up during the early revolutionary period, recalled. Another older woman, already married during that time, explained that, if a woman found herself divorced or widowed, she would not necessarily keep the marital tent she had been given by the state-movement—as was the right in pre-exile circumstances of a formerly married woman to maintain her marital tent, even if she moved back to her natal *frīg*. Instead, the divorced or widowed refugee might move back in with her natal family, giving her tent back to the state-movement so that it could be redistributed to someone else. Even domestic space could be reconverted back into the public domain from which it had been materially sourced.

I heard so much about "the good old days" of the 1980s that I almost stopped listening to stories that I thought I already knew. In fact, these stories carry an important yet subtle message. They tell of a consistent push to shift the activities of the prerevolutionary household—education, health care, the basic activities of production and consumption, including domestic labor—from the *khaymah* and *frīg* into the newly forged public domain of the state-movement. All citizens could make claims on this public domain, and all also were expected to participate therein. Crucially, the significance of these transformations goes beyond the practical need to reorganize households' survival in a context of dispossession and exile. The transformations were also ideologically important for producing persons with dispositions suited to the revolution. In addition, by moving activities out of the *khaymah* and into the public domain, the state-movement created a tangible public domain. In the schools, hospitals, child care centers, and work groups for weaving, sewing, or other tasks, refugees could "see" and "touch" the state-movement. The forging of this public domain also laid the foundations for the expansion of the public domain and ministerial work in the late revolutionary period. This expansion would seek to provide jobs for men demobilized from the front after the cease-fire (Gimeno Martín and Laman 2007).

The shift in the early revolutionary period toward the production of persons with social dispositions suited to the state-movement can be observed through changes in the means of identifying others. In the early revolutionary period it was forbidden, and according to some of my interlocutors punishable by penalties of physical labor, to use words such as *'abd* (male slave), *khādim* (female slave) or *mu'allim* (artisan), just as it was prohibited to ask about the *qabīlah* to which someone belonged or to introduce oneself by giving one's extended genealogy. Similar prohibitions of the mention of tribes under socialism in Somalia led to sometimes inventive circumlocutions (Lewis 1979). As I still heard in the 2000s, Sahrawi refugees' alternative means of identifying each other usually combined a first and second name with information about place of residence or work, for example, Khadijetou mint (Hassaniya form of *bint*, here meaning "daughter of") Hamīda, living in Farsia, neighborhood number three. Since the tripartite name is considered necessary to identify someone's *qabīlah*, these kinds of relations were remarkable for the fact that they were discussed without the possibility for recognizing someone's *qabīlah*, did not necessarily entail mutual knowledge about the *qabīlah*, and indeed often did not. The bearing of the identity of a *qabīlah* was no longer meant to be reproduced. Instead, changed households and a new public domain helped produce dispositions suitable for refugee citizens who lived, worked, studied, and shared as members of the state-movement.

## Reconfigured Participation and Representation

The tendency for the social relations of state power to overwrite the social relations of the *qabīlah* worked in tandem with a contrary tendency. Some aspects of *qabīlah* relations, perceived as a precursor to the aims of the state-movement, were meant to be preserved. For instance, officers of the state-movement, as well as "lay" refugees, opined that, thanks to the existence of the *jamā'ah* and the *ait arba'īn* (see Chapter 1), Sahrawis were "democratic before democracy." The *jamā'ah* and the *ait arba'īn* were therefore meant to be replaced in ways that did not obscure *qabīlah* legacies but allowed for them to be recognized and "show through" the palimpsest. Before addressing the implications of claims that these structures promoted "democracy" and continued a legacy from *qabīlah* relations, I examine first the state-movement's structures of participation and representation. (These may be familiar to readers already well acquainted with the state-movement.)

As noted above, the approach to democracy in the camps in the early revolutionary period took inspiration from Gaddafi's Popular Revolution in Libya, and accordingly favored direct participation rather than representation. The Popular Committees (the administrative organization) facilitated direct participation, allowing the people—in theory—to be directly in control of offices and public services. Again echoing Libya (and ironies within its Popular Revolution), the state-movement interwove direct participation with a system of representation. Some elements of this system underwent reforms in the mid-1990s. In the late 2000s, following several rounds of reforms and in the context of the relaxation of the state-movement's levels of intervention in refugees' daily lives, interlocutors often struggled to describe the past and present structures of the state-movement. My description is therefore as accurate as the accounts gathered from administrators, office holders, and lay refugees allow.

Throughout the revolutionary period, the most important form of representation-cum-participation was the Popular General Congress (PGC) of the Polisario Front as a liberation movement (note that this is explicitly not a SADR event). The fourteenth PGC was held in December 2015 in Tifariti in the Polisario-controlled areas of Western Sahara. Prior to that, I observed the preparations for, and the inauguration of, the twelfth PGC in December 2007. In the late 2000s, the preparations for a PGC consisted of several stages. Dossiers to stimulate discussion were prepared by the state-movement covering (1) an evaluation of the period elapsed since the last PGC; (2) a program for the forthcoming period until the next PGC; (3) "Basic Law" (Polisario statutes and SADR constitution); and (4) defense and foreign policy. The dossiers were circulated in advance to open discussion meetings, which, in the late 2000s, were called *nadawāt siyāsīyah*.

I attended one such preparatory meeting in a *dairah* in Smara camp in November 2007, held in the *dairah*'s centrally located meeting room. In the presence of the (male) head of the *dairah*, women from the administration took turns to sit on a chair beside a simple table and to read out the dossiers to the audience, who were sitting on the floor. As was the case in most *dairah*-level meetings that I attended, the audience was composed mostly of middle-aged women. (As discussed below, men often had other affiliations to Polisario, such as the army, and attended meetings organized for that constituency. Younger women were often left in charge of a household while their mothers attended meetings in person.) The women sat on the floor in the carpeted room and, when discussion from the floor was invited, stood up to voice suggestions, criticisms, or observations. These comments were collated by a secretary, to be passed on as feedback at the actual PGC. The atmosphere of the meeting I attended was sedate. I heard from a male interlocutor, a middle-aged father who had returned from Spain to attend the preparations and the PGC, that at the *wilāyah*-level meeting he had attended, discussion had been rousing. "In the *wilāyah*, you find people with more ideas. That's where you can find real discussion," he opined.

Such meetings were held wherever electoral constituencies were formed. The constitution of electoral constituencies was unusual and demonstrates the principles of the construction of citizenship in the state-movement. For the twelfth PGC in 2007, electoral constituencies were drawn up in the following sectors:

Figure 4. Pre-electoral discussion meeting (*nadwah*) in Auserd, 2012 (photo by Alice Wilson).

1. Residential Districts (*dawāir*)
2. Ministries
3. The Army
4. Diaspora Communities (migrants and students) (*jālīyāt*)
5. The "Occupied Territories."[6]

Thanks to the inclusion of diaspora communities, Sahrawis who lived abroad (in Spain, France, Italy, Belgium, and elsewhere)—who had migrated either from the camps or from areas under Moroccan control—were invited to gather together *in situ* to discuss documents in exactly the same way as refugees in the camps.[7] Their views, comments, complaints, and suggestions, like those of refugees in the *wilāyāt*, were recorded by the government official appointed to run the meeting. Diaspora Sahrawis also elected a representative(s) to attend the PGC as a delegate with the right to vote. Work commitments might make it difficult for a Sahrawi abroad to consider attending the PGC as a representative, though. In the case of the diaspora meeting in Mantes-la-Jolie, near Paris, in 2007, a member of the Ministry of Information who had been sent to chair the meeting told me that, while the meeting had been well attended, hosting both Sahrawis from the camps and from the Moroccan-controlled areas, he had been obliged to "force" someone to attend the PGC, as initially no one had come forward to make the trip to Tifariti for the PGC.

In sum, there were three elements to the construction of citizenship for the state-movement: ethnic, political, and activist. One had to be Sahrawi—wherever one happened to be in the world (the "ethnic" criterion). One also had to be incorporated into the pro-self-determination political community along the lines of the administrative and political organizations described above (the "political" criterion). A voter was assigned to a constituency according to the place of activity for the state-movement, whether this was in a ministry, on the "home-front" in a *wilāyah*, or as a worker or student abroad (the "activist" criterion).

Those elected at the discussion meetings as PGC delegates (in 2007, some 1,050 people) went on to discuss again, over three or four days at the PGC, the themes that were raised in the documents and preparatory discussions and voted on major policy decisions. In addition, PGC delegates voted to elect the most senior positions in Polisario, some of whom by virtue of that position took on, or became eligible for, senior positions in SADR. PGC delegates elected the secretary general of Polisario, who, from 1982, constitutionally served, by virtue of that office within Polisario, as president of SADR. Since the death in 1976 of the first secretary general of Polisario, alWali Mustafa Bashir, Mohamad 'Abd al'Azīz has been consistently reelected and reappointed to both positions.

PGC delegates also elected the senior ranks of Polisario. In the 1980s, this was the Political Bureau (PB) (twenty-one members) (see Figure 5). The seven candidates with the most votes from among them would in turn form the Executive Committee (EC). At that time, the EC held executive power, rather than the president. The EC acted as the Council for the Command of the Revolution (CCR), which was considered the highest instance of SADR. The EC also appointed the Council of Ministers for the SADR. The Sahrawi National Council (SNC) (the Parliament) consisted of the twenty-one members of the PB and the twenty heads of the *dawāir* (who were directly elected). But it had little real power in this period (Bäschlin 2004: 140). In addition to these national institutions, in line with the Libyan model, in the 1980s, there were congress-like events on a subnational scale. Those concerning the mass

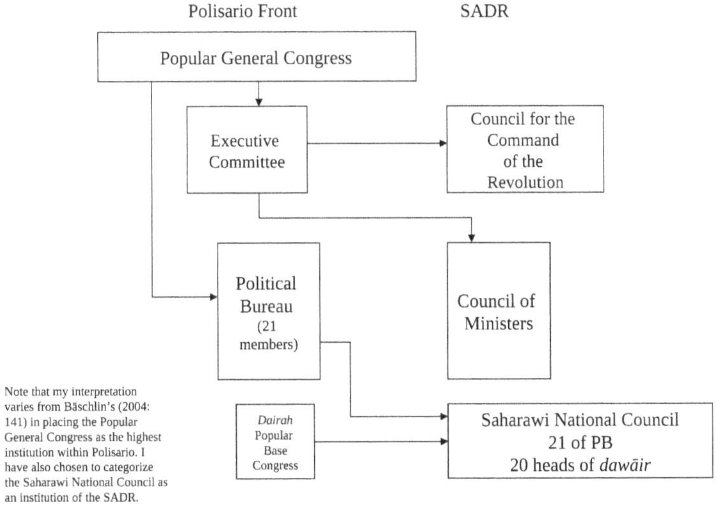


Figure 5. Principal organs of Polisario and SADR, 1976 constitution.

institutions—the Workers', Women's, and Youth's Congresses—continued to the late revolutionary period. But in the early revolutionary period, there were also annual *dairah*- and *wilāyah*-level congresses. In the late revolutionary period, they were recalled with nostalgia by refugees who had known them as contexts in which issues in running public services were discussed with vehemence and effective pressure on government officials perceived to be all too rare in the late 2000s.

With the exception of the PGC, the main structures of direct participation and representation were overhauled in the 1990s. Over the course of the early revolutionary period, the articles of the Sahrawi democratic creed of face-to-face discussion and direct participation in decision making and governing had met with formidable stumbling blocks. Despite its participatory stance, the state-movement's governance had been prone to authoritarianism (Bäschlin 2004: 152). We might add that the very structures of participation may also have served as structures for the tight grip of the state-movement's social and political control, as is indeed a vulnerability of "participatory techniques" (Cooke and Kothari 2001). In October 1988, refugee protests against abuses of power were violently put down by the state-movement.[8] A political crisis ensued. The PGC of 1989 that followed these

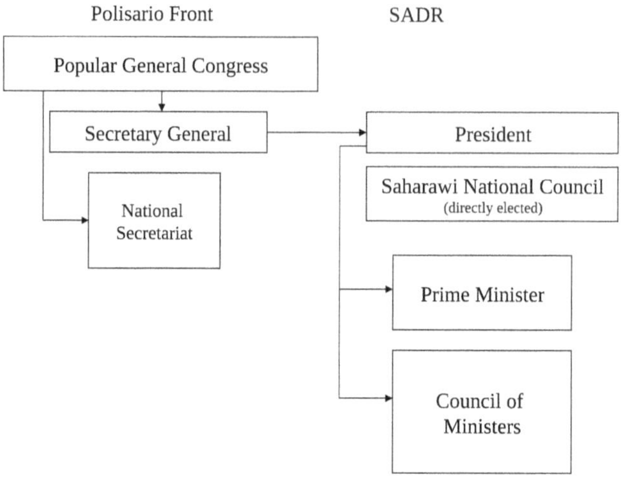


Figure 6. Principal organs of Polisario and SADR, 1991 constitution.

events marked the beginning of a trend toward expectations of public accountability and curbs on central power. Anticipating an imminent postcease-fire return to the homeland, the PGC of 1991 passed further reforms, including a new constitution that guaranteed certain freedoms and reformed the structure of Polisario and SADR. The EC and the CCR were abolished, and the Political Bureau was expanded and renamed the National Secretariat (see Figure 6).

These changes, and further reforms in the 1995 and 1999 PGCs, concentrated powers in the hands of the president of SADR. The president became the head of state, acquired the role of appointing the head of the government (the prime minister), appointed the government with the advice of the prime minister, was head of the army, could dissolve the Parliament and the government, and held various other powers (Es-Sweyih 2001: 71–72). The role of the SNC also changed to increase its powers to hold government to account (see Chapter 7). The year 1999 also saw the establishment of a council for the *shuyūkh* or tribal leaders. *Shuyūkh* gained importance in the early 1990s during voter identification for a potential referendum on self-determination. Their expert knowledge was sought out to assess the applications of those registering to vote (see Jensen 2005: 15). The official name of the council composed of *shuyūkh* is *al-majlis al-istishārī*, the Consultative Council (CC). Its role was undefined in the 1999 constitution (article 128). For Mohamed-

Fadel Ismaīl Es-Sweyih (2001: 80–81), the CC might have a future role as a second chamber of the parliamentary system. In the meantime, the CC met only once a year unless convened extraordinarily by the president. It is not clear that the CC had any real political power by the late 2000s. The late revolutionary recognition of *shuyūkh* as part of SADR structures is significant in itself, however, as an indication of the shift toward the accommodation, rather than the exclusion, of the *qabīlah* within the state-movement's aspirations for state power.

Another major change was the disbanding of the Popular Committees, reduced and renamed as councils (*majālis*) in 1995. From the point of view of the management of public services, the council maps neatly onto the old Popular Committee; this may explain why the dissolution of the Popular Committees has received scant attention in most accounts of the camps. From the point of view of the lived experience of the refugees, however, the change was immense. There was no longer any conscription of female unpaid labor to the various areas of public service. This impacted greatly on the state-movement's potential to "extract" labor from refugees (see Chapter 4). The loosening of the grip of the administrative organization was paralleled in the weakening of the political organization. Most women whom I questioned in the late 2000s did not know to which cell of political orientation they belonged or who their *'arīfah* was. By all accounts, this would have been unthinkable in the 1980s. The double principle of incorporation into the state-movement was still marked in the 2000s. The electoral system was one vestige: one could vote only if one was affiliated (*tābi'*) to an organ of the state-movement. But the 1980s joke about the dispute between the heads of the political and administrative organizations would make little immediate sense to Sahrawis who grew up in the 1990s and were young adults in the 2000s.

## Suggestions of *Qabīlah* Legacies

The state-movement's structures of participation and representation reconfigured the *qabīlah*'s political institutions of *shaykh*, *jamā'ah*, and *ait arba'īn* (see Chapter 1). Initially, the figure of the *shaykh* disappeared altogether from public life. In practice, according to the accounts of some interlocutors, in the early revolutionary period, those *shuyūkh* who found themselves among the refugee population tended to be appointed as heads of the *dairah* within the administrative organization. I was not able to confirm this as a policy with state-movement officials. If it was indeed the case, it adds greater poignancy to the joke about the dispute between the administrative and the political heads of the *dairah*. The clash between the politicized cadre of the political organization and the former figure of *qabīlah* authority represented not merely the potential clash of personalities or priorities in the context of exile, but also the clash of the prerevolutionary and the revolutionary.

The early revolutionary placement of *shuyūkh* in the state-movement administration as officers of the latter, rather than representatives of a *qabīlah*, is indicative of a preference to transform vestiges of *qabīlah* political institutions. A *shaykh* may well have had experience in leadership and decision making that could be useful to the state-movement. In the early revolutionary period, the usefulness of the *shaykh* had to be incorporated via his revolutionary transformation into an officer of the state-movement. In contrast, in the late revolutionary period, *shuyūkh* came to be incorporated into the state-movement as *shuyūkh* in the CC. Officials in the camps often cited the importance of the *shuyūkh* for voter identification as the motivation for the "rehabilitation" of *shuyūkh*. In the light of the shifts to be discussed in Part II in dispute resolution (Chapter 3) and marriage regulation (Chapter 5), the move to incorporate *shuyūkh* into the state-movement in that capacity, rather than in another guise, bespeaks a wider trend in the late revolutionary period: the state-movement shifted toward utilizing explicitly the social relations of the *qabīlah* for its own projects of governance.

As for the *jamāʿah* and the *ait arbaʿīn*, the intra- and intertribal councils respectively, they have arguably been reconfigured in the form of the public discussion meetings and the SNC.[9] In fact, refugees would voice explicit claims that it was in their "culture" for there to be widespread participation in decision making. Many refugees would proudly explain that the *jamāʿah* was a precedent for their discussion meetings in the camps. A similar argument was made by the serving head of Political Orientation, Bashir Mustafa Sayed, longstanding leading member of Polisario and brother of the deceased former leader elWali. In an interview in February 2008, he linked the origins of Sahrawi democracy to the practice of holding a *jamāʿah*. He further supported the thesis of Sahrawis' inclinations toward democracy with reference to the importance of the notion of *jamāʿah* in Islam:

> In our culture, in our traditions, men and women are educated in the sense that opinion shared by various people is accepted, and [an

> opinion held by one person] is not accepted. In Islam, which is the main part of our culture, we find the phrase: *yad Allah maʿ al-jamāʿah* [God's hand is with the group/gathering]. The meaning of this is that, when persons are assembled to work, it depends on the number of persons to do that work. When work is for one person, then they will have difficulty in doing it. *Al-jamāʿah* can inspire more, in the sense that, when more persons confront an idea, this indicates the right way. In implementation, then, you have to gather numerous persons. Here I cite the proverb *yad wāḥida . . .* [*mā tuṣaffiq*, one hand alone cannot clap]. These are the faraway origins of democracy. (Interview held in English, Rabouni, February 11, 2008)

In parallel to arguments made about the preservation of the *jamāʿah* tradition, the SNC came to be seen, especially from the time of the reinvigoration of its mandate during the 1990s, as a continuation of the *ait arbaʿīn* (Pazzanita 2006: 379).[10] For instance, in the run-up to the SNC elections in 2008 (see Chapter 7), the state-movement circulated papers at the pre-election discussion meetings in which it presented its vision of the SNC as harking back to the tradition of the *ait arbaʿīn*. These papers were read aloud at the *nadwah* that I attended to nods of consent from the floor. Thus, in the cases of the *jamāʿah* and the *ait arbaʿīn*, the legacy of the *qabīlah* was not meant to be rendered unseeable and unknowable but as seen, known, and celebrated as an alleged prototype of democratic practice.

In North Africa, convictions that, in certain respects, tribes, along with a claimed notion of "Islam," equip persons to participate in democratic political relations are by no means unique to Sahrawis. On coming into contact in Kabylia, Algeria, with institutions of decision making at village level, known as *tajmaet* (the Berber cognate of *jamāʿah*), French colonial authorities claimed on these communities' behalf that they were "democratic"—albeit without, in the Kabyle case, these perceived democratic tendencies being attributed to Islam (see Hanoteau and Letourneux 1872: 1). For Pierre Bourdieu, Kablyes' was a "gentilitial democracy," that is, a democracy incorporating the participation of the male heads of land-owning households (Bourdieu 1962: 16–24). Claims about the democratic nature of *tajmaet/jamāʿah* institutions have been voiced not only by external observers but also by local adherents of these institutions—although some local projections have been analyzed as obfuscations of how councils may operate as an elite entity (Scheele 2009).

If local and external observers have claimed the existence of indigenous "democratic" structures in North Africa, the claimed relationship between these structures and state power has varied. Local enthusiasts may take the institution about which they make these claims to be part of the apparatus of the state (Scheele 2009). It is less clear, though, at least in the cases of independent Morocco and Algeria, that state authorities have sought to incorporate such institutions within their own state apparatus while making claims about their own democratic practice thanks to this incorporation. Indeed, quite the contrary, the central state apparatus in Algeria and Morocco has had, at least in the early decades after independence, a policy of failing to recognize local council institutions (Hatt 1996; Mahé 2000).[11] Debates about *tajmaet/jamāʿah* in either Algeria or Morocco thus seem to lack the dynamic found in the case of the state-movement, whereby state power claims to incorporate a *jamāʿah* legacy into its apparatus of government as a means of furthering its claimed practice of democracy.

The closest North African parallel for the state-movement's claimed incorporation of local councils into its own structures is perhaps Gaddafi's Libya. Although Gaddafi reportedly took inspiration for his Popular Revolution, which introduced Popular Committees, from Mao's Cultural Revolution (Fathaly and Palmer 1980: 117), his ideas about direct democracy are generally understood to have been more influenced by his views on Islam and his upbringing in a "tribal" setting (Bleuchot 1982; Joffé 1995: 150). Gaddafi's attitudes toward Islam were contradictory (Joffé 1995; Mayer 1995), but at least with regard to direct democracy through committees, he understood this as having a religious basis in the Islamic tradition of *shūrā* (consultation). He saw his volume I of the Green Book, which deals with direct democracy, as an interpretation of the line in the Qur'an: "and their affairs are decided through consultation [*shūrā*] among themselves" (Ayoub 1991: 35) (but note that neither this line, nor any other from the Qur'an, is cited in the Green Book). Attention has likewise been drawn to how what has been called, rather unspecifically, a "tribal ethos" influenced Gaddafi's emphasis on "egalitarianism and lack of hierarchy" (Vandewalle 2006: 103). Again, without mentioning tribal councils in particular but having depicted for his reader Gaddafi's upbringing in a Bedouin tribe, Bleuchot (1982: 147–48) elaborates that, for Gaddafi, the "only valid model" of direct democracy was "his own warm enveloping democratic egalitarian and austere society."[12] If, for Gaddafi's Libya, the case is not explicitly made that tribal councils were a model for popular committees, this possibility is not excluded. It would be compatible with the wider point made that Gaddafi legitimized his ideas for direct democracy with reference to tribes. In the case of the state-movement, the appeal to tribal councils as a model and precursor of direct democracy was explicit.

## Trompe-l'Oeil

The convictions of Sahrawi refugees and their leaders that they were qualified to participate in democratic political relations thanks to a *jamāʿah* (and *ait arbaʿīn*) heritage must be scrutinized. For Sahrawis (and other North Africans), it must be asked (1) whether the *jamāʿah* (or an equivalent institution) was "democratic" in the first place. In the case of the state-movement's explicit claims that its own governance was democratic thanks to the incorporation of a *jamāʿah* legacy, it must also be asked (2) to what extent the state-movement's institutions were a continuation of the *jamāʿah* and related institutions, and (3) whether the state-movement's institutions were indeed "democratic." It does not follow that an answer in the affirmative to any of these questions implies affirmation of any of the others.

To answer these questions is by no means as straightforward as asking them, however. As discussed in the previous chapter, we know relatively little about the workings of either the *jamāʿah* or the *ait arbaʿīn*. There are considerable gaps in the knowledge available to outsiders about *nadawāt* and the SNC, the structures in the camps alleged to have taken up the legacy of *jamāʿah* and *ait arbaʿīn*. Crucial moments in the allegedly democratic process in the camps are closed to outsiders, as is indeed the case for the PGC itself. Able to attend a grassroots pre-PGC meeting, I was unable to follow persons or ideas through the system thereafter. This means that the impact of popular participation prior to and during the PGC on outcomes cannot easily be evaluated by an external audience. Even if such data were available for the refugee camps, it would only make sense to appraise (potential) engagement in democratic political relations in a broader context, including questions of freedom of movement, freedom of association, freedom of expression, and accountability. While I address political freedoms in the camps in Chapter 7, a full treatment of these questions (see Human Rights Watch 2014) would be quite a different object from my present purpose.

Yet it is not only features of life in the camps, such as lack of transparency for external observers about political processes in the camps, and the effects of the conflict setting on freedoms of expression and association, that complicate analysis of the nature of (potential) democratic engagement in the camps. It is not clear against which standards the "democratic" qualifications of the camps (or, for that matter, the *jamā'ah* and *ait arba'īn*) should be "measured." There is no scholarly consensus, either in anthropology (see Paley 2002) or beyond (see Whitehead 2002), on the definition of "democracy" (see Chapter 7).

Although the conceptual and empirical difficulties at stake may prevent a full discussion of Sahrawi refugees' claims to have been "democratic before democracy," some observations about the state-movement's and refugees' claims can be made. If we cannot be sure of the extent to which *nadawāt* and the SNC are a continuation of *jamā'ah* and *ait arba'īn*, we can at least observe some differences between them. Whereas, within a given *qabīlah* (or section thereof), the *jamā'ah* and the *ait arba'īn* were exclusive to persons of particular age, gender, and status, the *nadawāt* were open to all citizens who fell into the administrative sector for which a particular *nadwah* catered. In this sense, the institutions of the state-movement differed from their alleged prerevolutionary equivalents in having "democratized" the criteria for participation.

What grounds might support refugees' linking of *jamā'ah* with the state-movement's institutions of direct democracy? Grounds for similarity perhaps lie in a preference for decision making, especially when dealing with difficulties, through group consensus (however the "group" is defined), to the point of finding it improper if decisions are made otherwise. Māghalāha's son, 'Abdi, explained the high regard in which Sahrawis held the practice of discussing difficulties and agreeing on a decision to deal with them in a group setting. Even on the level of family problems, he explained, the discussion and taking of decisions should be taken as a *jamā'ah*:

> If I notice that my cousin is not behaving well, that he is working and earning money but that he is not helping his family, he is spending it all on himself, on cigarettes and on women, then I might go to his aunt and say to her: "I've noticed that so-and-so is doing this and that." We will gather together a group of our relatives to discuss the problem and to see what we should do. It would be wrong for me to discuss it with her on our own. We have to discuss it as a group (*jamā'ah*) and decide together what we should do.

ʻAbdi's point was that a decision should not be taken without group deliberation. This surely resonates with what we know both about *jamāʻah* and *ait arbaʻīn* in the precolonial or colonial setting and about *nadawāt* and the SNC.

To note a continued expectation of group discussion in decision making is still not an answer to the broader questions of whether the *jamāʻah* was democratic or whether the institutions of the state-movement were democratic thanks to the incorporation of a *jamāʻah* legacy. But perhaps such answers are not needed for contemplation of the techniques through which the social relations of sovereignty were being remade in the camps. In contrast to the techniques of overwriting, examined earlier in this chapter, when *qabīlah* relations were being claimed as a precursor to democratic practice, a different effect was at play: one of trompe-l'oeil. Trompe-l'oeil is a technique of representation in painting and drawing whereby an image is created in such a way as to suggest an illusion of underlying depth. A trompe-l'oeil painting "tricks us into seeing a number of objects that apparently stand out of the picture plane and invade our own physical space" (Corsín Jiménez 2013: 58). For instance, a figure may appear to "come out" of the painting toward the viewer, away from a suggested background that in reality is no farther from the viewer than the apparently protruding figure.

In their ideas about their past and present engagements in democratic relations, Sahrawi refugees and their government were engaged in an act of trompe-l'oeil. They presented to themselves, and to others, their vision that the institutions of their state-movement referred back to and incorporated something deeper, the allegedly democratic legacy of the *jamāʻah* and *ait arbaʻīn*. If there was not quite a strict parallel to this operation in the governance of other North African states, then there is a close parallel on the other side of the continent. In Botswana, Molutsi and Holm note (1990: 325) that *kgotla*, "a gathering . . . of adult males to consider issues raised by the chief of the tribe or a local headman," has been portrayed as a precursor of post-independence democracy. Nevertheless, having the benefit of access to historical ethnographic accounts that offer greater detail than those available for the *jamāʻah* among Sahrawis, Molutsi and Holm go on to stress that the precolonial forms of *kgotla* were among the most "authoritarian" systems in precolonial Africa, with *kgotla* being "for the most part . . . a vehicle to mobilize public support for decisions already made by the community's political elite. Ordinary citizens were left largely outside the struggles determining policy" (Molutsi and Holm 1990: 326).

In the case of Botswana, at least for Molutsi and Holm, the trompe-l'oeil may project the suggestion of something that was never "there" in the first place. For the state-movement, it is hard to know either the ostensible foreground or the suggested background of the trompe-l'oeil. But the trompe-l'oeil effect itself is there. It completes the aspirations of the state-movement's palimpsest: both to obscure the *qabīlah* by overwriting with the social relations of the state-movement and yet at times to let the *qabīlah* show through by summoning it as a claimed background. In both scenarios, the state-movement sought to take over the former place and role of the *qabīlah*. An experience of its success was voiced by Fanna when she spoke of how "the state was [her] father."

The aspirations of the state-movement to replace and displace the *qabīlah* met, however, with compromises and dilemmas. They form the subject of Parts II and III of this book.

# PART II

## Compromises

CHAPTER 3

# Unpopular Law: Tribal, Islamic, and State Law, and the Fall of Popular Justice

> We must ask whether such acts of popular justice can or cannot be organised in the form of a court.
>
> —Michel Foucault, "On Popular Justice: A Discussion with Maoists"

Part I explored how Sahrawis (and others) envisioned their past as one in which tribes opposed and resisted state power; they likewise premised the success of a Sahrawi state power on the attempted displacement of tribes. Part II assesses the compromises that arose in exile over time, whereby the initial attempted displacement of the *qabīlah* by the state-movement was modified. The social relations of the *qabīlah* came to be tolerated or at times even courted by the state-movement to further its own goals of governing the refugee population. Such courting as the result of compromise often occurred covertly; as such, it is distinct from the previously discussed trompe-l'oeil effect of direct appeals to an implied legacy of *qabīlah* relations (see Chapter 2). Although this reorientation came in the wake of an early revolutionary antitribalist outlook, such compromises are not necessarily paradoxical. In this book, I apprehend the *qabīlah* (in certain historical forms) and the state-movement as projects of sovereignty (see Chapter 1). The fact that the state-movement drew on the social relations of the *qabīlah* by, at times, instrumentalizing them, bespeaks the potential for compatibility between the social relations of the *qabīlah* and those of the state-movement for animating projects of sovereignty.

Across Part II, I trace the modification of the relationship between *qabīlah* and state-movement over three areas of the social relations of sovereignty. This chapter and Chapter 4 consider areas of governance that have been widely approached as constitutive of sovereignty: deciding on law, and the appropriation of resources. Chapter 5 suggests that a further arena of the social relations of sovereignty is the organization, legitimization, and reproduction of social (in)equalities, which I explore for Sahrawi refugees through marriage practices.

## An Unknown Thief

When I was staying with Sumaya and her family in the center of February 27 camp in early 2007, Sumaya warned me that I should be careful in case some of my possessions were stolen. February 27 had the reputation of being the most "urban" of the camps. Neighbors were less involved in each other's lives, and many people moved in and out of the camp—conditions perceived by some refugees to favor theft. Some weeks into my stay, though, it was Sumaya who one morning let out a cry of distress as she discovered that money she had left in a purse in the front of her two mud-brick rooms had been stolen. A commotion broke out. Later, as her mood calmed, family members exchanged other stories of theft in the camps. Her husband, Fadili, explained to me how one morning he had awoken to find that a new pressure cooker he had brought back from Spain was gone from the kitchen. Fadili had traced and followed the steps of the intruder in the sand. (I would one day benefit from this technique, as interlocutors literally tracked down stray family members with whom I wished to talk.) He recovered the dish. Sumaya was not so lucky, however. Too many people had walked over the sand around the crowded area in which her family lived. With no clues to follow, she gave up on trying to track the thief. The money was never recovered. I asked Sumaya and Fadili what happened to thieves in the camps. "They go to jail" came the reply. I would later learn from another interlocutor, who worked as a teacher in the men's prison (not far from February 27), that the most common crime for which inmates were detained was theft. Violent crime, though not unknown in the refugee camps, was perceived as much rarer and deeply shocking.[1] Notably, the jail to which refugees referred was a SADR, not an Algerian, prison. Prisoners serving time there had contravened SADR laws and were tried and condemned in a SADR court.[2]

If convicted criminals in the Sahrawi refugee camps served sentences in SADR prisons, this was a relatively novel situation for hassanophone northwest Sahara. Criminals had by no means always gone to prison there or even had prisons to go to. The state-movement had introduced sweeping legal reforms in the camps that eventually instigated a set of state laws, the penal code of the SADR. The state-movement likewise established the prisons to which the transgressors of these laws could be sent. This chapter places the existence of these new SADR laws within the context of the state-movement's attempts to present itself, to internal and external audiences, as a state power that decided on and enforced laws. Interested in how the state-movement decides its own laws, this chapter focuses on the elaboration of SADR laws, rather than SADR's ratification of international legal agreements in the context of its membership in the African Union.[3] Initially, the state-movement set up a detribalized "popular" justice system in the camps. Over time, though, the legal administration was professionalized and, incidentally, partially "retribalized." This partial reemergence of *qabīlah* relations proves illuminating for the relationship between sovereignty and law.

## Sovereignty and State Law

The imposition of laws has come to be seen as integral to, and constitutive of, the sovereignty expected of centralized, territorial state power. For Carl Schmitt (1985), the monopoly on deciding the state of exception to laws is intrinsic to the sovereign power of states: "Therein lies the essence of the *state's* sovereignty, which must be juridically defined correctly, not as the monopoly to coerce or to rule, but as the monopoly to decide (Schmitt 1985: 13, emphasis added). As Wendy Brown (2010: 22) observes, a (Schmittian) model of inviolable sovereign state power has come to be perceived as a "fiction"—but a "potent fiction." Its potency surely lies in the extent to which the enjoyment of a monopoly over the state of exception—what I shall call the deciding of when laws hold—reinforces broader claims for state power. The very capacity of deciding when laws hold has been presumed, at least according to Schmitt (1985), to be constitutive of the sovereignty of state power. A monopoly on deciding laws also reinforces nation-state power more specifically, through the nationalist vision of one set of laws for one nation. Pretensions to democratic state power may likewise be strengthened by the notion of one set of laws for all subjects. For the state-movement, then, appropriating the power to decide when laws hold offered the attractions of performing state power, reinforcing the idea of a Sahrawi nation, and claiming to be democratic.

The establishment of state law also promises potential internal and external political advantages for a polity in quest of international recognition as a state. By promoting state law centering on and emanating from itself, the state-movement consolidated its own claims to be the legitimate center of state power. At the same time, the long-term legitimization of the liberation movement—the internationally recognized right of the Saharawi people to self-determination—inhabits the same international legal framework as the notion of state-centered legality. The state-movement's emulation of standards of "good governance," such as democracy and the rule of law, thus reaffirmed its commitment to the legal norms from which it derived legitimacy.

Beyond its attractions for state power in general, and more specifically for a liberation movement seeking recognition as a state, the establishment of state law held further appeal for the Sahrawi liberation movement. Sahrawis historically operated under legal regulation specific to *qabā'il*: tribal law, *'urf* (pl. *a'rāf*). Each politically dominant *qabīlah* had its own *a'rāf*, operating as its own penal code. For the state-movement, setting up state law, therefore, entailed repressing and superseding *a'rāf*—the latter, by their very nature, pertaining to *qabā'il*. Legal reform was thus a feature of the palimpsest whereby, as part of the state-movement's efforts to establish itself as a state power, the social relations of the state-movement were to overwrite and obscure those pertaining to the *qabīlah*. Yet over time the state-movement's attempts to overwrite the social relations of the *qabīlah* in legal administration met with compromises.

## (Pre)Colonial Perspectives

What were the legal arrangements and institutions the state-movement set about reforming? There has been considerable attention to tribal law in MENA (Middle East and North Africa) (e.g., Dresch 2006; Scheele 2008), in relation to Bedouin in particular (e.g., Chelhod 1971; Bailey 2009). Yet, as Frank Stewart (2006, 1987) notes, there has been a paucity of detailed studies for Saharan northwest Africa. Drawing on fieldwork in the early 1950s, Julio Caro Baroja (1955) describes some aspects of legal regulation among those who would come to be known as Sahrawis.

*'Urf*, Caro Baroja explains, is a body of rules that are particular to one *qabīlah* and only to be found in connection with specific *qabā'il*, which he goes on to name (1955: 43–45).[4] Those named are all politically dominant *qabā'il* who would have been in the position to extend protection to client tribes, and/or collect tribute from them. Indeed, Caro Baroja (44) explains that those tribes under the protection of others cannot be said to have *'urf*. He continues (43) that *'urf* is decided by the *jamā'ah* (council) of a particular tribe (see Chapter 1). According to Caro Baroja's interlocutors, *'urf* deals with crimes such as killing, stealing, and injury.[5] The punishments specified vary from *qabīlah* to *qabīlah*. They might comprise the sacrifice of a sheep or camel in reparation, as well as material recompense to be paid to the victim. From Caro Baroja's (1955: 44 n2, 439–42) examples, for instance, we find that, among the Rgaybāt and Izargiyen, a thief has to pay back four times the value of property stolen (440, 441). Among the Ait Lahsen, the property stolen must be returned along with a sheep or goat suitable for slaughtering (434).

Caro Baroja conducted his research within the colonial period, but at a time (1952–1953) when, only a few years earlier, it had been noted that there were very few sedentarized people in the Spanish Sahara (Flores Morales 1946). Within fifteen years of his fieldwork, however, Caro Baroja (1966: 61) would write of how the world that he had observed then had almost disappeared. The way of life portrayed by Caro Baroja's work from the early 1950s may be used with caution to offer insights into both the precolonial world in which his interlocutors would have grown to adulthood ("pacification" having only been enforced in 1934) and the altered colonial world that they were already experiencing.

In precolonial times in what would later become Spanish Sahara, where there was no single central source of political authority, a dominant *qabīlah* (according to Caro Baroja working through the institution of the *jamā'ah*) decided its own *a'rāf*, that is, which laws would apply (its own). Once a person left the sphere of that dominant *qabīlah*'s project of sovereignty, those *a'rāf* no longer applied. As long as one remained within what Paul Dresch (1989) has called the moral community of tribes—where fellow tribesmen recognize, across different tribes, membership in the same moral community—another set of *a'rāf* would hold.

If, for Schmitt (1985), sovereignty—for him, specifically that of state power—is defined by the exertion of a monopoly on deciding when laws hold, it would seem that, in precolonial times in the future Spanish Sahara, the power to decide when laws hold was not absent. Rather, it was exerted not by a state authority but by a different project of sovereignty: a dominant *qabīlah* deciding its own *aʿrāf*. This brings into question Schmitt's expectation that the monopoly to decide when laws hold is specific to the sovereignty of states and suggests that it might pertain to projects of sovereignty more broadly.

My argument is not that the imposition of *aʿrāf* per se denotes that a *qabīlah* is operating as a project of sovereignty. Historical context is crucial: to the extent that in the precolonial period there was no single central source of political authority in what would become Spanish Sahara, the presence of *aʿrāf* indicates a project of sovereignty. In the altered historical context of colonial rule in Spanish Sahara, *aʿrāf* still operated but cannot be apprehended as the markers of a project of sovereignty. For, despite the "myth" (San Martín 2010) of Spain's "benevolent" colonialism in the Sahara, the Spanish colonial authorities reserved for themselves the right to decide when laws held, introducing their own laws, which created exceptions to indigenous practice. For instance, no indigenous inhabitants of the Spanish Sahara other than those in the armed service of the Spaniards could carry firearms (Caro Baroja 1955: 33).

The common colonial scenario whereby one legal regime, that of colonial powers, encompassed and allowed to operate within it another legal regime, here, that of *aʿrāf*, evokes the contested (Tamanaha 2008) term legal pluralism in its "weak" form (Griffiths 1986; Merry 1988). Yet in what became the Spanish Sahara, legal pluralism, understood as one legal sphere resting and operating within another encompassing legal sphere, predates colonialism. Long before Saharan northwest Africa had Arabized, it had Islamized (Norris 1986). From at least the region's Islamization around the ninth century CE, spheres of religious (Islamic) law coexisted alongside *aʿrāf*. For Frank Stewart (2006), tribal law (in his terms, customary law) generally takes precedence among Bedouin over Islamic law. He suggests that each would normally be dealt with by a different legal specialist.

While Caro Baroja's (1955) account highlights the importance of the *jamāʿah* for deciding *aʿrāf*, it does not specify who—whether a council or an individual—was responsible for pronouncing legal decisions between parties to a conflict.[6] At the very least, it can be said that, in the areas addressed by *aʿrāf*, the punishments defined therein were preferred to punishments specified in Islamic law. The corporal punishments and mutilations of the latter have not been practiced historically in the northwest Sahara (Bonte 2007: 47). This should not be taken as a sign of lax adherence to or interest in

Islamic law. In other spheres, hassanophone northwest Africa has been noted for a stricter adherence to Islamic law than is sometimes found in other areas of MENA. For example, in some Arab contexts, both sedentary (e.g., Moors 1995) and mobile pastoralist (e.g., Peters 1990), women routinely forgo their rights to inherit as prescribed in Islamic law to maintain the right to make claims for protection on their natal kin. In hassanophone northwest Africa, nevertheless, women's rights to inheritance are routinely respected (Tillion 1966: 157–58), with women continuing to make claims on their own kin if need be. We should nonetheless note that, in a different aspect of family law, the possibilities envisaged by Islamic law have typically been avoided by Hassanophones. In marriage contracts Hassanophones have tended to include a clause precluding polygamy (Tillion 1966: 156; Bonte 2008: 102).

Whilst legal pluralism was by no means brought to the hassanophone Sahara by colonialism, colonialism nevertheless shifted the terms of preexisting legal pluralism in significant ways. It introduced a new project of sovereignty that placed the prerogative to decide when laws hold in the hands of the colonial authorities. Colonialism also introduced the notion of a set of laws applying to all persons within a fixed territory.

In both precolonial and colonial contexts, legal expertise, in *aʿrāf* as well as other legal spheres, was produced through the social relations of the *qabīlah*. Specialist knowledge about *aʿrāf* would be produced and disseminated by members of the particular *qabīlah* concerned. The production of religious knowledge, including Islamic law, was concentrated in the hands of families from *qabāʾil* in the status group of elite religious specialists (see Chapter 1). It is also useful to consider the social context in which legal proceedings would be undertaken. The holding of a formal *jamāʿah* would clearly take place within the context of a specific *qabīlah*. Yet there were also forums for dispute resolution, *ṣulḥ*, a term often translated as reconciliation. These were likewise staged within the social relations of membership in a *qabīlah*, taking place in a "*jamāʿah*" of a more informal nature.

*Ṣulḥ* is practiced throughout the Arab Muslim world. According to Ben Hounet (2010), the purpose of *ṣulḥ* is to bring about reconciliation in the social relations between the parties affected by an incident or conflict that has led to a compensation payment (*diyah*) being due. Any material transfer *ṣulḥ* entails is thus distinct from a *diyah* payment. Even where a crime is dealt with in a state penal system to the point of obviating a *diyah* payment, *ṣulḥ* may still be carried out in parallel and outside the state system. It can "complete" (Ben Hounet 2010) the state system's sanctions to the extent that it recognizes the collective responsibility of the agnates of the perpetrator and the need to renew social relations between the parties to a conflict.

Although *ṣulḥ* is not discussed by Caro Baroja (1955), my interlocutors were emphatic about its prominence as a means of dispute resolution, both historically and in the camps in the late 2000s, in settings where a compensation payment for an injury, killing, or marital dispute resolution might be due. In fact, *ṣulḥ* was one of the themes refugees most enjoyed talking about in response to my questions, whether my interlocutor was younger than me or two generations older. As one young man put it, *ṣulḥ* was "the most important thing" for Sahrawis. He added in the same breath that *ṣulḥ* was an event that took place around tea. The unforgettable words of an elderly male interlocutor concurred in the importance of tea for *ṣulḥ*: "If there was no tea-set, there could be no *jamāʿah*. If there was no *jamāʿah*, there could be no *ṣulḥ*." The term *jamāʿah* was used by my interlocutors in several senses that are more informal than Caro Baroja's sense of a "tribal council." Any social gathering (to drink tea in particular) could be called a *jamāʿah*. Yet, if a group of persons were gathered together to discuss a problem needing a solution, this was also known as a *jamāʿah*. The importance of tea for *ṣulḥ* lies, in addition to tea's status as the quintessential marker of hospitality and honoring of guests, in the fact that Hassanophones' ritualized consumption of tea is a potent tool of communication in its own right. The delaying strategies between the three (or, if there was a desire to extend conversation, four) cups send signals to those gathered in conversation about its progress. (When I was conducting interviews in the camps, I came to understand the vicissitudes of tea drinking as invaluable indicators of the interview's progress.)

In my interlocutors' descriptions, tea drinking and discussion in a *jamāʿah* for *ṣulḥ* took place among the important elderly male figures of a *qabīlah* or a section of a *qabīlah*, who would meet with their equivalents from the other party. Such an event was described to me by Khadīja as she recalled the occasions on which she became "angry" (*mughṭāḍah*) with her first husband. When a hassanophone wife becomes *mughṭāḍah* with her husband, he is required to make material gifts to her in order to regain favor and resume marital relations.[7] On the first occasion when Khadīja became *mughṭāḍah*, her husband's reparations culminated in a *ṣulḥ* in the pasturelands of Spanish Sahara in the late 1960s. Khadīja described how the male elders of the relevant *qabīlah* section were gathered together for the *ṣulḥ*:

> I got angry with my husband [*mughṭāḍah*] on two occasions. The first time [before the revolution], he had just married me, but I was still living with my family in the pasturelands [*badīah*]. We had not been to pay the first visit to his parents [*faskhah*—see Chapter 5]. My husband went to work in the city for some months. He didn't visit. I had my first son. My brothers went to work in the city, and they came and told me he had married another woman. I got *mughṭāḍah*. When my husband came back, he slaughtered a camel for me, and brought lots of the elders [*kūlah*] from the family. He did all this to satisfy me. But I didn't want to have him back. I cried. But in the end, my family persuaded me to have him back.
>
> The second time I got *mughṭāḍah* with him was at the time of the uprising. By that time we had four children and were living together in a house in Elayoune. But because of the uprising, everyone told me to go back to him, and in any case he didn't have any [material things] to satisfy me. So nothing really happened.

While the advent of colonialism brought significant changes for legal regulation for Sahrawis, in both precolonial and colonial contexts legal affairs were imbued with the social relations of the *qabīlah*. The close association of the social relations of the *qabīlah* with legal affairs posed a challenge to the state-movement and its aspirations to establish itself as law maker and arbiter. This challenge was initially met with attempts to "detribalize" legal spheres.

## Popular Justice and "Legal Detribalization"

In the early revolutionary period, when services in the camps were run primarily by the Popular Committees (see Chapter 2), the Committee for Social Affairs and Justice—often referred to as the "Justice Committee"—was charged with a number of legal responsibilities. In late 2008, I came to know Yaḥḍi, by then in his late sixties or older, who had been one of the Justice Committee's legal advisors. Questioned about the Justice Committee, he reflected meditatively: "The Justice Committee did a very important job—a very important job." Its importance, I suggest, includes that it was responsible for wresting the production of laws, legal expertise, and the social context in which legal regulation took place away from the social relations of the *qabīlah* and resituating them in the social relations of the state-movement.

Like all the Popular Committees in the camps (see Chapter 2), the Justice Committee was composed of adult women. Yet the Justice Committee was the only Popular Committee to which a man was also assigned, in the role of specialist advisor (*mukhtaṣṣ*). He was charged with bringing expert legal knowledge to the committee. It is likely that only men would have had the necessary training in religious law to prepare them for this role. Yaḥḍi was one such former *mukhtaṣṣ*.

One morning in November 2008, Māghalāha's son 'Abdi accompanied me on foot across the *wilāyah* of Auserd to meet Yaḥḍi at his home. We spent the morning sitting comfortably on the floor in one of the rooms of Yaḥḍi's home, with his son making tea for us all. Yaḥḍi explained that, before going into exile, he had studied the Qur'an and Malikite Islamic law in a religious school (*maḥḍarah*), first in the Spanish Sahara and then also in Mauritania. When he arrived in exile, Yaḥḍi was thus already trained in legal expertise. He recalled working first with the administrative department in charge of justice in Rabouni (the administrative "capital" of the camps), before later working as a judge (*qāḍī*) in a residential camp. When I questioned him about any qualifications required by the state-movement, Yaḥḍi said he had not taken an exam to qualify for either role. Another former *mukhtaṣṣ* for the Justice Committee whom I met and interviewed on another occasion recalled taking an "exam" with the state-movement to qualify as a *mukhtaṣṣ*. The judge in question was inconclusive in response to my questions as to the content of this exam, whether religious, ideological, or of some other focus. The contrasting memories of the two men who served as a *mukhtaṣṣ* perhaps suggest that, through a combination of formal selection and in-house training, the state-movement vetted those who went on to hold legal offices in the camps.

As well as registering births, marriages, and divorces (Firebrace and Harding 1987: 15–16), the Justice Committee operated as a lower court (Bäschlin 2004: 144), in which capacity it was expected to resolve marital disputes at the level of the *dairah*. The role of the women—of whom Yaḥḍi recalled there being 160 on the committee with which he worked—has been reported as one of advising the *mukhtaṣṣ* so that he was sure to take into account the female point of view in dealing with a dispute (Lippert 1985: 19). In Yaḥḍi's account, the women led discussions to resolve a dispute, and his role was to ensure that any decision to which the women came did not contravene Islamic law. Female interlocutors who had served on a Justice Committee also recalled that their role had been to hold discussions as a group, reason with both parties, and try to suggest what was best. Certainly, in Yaḥḍi's recollections, the women did not neglect the opportunity to express their views. "It was very difficult for me at times," he recalled, laughing, "because I was the only man there. Every time a problem came up about marriage, the women would turn to me and blame 'you men'. I would tell them 'you can't blame it all on me personally!'"

According to Anne Lippert (1985: 19–20), in a context of prolonged separation between spouses because of the war, which could lead to "misunderstandings," emphasis was placed by the Justice Committee on the avoidance of divorce. When asked what sorts of problems the Justice Committee dealt with, Yaḥḍi mentioned situations in which a man had left a wife but would not divorce her, a divorced husband was not helping his children enough, and a man wanted to take a second wife.[8]

The Justice Committee might seem a humble candidate indeed for the "very important job" of displacing the social relations of the *qabīlah* from judicial administration and replacing them with those of the state-movement. Yet the Justice Committee was key to unseating the social relations of the *qabīlah* in judicial administration. When political scientist Stephen Zunes visited the camps in 1988, he praised the means by which the Justice Committee sought to resolve disputes by consensus-driven arbitration and reconciliation at the community level between the conflicting parties (1988: 143). These activities—consensus-driven arbitration and reconciliation at the community level—sound strikingly familiar. What the Justice Committee was doing was surely *ṣulḥ*—but with a difference. *Ṣulḥ* had been removed from its social context within the *qabīlah*, thanks to the replacement of a *jamāʿah* of elderly male *qabīlah* notables with the women of the *dairah*'s Justice Committee. In fact, *ṣulḥ* had been "detribalized," and this detribalization was achieved through its "popularization."

For Michel Foucault (1980), popular justice movements seek liberation, all too often in vain, from the coercive ideological underpinnings of the judicial system that developed from late medieval times in Europe. This system enshrined bourgeois priorities such as the inviolability of private property and punishment of those who did not submit to the discipline of the proletariat. In the Arab Muslim world, projects to popularize justice have most commonly occurred in connection with revolutionary governments or liberation movements (e.g., Libya, the People's Democratic Republic of Yemen, and the PLO). Nevertheless, there are limitations to the depth and research access with which principal cases have been studied.[9]

We find a richer record of the operation of popular justice forums in other settings (Salas 1983; Hayden 1984; Clark 2007). Salas's (1983) study of popular tribunals in Cuba emphasizes how both the social actors and the institutional form of the administration of justice were popularized. This proves to be the case for Sahrawi exiles' popularized *ṣulḥ*. The role formerly played by a gathering of elders from each *qabīlah*, or part thereof, representing a party to a dispute, was placed into the hands of "the people," the women assigned to the Justice Committee. They voiced their opinions as to how disputes brought before them should be resolved and negotiated a resolution between the parties to a conflict. The popularization of the actors encompasses the popularization of *ṣulḥ* itself. It was transformed from reconciliation negotiated between two parties represented through the elders of the respective *qabā'il* to reconciliation negotiated by women representing an administrative unit of the state-movement. Similarly, the *mukhtaṣṣ*, even if he had acquired his legal expertise in the prerevolutionary period through his position in *qabīlah* hierarchies, was incorporated into the Justice Committee through his trajectory in the organs of the state-movement. The demographic profile and atmosphere of the Justice Committee's *ṣulḥ* could hardly have been more different from practices a few years earlier.

The extent to which popularized *ṣulḥ* was detribalized is highlighted through a comparison with *ṣulḥ* as operated by the PLO when it ran refugee camps in Lebanon autonomously (1969–1982). One of Julie Peteet's (2005: 140–41) interlocutors recalls how during that period the PLO would encourage disputes to be resolved through the negotiation process "*sulha.*" In doing so, however, the PLO called on tribal elders to operate negotiations under the supervision of a PLO representative. The Sahrawi refugee case went even farther, popularizing and detribalizing the very actors involved in *ṣulḥ*.

The Justice Committee, with its popularized, detribalized *ṣulḥ*, had a restricted legal remit. Interlocutors recalled of the early revolutionary period that, in other areas of governance, the Council for the Command of the Revolution (see Chapter 2) tended to rule by decree. Rule by decree may also be seen as a form of detribalization whereby state law, emanating from the state-movement, further undermined the notion of there being *a'rāf* for particular *qabā'il*. The Justice Committee can thus be seen as a popular vanguard of a broader phenomenon, whereby the early revolutionary state-movement detribalized both laws themselves and the social context in which legal expertise and procedures took place.

## Professionalization (and Depopularization)

Following the cease-fire of 1991, the priorities of the state-movement changed. Increasing emphasis was placed not on the running of the camps through Popular Committees but on the professionalization of public services. Official rhetoric stresses how this shift supported the setting up of institutions suitable not so much for the "temporary" circumstances of exile but for a long-term future in an anticipated independent Western Sahara. Yet at the same time the professionalization of public services also provided occupations in which to redeploy men returning from the battlefront (Gimeno Martín and Laman 2007). In this context, the Popular Committees were reformed in 1995 and reinstated as councils engaged in the same areas of activity (education, health, rations, and production). There was one exception, however: the Justice Committee. Its dissolution marked the end of popular justice in the camps.

The professionalization, and thus depopularization, of judicial administration in the camps had begun a few years earlier. Whereas in the early revolutionary period there had been a Department of Justice within the Ministry of the Interior, the eighth PGC in 1991 set up a Ministry of Justice in its own right (later to become the Ministry for Justice and Religious Affairs at the tenth PGC in 1999). At the ninth PGC in 1995, when the committees were reinstated as councils, the work of the Justice Committee was transferred to a state justice system comprising law courts and legal professionals. In this new system, each *dairah* had a judge trained in Islamic law. He was responsible for overseeing marriage contracts in the *dairah* and initial attempts to resolve marital disputes—but there was no committee of women to assist him (or for him to assist).

Disputes between spouses and about work contracts were referred to the Court of First Instance, *al-maḥkamah al-ibtidāʾīyah*. In 2008, there were three Courts of First Instance, located in the *wilāyāt* of Auserd and Dakhla and in Mijek in the Polisario-controlled areas of Western Sahara. (To ease refugees' access, a Court of First Instance was later opened in each *wilāyah*.) In Auserd, which, in the late 2000s, served the biggest population of the three Courts of First Instance then in existence, there were at least three judges, with one holding the position of president (*ra'īs*). The court's archive of cases dated back to 1997.

The Court of First Instance had no authority to deal with crimes coming under the penal code of the SADR. Such cases were dealt with at the Criminal Court, *maḥkamat al-jināyāt*, in February 27 camp. The Criminal Court also dealt with appeals from the Court of First Instance. Finally, there was the Court of Appeal, which, in 2008, had no fixed location but convened upon demand.

The Criminal Court and the Court of Appeal each had judges assigned to them, trained in state law rather than Islamic law. As some judges explained to me, those who took these positions were required to hold degrees in law, but these qualifications could be from any country (such as Algeria, Libya, or Cuba). The legal personnel working in the SADR system, having per force trained elsewhere, learned its laws in situ.

The upper echelons of the SADR legal system consisted of a Council of Magistrates and attorney general, established in 1991 (Bäschlin 2004: 146), and a Constitutional Council, which was responsible for ensuring that any laws passed in the SADR were in line with the constitution. The Ministry for Justice and Religious Affairs in Rabouni received members of the public in order to provide them with legal documentation, such as marriage certificates for those traveling abroad.

Keen to attend one of the courts in action, with the help of Māghalāha's family, I visited the *qāḍī* of their *dairah* at his home in Auserd camp. This *qāḍī* was also the serving *ra'īs* of the judges in Auserd's Court of First Instance. I was invited by him to attend the Court of First Instance on one of the days when it was in session. One chilly morning in October 2008, 'Abdi accompanied me on foot across the *wilāyah* to a centrally located but tired-looking mud-brick building that, if no more dilapidated than other sand-whipped structures, was certainly not the smartest. Some two decades earlier, it had hosted literacy classes for adult women, including 'Abdi's mother, Māghalāha.

The building showed no signs of life as we approached. Calling out and eventually following the sound of answering voices, we entered the building and followed a corridor until we came across two judges seated in a simple room furnished only with flat cushions around the edge. Both men were senior in years, and each wore a clean, fresh-looking robe (*ẓarā'ah*). Most men in the camps only wore this clothing on formal occasions. When older men wore it every day, they usually had a well-worn robe for daily use and kept a pristine robe, such as that worn by these men, for special occasions. The men were making tea. I explained my presence, my interests, and my invitation. While the judges gave their impeccably polite replies, 'Abdi was called outside by another male voice. When he returned, he explained that the head of "security" had ordered me to leave. The owner of this voice conveniently made himself scarce, so there was no possibility of inquiring what steps could be taken to rectify the situation.

Those of us who remained agreed that I should wait to greet the senior judge, without whom procedures could not begin anyway. In this way, he would know that I had accepted his invitation, and I hoped—in vain, it would prove—that some light might be shed on how, in another visit, I might learn more about the court's actual functioning. Eventually, the senior judge arrived. Of a similar generation, he was dressed in a startlingly white robe and carried a brief case (a rare sight in the refugee camps). His face was wrapped in a smart black turban, and the final touch was the black kohl drawn around his eyes. Here was an old man at his most formal. The arrival of this impressive figure was the cue for some men who had been gradually gathering outside the court to filter in. Regrettably, it was also the cue for my departure. Under the piercing gaze of the senior judge, the hearing—tea set and all—would soon be in full swing.

One of the judges—indeed, the very Yaḥḍi who would lend such a generous ear to my questions some weeks later—showed me and 'Abdi around as we left the court. We saw the main audience room, vacated, we learned, for renovation. The room in which that day's audience would soon begin was really the judges' room for resting between sessions. For the moment, the tired walls and ceiling of the audience room looked down on a vacant dais at the far end of the otherwise empty, unfurnished former classroom. Did the judges take their seats on this dais when proceedings were held in this room? The corridor leading away from the audience room through which we passed on our way out was lined with offices, labeled Secretariat (*al-kitābah*), Administration (*al-idārah*), Public Prosecutor (*al-mumaththil al-niyābī*), Guardroom (*al-darak,* for the military police) and Police (*al-shurṭah,* a civilian service).

These were to be my final glimpses of inside a SADR law court. Thereafter, individual judges in Auserd and Rabouni, as well as two lawyers in Auserd and Smara camps, gave generously and patiently of their time to me in interviews. But none of the judges' much-repeated assurances that I could visit a law court during its functioning ever led to a successful visit, nor was

I granted authorization to look at any of the court archives. The interest of a foreigner in the kinds of problems that led camp residents to resort to legal intervention was met with caginess by enough of the invisible voices of "security" to prevent research access beyond interviews with legal professionals. If, in the circumstances, a range of questions about the workings of the administration of justice in the late revolutionary period must remain unaddressed, some effects of the professionalization of the legal system can, nevertheless, be discerned.

## Reconfigurations of State Law, Islamic Law, and Tribes

The attempt to set up a state justice system that could serve in an independent SADR took the form of a Western-inspired model of law courts (emulated via the more immediate reference of the Algerian system, the latter modeled in turn on the French). With this aim taking priority, the participation of nonlegal specialists that characterized the Justice Committee as a form of popularized justice was replaced by a professionalized body of judges, lawyers, and other legal officers. This is very much a parallel to Cuba's eventual replacement of popular tribunals with legal specialists (Salas 1983).

Professionalization brought depopularization, then. Yet, drawing on the image of the Court of First Instance, it is clear that professionalization also brought what, paraphrasing Harri Englund's (2002: 173) "paraphernalia of democracy," we might call the "paraphernalia of state power." From its name to its component offices of military and civilian security, archives, and public prosecution, the court was steeped in the language of state power. Its promotion of state power notwithstanding, professionalization also had other effects that perhaps reinforced the need for the parading of the paraphernalia of state power.

In fact, the Court of First Instance (like the Justice Committee before it) dealt with a limited range of disputes: marriage, divorce, inheritance, sales, and contracts. Yet it dealt with these exclusively through Islamic law, these being the areas in which, in the absence at that time of civil codes of its own covering with these areas, the SADR deferred completely to Islamic law. Yaḥḍi, the senior judge, and their colleagues dealt only with Islamic law, Yaḥḍi assured me in our later interview. The paraphernalia of state power might make the court look like an institution that was dealing in state power. But in fact in the areas addressed in that court, the state-movement had no laws of its own making to apply. If Sahrawis have long been dealing with the areas in question (marriage, inheritance, contracts of sale) through Islamic law, the SADR Court of First Instance was, for exiled Sahrawis, perhaps the first physical institution that could be pointed out as a place that dealt with Islamic law and no other forms of law.

Professionalization also affected the detribalization of the administration of justice. With the exception of the senior judge's briefcase, which was a firm nod toward bureaucracy, the judges themselves seemed to personify expert legal knowledge as it might have manifested itself in a *jamāʿah* hosted in the social relations of the *qabīlah*. The tea set confirmed my impression that, whereas the shell of the law court sought to impose a language of state justice on proceedings, the actual ambiance, had I been able to stay, might have felt much more like a *jamāʿah* dominated by male elders. In the new style of courts, the detribalization of the administration of justice became clouded.

This reading of the Court of First Instance underscores how the professionalization of the SADR legal system entailed multiple trends. It not only comprised depopularization, and thereby the promotion of the notion of the state-movement as the source and enforcer of state law, but there had also been both a subtle increase in the profile of Islamic law (in the form of a state-sponsored physical institution specializing in Islamic law) and an implicit undermining of the earlier detribalization (the return of *ṣulḥ* dominated by elite elderly males). Might these trends speak to broader phenomena at work in the camps?

The rejection of tribal law seems fully complicit with an overall aim of centralizing the regulation of legality in the hands of the state-movement. Yet the rejection of tribal law can be said to have had an additional effect of raising the profile of Islamic law. With the rejection of tribal law, religious law became in its stead a point of reference and inspiration for state law. This becomes apparent from the SADR constitution and penal code. Article 2 of the constitution states that Islam is the "source" (*maṣdar*) of law for the SADR. An examination of some articles of the SADR penal code shows how, in a context of *aʿrāf* no longer serving as a reference point for dealing with certain crimes, Islamic definitions of these crimes have acquired a more immediate influence on the SADR manner of dealing with them.

Crimes dealt with in the SADR penal code such as theft, murder, and rape are staples of both *aʿrāf* and Islamic law. As noted above, the mutilations and corporal punishments with which these crimes are sanctioned in Islamic law have not been readily applied in hassanophone northwest Africa, whether in precolonial, colonial, or postcolonial times (Bonte 2007: 47). In precolonial and colonial times, such crimes were dealt with through *a'rāf*, which imposed material punishments for infringements. In the late revolutionary period, these crimes came to be sanctioned under the penal code of the SADR. But, although ostensibly an expression of state law, the SADR penal code, we shall see, can express the influence of Islamic legal definitions of these crimes. This is not distinctive to SADR—other states' penal codes have been influenced by Islamic law (see Dupret 2006).

An example of this phenomenon in the penal code of the SADR is the treatment of sexual relations classified as crimes. Sexual relations taking place outside marriage, *zinā'*, are subject to punishment in Islamic law.[10] There is also evidence of such acts being subject to punishment in *a'rāf*. The *a'rāf* of the Izargiyen defines a punishment of the payment of the bridewealth for "rape" (*estupro*, Spanish), and the *a'rāf* of the Rgaybāt prescribes the same punishment for "touching another man's wife" (Caro Baroja 1955: 441). The treatment of extramarital sexual relations in the SADR penal code introduces an explicit distinction in punishment on the grounds of the question of consent or nonconsent. It also introduces a reference to Islamic jurisprudence of the Malikite school.

As concerns consensual extramarital relations, article 169 of the SADR penal code defines as prohibited all sexual relations taking place outside the context of a married couple. Article 170 further specifies that the punishment for *zinā'* is between one and five years of imprisonment, applying to both men and women. Article 170 goes on to add that this punishment applies to a woman found pregnant outside marriage. These articles' definition of consensual extramarital relations as criminal complies with Islamic law definitions of *zinā'*. *A'rāf* are not explicit on the question of consent or nonconsent for extramarital relations incurring penalty. In practice, Hassanophones have preferred discretion, such as hiding pregnancy outside marriage, rather than sanctions. Such discretion might take the form of marrying the woman as soon as possible to her father's brother's son, who, as her agnate, bears the responsibility to hide the shame arising from the pregnancy not only for the woman but also for her—and, therefore, also his—agnates (Fortier 2000: 450). The additional specification in Article 170 that pregnancy outside marriage is proof of *zinā'* arises directly from the Malikite school of Islamic law. This school is distinct in stating that pregnancy can be taken as proof of *zinā'* (Miller 2007: 75).[11]

If the treatment of consensual extramarital relations in the SADR penal code adheres more to Islamic precepts than those of *a'rāf*, a similar trend pertains to the treatment of nonconsensual sexual relations. Article 165 of the SADR penal code specifies a punishment of between two and five years of prison for committing rape, and in the case of the use of violence against a minor, between five and ten years. Article 167 specifies that, if the rape is committed against a virgin, then the punishment is also between five and ten years of prison. It is not clear that the treatment of nonconsensual sexual relations in *a'rāf* differs according to whether the woman in question is a minor or a virgin. A distinction for the rape of a virgin has been claimed for Islamic jurisprudence.[12] In sum, in its definition and routinization of punishment, the SADR penal code grants a greater prominence to Islamic law than was previously known among Sahrawis.[13]

It is no novelty arising from the state-movement that certain areas of Sahrawis' life have been governed through Islamic law. We saw that, in personal status law, as well as contracts and sales, Sahrawis have long followed Islamic prescriptions. Ironically, though, in one of the areas where Sahrawis, along with other Hassanophones, were known for avoiding the possibilities of Islamic law, namely, in polygamy, the attempts of the state-movement to impose its own law resulted in increased emphasis on Islamic prescription, rather than the formalization of an existing local preference for its avoidance. As noted above, in precolonial and colonial hassanophone northwest Africa, the inclusion in a marriage contract of a clause against polygamy ("neither a preceding [wife] nor following [wife]," "*lā sābiqah wa lā lāḥiqah*") was so routine that it has been seen as offering an effective guarantee against polygamy (Tillion 1966: 156). In the state-movement's early years, several reforms took place with regard to marriage. It was required that both marriage partners give their consent to the marriage, and a minimum age of sixteen for women and eighteen for men was introduced (Lippert 1985: 19). This was a departure from the Malikite school, in which there is no minimum age for marriage, but it is held that a spouse must have reached puberty. At one of the early PGCs, a debate was also held about whether polygamy should be banned, as one of the officers involved in this debate recalled to me. It might have been expected that, in a context where other reforms circumventing that which was permitted in Islam, such as a minimum age for marriage, had been achieved and with such a cultural preference in the region for polygamy's effective prohibition, it would not be difficult to prohibit polygamy. Not so. As the interlocutor who had been present at that debate recalled, it was rejected that the state-movement could forbid something permitted in Islam. State law proved unable to achieve de jure the de facto prohibition of polygamy the moral community of the *qabā'il* had achieved.

To clarify, it is not my intention to suggest that the increase in the profile of Islamic law signals an "Islamization" of governance, such as has been pursued in revolutionary Iran, Gaza under Hamas, or Sudan under Omar al-Bashir. The increase in reference to Islamic law was subtle, taking the form of greater formalization and precision in state law than had previously existed in *a'rāf*. The underlying concerns not to disallow something permitted in Islam (such as polygamy) nor to allow something forbidden in Islam (such as sexual relations outside marriage) were not new on the part of the state-movement but chimed fully with *a'rāf*. It would also be hard to argue that a broader Islamization was at stake in the camps. The state-movement, eager to court potential supporters among Western nations, sought to distance itself from Islamist politics.[14] Islamist religious practice was not unknown in the refugee camps, there being a few men and women (usually young adults) who had adopted Islamist piety practices (such as distinctive modest clothing, avoidance of contact with unrelated members of the opposite sex, and intensive attendance of prayers at the simple mosques that, by the 2000s, had been built in each *dairah* in the refugee camps).[15] The few so engaged were openly discussed as "odd" by other refugees, though; far more commonly Sahrawis, like their Bedouin peers the Awlād 'Ali in Egypt's western desert (Abu-Lughod 1999: xiii–xiv), believed that their "everyday religiosity" qualified them as "good Muslims."

On the question of legal detribalization, how far did the reforms go in demoting *a'rāf* and detribalizing the social context of legal administration? While the SADR penal code replaced *a'rāf* in the specification of punishments for particular crimes, in one area a Sahrawi jurist found grounds for arguing that *a'rāf* had not been made fully obsolete. In the last chapter of the penal code, Article 220 specifies that, in the cases of homicide and injury, indemnization must be paid in accordance with the principles of *diyah*. As one of the judges specializing in state law highlighted to me, SADR law refers explicitly to Islamic law (*sharī'ah*) in this article. But, the judge continued, since *sharī'ah* does not specify the amount to be paid as *diyah*, in his opinion this article also referred obliquely to *a'rāf*, for any judge applying that article would be obliged to refer to *a'rāf* in order to set a *diyah* amount.[16]

If this judge's reasoning is convincing, then even the penal code of the SADR did not wholly sever links with the *a'rāf* that the state-movement had sought so hard to erase. Any lingering presence of *a'rāf* was, however, minor, even tenuous. The vast majority of the punishments specified by *a'rāf* were replaced by SADR punishments as specified in the penal code. But a more serious disruption of the thrust of the state-movement's original reforms has arguably occurred in the late revolutionary "retribalization" of social relations in which some administration of justice took place. Specifically, the *qabā'il* began once again to host *ṣulḥ*.

In the summer of 2008, Salek, a lawyer in his late twenties specializing in state law, explained to me that families would try to resolve their disputes in the first instance among themselves before going to "the state." Salek used the term *ṣulḥ* directly and explained it as a process whereby the elders of the two concerned parties would gather together to try to find a solution to a dispute. I was able to collect a number of testimonies in which attempts at a resolution were brokered between the elders of the two different *qabā'il* implicated in a conflict. Some of these were attempted resolutions of marital disputes that were described to me as meetings between the elder men of the *qabā'il*, or sections of *qabā'il*, involved. Two examples follow of *ṣulḥ* in the wake of an injury and a killing respectively. For the sake of anonymizing the stories, I have removed the names of the *qabā'il* involved, although both stories were told to me with the speaker using the name of each *qabīlah* involved.

Khanātha, Māghalāha's second daughter, recounted to me a case of *ṣulḥ* in Māghalāha's family in the mid-2000s:

> [Our relative on our mother's side] was in a car accident with another car, a man selling water for making tea. He didn't have mirrors and drove into [our relative]. He was sent to [the hospital in] Tindouf and then to Algiers. He couldn't move anymore. They [the *qabīlah* of the man who had been driving the car without mirrors] went to the others [the *qabīlah* of our relative] and asked them what they would like. They said that they would like some help. They [the *qabīlah* of the man who caused the accident] understood that they wanted something, and so they gave a car and some money. [Our relative got better] and now he drives that car.

A young male civil servant from Elayoune camp recounted to me one of his own family's experiences of *ṣulḥ* in the mid-2000s:

> My *mint 'amm* [father's brother's daughter or classificatory equivalent] was walking along with her son, who was young, about two, and a car came past without breaks and ran over the boy. He died. The old men from those people [the *qabīlah* of the man who had been driving] came to see our old men [from our *qabīlah*], and they sat together and had tea. They [the elders of the other *qabīlah*] asked us [the old men from my *qabīlah*] what they would like, and they [the elders from my *qabīlah*] told them that they didn't want anything, that it was an accident. That was all.

Salek, the lawyer, had been keen to impress upon me that the state-movement encouraged parties to a dispute to seek solutions in the first instance through *ṣulḥ* conducted between *qabā'il*, before resorting to formal legal procedures in a court setting. In this light, the shadow of the social relations of the *qabīlah* that I discerned in the gathering of the elderly male judges in the Court of First Instance was not an isolated incident but bespeaks a broader late revolutionary resurgence of the social relations of the *qabīlah* for judicial administration.

It does not follow, though, that there had been a straightforward "return" of the past. First, it is not clear that late revolutionary *ṣulḥ* was a "return" to prerevolutionary *ṣulḥ* conducted in the context of *qabīlah* relations. The role of the *qabīlah* varied between precolonial and colonial settings; the *qabīlah* could be different again in its own right in its late revolutionary manifestations.

Second, while the state-movement may have encouraged a narrative emphasizing its own initiative in reopening a role for the *qabīlah* in the regulation of social life, it is unclear how much the state-movement was acting to legitimize a tendency that was already springing up anyway in the refugee camps. The reasons behind the onset of *ṣulḥ* within the *qabīlah* are open to speculation. The professionalizing legal reforms, unlike the earlier popularizing reforms, omitted to institutionalize *ṣulḥ*. Given Sahrawis' overwhelming enthusiasm for *ṣulḥ* ("the most important thing") and given that the state-movement had ceased to provide its own institutionalization of *ṣulḥ*, perhaps refugees reintroduced it in the more tolerant climate of the late revolutionary period. The state-movement might have merely co-opted what was a *fait accompli*. Yet the very fact that the state-movement was endorsing *ṣulḥ* taking place within the social relations of the *qabīlah* creates an association between this form of *ṣulḥ* and the state-movement. This situates *ṣulḥ* in the late revolutionary period in a gray zone that is neither wholly within nor outside the state-movement.

Third, late revolutionary *ṣulḥ* should not be assumed to exclude the state-movement other than in a role of providing external legitimization. On one occasion during my fieldwork, I was able to attend the climax of a *ṣulḥ* process, the conspicuous consumption paid for by a husband signifying reconciliation with his estranged wife. This event was, in a sense, an exilic equivalent of the reconciliation in the pasturelands recalled above by Khadīja. Māghalāha's youngest sister was being reconciled with her husband. Together with Māghalāha's female relatives, I helped serve the meal to family, friends, and neighbors to mark the reconciliation. As it was Ramadan, everyone gathered near Māghalāha's mother's home after sunset. The women (who were more numerous than men) were outside and the men in a nearby tent. As I moved between the female guests, bending over to pour water for washing hands or to set a dish down, I recognized among the guests both those invited because of shared relationships through the social relations of the *qabīlah* and those invited because of shared relationships through the social relations of the state-movement as fellow workers, councilors and "fighters" (*munāḍilāt*). The *ṣulḥ* of the late revolutionary period hosted within the social relations of the *qabīlah* was also, at least at the moment of the crowning conspicuous consumption, criss-crossed by the social relations of the state-movement. Thus, while it is helpful to recognize how late revolutionary *ṣulḥ* has "retribalized," the very notion of retribalization must itself be qualified.

## Sovereignty and Law Revisited

I began this chapter by evoking a scene and discussion about theft, which foregrounded that Sahrawi exiles were subject to SADR laws. My concern in the ensuing analysis was less to assess how strictly these laws were applied (although it can at least be said that SADR laws did see some refugee criminals convicted and serving sentences in prison). Rather, I interpreted the existence of these laws and their attendant apparatus as a sign of the state-movement's considerable efforts to configure itself in the image of the "potent fiction" of a supreme sovereign power that decides when laws hold.

I focused on how, in the case of the state-movement, its claims to having the power to decide when laws hold entailed overwriting *aʿrāf*, the penal codes specific to dominant *qabā'il*. I argued that this was because the existence of *a'rāf*, laws specific not to all Sahrawis but only to certain *qabā'il*, evoked precolonial *a'rāf*-imposing *qabā'il* as an alternative project of sovereignty to the state-movement. In line with the palimpsest metaphor that I pursue throughout this book, the making of the social relations of one project of sovereignty, the state-movement, entailed obscuring the social relations of another project of sovereignty, the *qabīlah* in its *a'rāf*-imposing form. But I also showed how, in the early revolutionary period, the state-movement's popularization of justice achieved an even broader range of forms of legal detribalization. The production of legal knowledge and reconciliation, which had previously taken place within the social relations of the *qabīlah*, were made to take place within the social relations of the state-movement, thanks to the appointment of SADR specialist legal personnel and women to the Justice Committee.

With the state-movement's decision in the late revolutionary period to professionalize its judicial apparatus, the state-movement's efforts to centralize legal regulation in its own hands revealed themselves more and more to be a reconfiguration of the relationship between state law, Islamic law, and tribal law. In this reconfiguration, I suggested how the ostensible promotion of state law and rejection of tribal law (*a'rāf*) led to an increased reference to Islamic law.

The rejection of *a'rāf* remained constant (perhaps with a faint echo in the SADR penal code as concerns compensation). But the broader detribalization of the social relations of legal administration came to fare very differently under professionalized justice. Late revolutionary *ṣulḥ* reemerged as taking place within the social relations of the *qabīlah*. The state-movement shifted from an attempted displacement of the social relations of the *qabīlah* (in popularized *ṣulḥ*) to the recruitment of the social relations of the *qabīlah* (in *qabīlah*-led *ṣulḥ*) as a means of pursuing its own goals, here to see disputes resolved effectively. The palimpsest changed gear, from overwriting so as to obscure, to compromise where *qabīlah* relations were tolerated to show through the palimpsest. Yet this occurred in a way that still allowed the state-movement to claim for itself aspects considered to be constitutive of sovereignty, here deciding when laws hold.

Of the reforms' various aims—to centralize legal regulation, to establish one set of laws for all (exiled) Sahrawis, to undo tribal laws, but, most of all, to affirm the state-movement as a sovereign power—how much was unprecedented? The colonial period had introduced state law and had undermined, if not *aʿrāf* themselves, the notion of dominant *qabāʾil* as projects of sovereignty. It had also introduced the new principle of the applicability of law to a territory (Spanish Sahara) rather than a group of people (members of certain *qabāʾil*, Muslims). Legal pluralism was long-standing throughout the colonial and precolonial periods. Was there, then, anything new about the state-movement's legal reforms, apart from their attempt to make *aʿrāf* obsolete?

Revolutionary novelty may lie in the fact that, previously, changes to the locus of the power to decide on laws had been driven by outside actors: colonial authorities had undermined dominant *qabāʾil* as projects of sovereignty, and the international legal confirmation of the right of the people of Western Sahara to self-determination had been endorsed by UN institutions. The state-movement's attempt to situate the deciding of when laws hold at the level of the state-movement was the first *internal* endorsement of the Sahrawi nation as a project of sovereignty. This was new and might be seen as the state-movement's grand project.

The legal reforms of the state-movement illuminate a number of wider themes in the anthropology of law: that reconciliation practices can be transposed from one social setting to another (here from tribes to popular justice); that "custom" is a plural field, the constituent parts of which can undergo divergent trajectories during legal reform, as was the case for *aʿrāf* and *ṣulḥ* here (Wilson 2015); and that different institutional forms, such as popular or formal justice, can have radical and sometimes unexpected effects on the relationships of ongoing legal pluralism. The legal reforms of the state-movement are perhaps of most interest for the present purposes for insights offered into questions of law, sovereignty, and state power.

As we have seen, an account of sovereignty as an inviolable power along the lines of Schmitt's proposed monopoly on the state of exception has been interpreted as a "potent fiction." Such an interpretation calls into question how law, its imposition, and the possibilities for its suspension might be useful for understanding sovereignty. But law continues to hold a place in discussions of governing authorities. Drawing on my reflections on the state-movement, I want to suggest two ways in which law is useful for discussions of sovereignty.

First, whether or not a monopoly on the state of exception is more fiction than key to understanding sovereignty, we can question Schmitt's assertion that such a monopoly is constitutive of the sovereignty of state power per se. In what is now Western Sahara, in precolonial times, decisions as to when laws held, which *a'rāf* pertained, resided in the authorities of dominant *qabā'il*. For this reason, I have suggested, the state-movement expended enormous efforts to undermine and obscure *a'rāf*, replacing them with its own laws. It remade the social relations of sovereignty, claiming for itself the prerogative to decide when laws held that had once resided with dominant *qabā'il*. To the extent that the deciding of when laws hold—that is, a monopoly on the state of exception—is helpful for understanding sovereignty, this may not necessarily pertain to the sovereignty of states, but may pertain also to other projects of sovereignty.

Second, attention to questions of law and sovereignty may shed some light on a bone of contention in discussions of legal pluralism. There has been disagreement as to whether the term "law" should be reserved for legal regulation backed by states (Tamanaha 1993), or whether it could be used more widely, on the grounds that there might be nothing distinctive about legal regulation when performed by states (Woodman 1999). My suggestion here is that this controversy arises in part from an asymmetry that has been neglected. Distinct from the question of whether there has to be a state for there to be law (the controversy in discussions of legal pluralism) is the reverse question of whether there has to be law for there to be state power—or, we might expand, some other project of sovereignty. Schmitt is not alone in suggesting that the existence of laws—in his account to be suspended or enforced at the will of the sovereign—is constitutive of state power. The Weberian notion of the state enjoying a monopoly on legitimate coercion within a given territory also presupposes that there must be laws (enforcing coercion) for there to be state power. Where the hegemonic notion of state power as a stratified political community in a fixed territory ruled by a centralized authority has been called into question, such as in David Sneath's (2007) reinterpretation of the state as a "state relation," rule making is retained in his conceptualization of the properties of the state relation (10). The controversy as to whether "law" should be reserved for rules imposed and enforced by state power can perhaps be alternatively understood as in part a struggle to register an asymmetry. If it is not necessary for there to be state power or another project of sovereignty for the work of defining and imposing rules to take place, it may, however, be necessary for there to be rule-making (and, for Schmitt, the potential cancelation of these rules) for state power or another project of sovereignty to know itself in that capacity and be recognized by others. It would seem that an expectation that a project of sovereignty entails rule making (and its suspension) may pertain as much to state power in the form idealized in the international system as to *a'rāf*-imposing *qabā'il*.

The asymmetrical relationship between law and sovereignty that I am suggesting here—that law may be essential for sovereignty when the reverse is not necessarily true—is highlighted in the legal reforms of the state-movement. To the extent that the state-movement sought to assert itself as engaging in the social relations of sovereignty, it sought to oust *qabīlah* relations from deciding when laws held. Thus it made *a'rāf* obsolete. To the extent that *qabīlah* relations were involved in aspects of rule making, such as the procedures for *ṣulḥ*, that did not pertain to deciding when laws held and, therefore, did not broach the question (of perceptions) of sovereignty, *qabīlah* relations were tolerated in the late revolutionary period.

Legal reforms in the state-movement suggest novel perspectives on some old questions about law and sovereignty. The next chapter considers how the appropriation of resources under the state-movement offers fresh insights into sovereignty and its relationship to taxation.

CHAPTER 4

# Tax Evasion: Appropriation and Redistribution Without Tax or Rent

The spirit of a people . . . is written in its fiscal history.
—Joseph Schumpeter, "The Crisis of the Tax State"

Rations days stood out in the camps. Word would spread from home to home that, on a designated forthcoming day, rations of a particular kind—for example, flour, sugar, oil—would be distributed in that district (*dairah*). For Sahrawis, as for Palestinian refugees in Lebanon (see Peteet 2005), rations collection was women's work. On a rations day, one of Māghalāha's three daughters would be assigned the task of bringing home the rations for the family. This daughter would have to make herself available all day, as the rations could arrive at any time. When the call from the *dairah*'s loudspeaker was heard, announcing the arrival of the rations truck, the designated daughter would fix her turban over her face, don her gloves, and, thus protected from the sun, set off.

I often went to the rations distribution too, in each of the three camps where I came to live. I was fascinated by the orderly management of distributions, which, in the late 2000s, were overseen by women from the local council for the Sahrawi Red Crescent (see Chapter 2). The women who counted out kilos of lentils, as well as those who collected their lot in the strong bag they had brought with them, were calm. Back in the tents, one might hear a woman praising another woman who was known for her distribution being fair—implying that other women might not merit such praise. In distributions themselves, though, women were confident that they knew their dues and would receive them. The most common disappointment, experienced with stoicism, was when the ration received for each household was far less than what was needed.

Stoicism also characterized distributions to the extent that they could entail exhausting hours of waiting, sometimes in the sun, or back-breaking work carrying heavy loads back home. Not all families could spare the cash to hire a wheelbarrow to carry a heavy load home, and not all families had a car whose driver might be persuaded to pick up a 50 kg sack of flour. Yet there could also be a sociable and joyful side to rations distributions. Women hailing from all four of a *dairah*'s neighborhoods would look out for friends at the distribution and catch up on news. Later, Māghalāha and whichever of her daughters had not been to collect the rations would grill the daughter who returned from the distribution for sightings and news. Families also enjoyed better meals in the days following a distribution. Fresh fruit and vegetable rations, typically potatoes, onions, carrots, and apples, brought rare luxury into poorer households whose scant cash income would seldom be spent on such items. In my visit in 2012, it became the talk of the camps when, for the first time ever, the fruit distribution included bananas. Māghalāha's family were delighted, and no one more so, they explained to me laughingly, than her husband, Tawwālu. He could enjoy bananas much more than the usual apples, for he had no teeth.

If rations were all these things—hard work, sociability, a reminder of exile and poverty, a fleeting taste of luxury—they were also a crucial constituent of the relationship between the state-movement and its refugee citizens. In this chapter, I analyze rations and related activities in the camps to reconsider an old trope of state power: the idea that state power entails a monopoly on legitimate coercion deployed in the appropriation of resources, such as through taxation or rent from natural resources. The state-movement initially appears unable to appropriate resources through either route. It could not extract property from dispossessed refugees. Nor could the state-movement benefit, in exile, from the phosphate, fishing, and other resources of Western Sahara.[1] I nevertheless take the state-movement as an unusual case that highlights underlying and hitherto neglected dynamics of appropriation and its relationship to redistribution and sovereignty.

I argue that the state-movement performed an "innovated taxation" comprising three strands. First, instead of appropriating (taxes) on a universal basis, the state-movement distributed (rations) on a universal basis. Second, through a supplementary, discretionary distribution system that drew on the politics of redistribution within *qabīlah* relations, the state-movement presented itself as a state power that let the "poor" tax the "rich." Third, the state-movement appropriated resources, in the form of conscripted labor. One of its most enduring forms of appropriation was a reconfiguration of labor pooling within *qabīlah* relations, transformed in exile to fit the state-movement. Yet over time—as I argued for the deciding of when laws hold (Chapter 3)—the attempted replacement of *qabīlah* relations was modified. In the palimpsest of the attempt to overwrite *qabīlah* relations, the latter came to show through the overwriting: *qabīlah* relations reemerged in appropriation and redistribution, and innovated taxation was eroded. By exploring the rise and fall of innovated taxation, I suggest how a familiar trope of state power—the presumed reliance on taxation and/or rent from natural resources—can be understood in broader terms of sovereignty, appropriation, and redistribution. Projects of sovereignty (not necessarily in the form of state power) may claim a monopoly on legitimate coercion for appropriation, but this appropriation is best understood in the light of its relationship to redistribution. I expand on Joseph Schumpeter's analysis, cited at the opening of this chapter, and suggest that the spirit of a people is written in its fiscal *and redistributive* history.

## Sovereignty and Appropriation

Every sovereign must find an answer, John Davis (1987: 15 n2) suggests, to the question of how the task of governing others will be financed. The notion that state power should appropriate resources has come to be taken for granted. Taxation in particular has become normalized as a means of appropriation—such as in Benjamin Franklin's saying that the only certainties in life are death and taxes (Guyer 1992: 42). Yet taxation has also been seen as constitutive of state power and of state power in particular forms. In a Weberian conception of state power, "the state has a double monopoly on taxation and the legitimate use of force" (Hylland Eriksen 1995: 170). A monopoly on legitimate coercion can indeed be said to collaborate intimately with a monopoly on taxation. The evasion of taxes attracts punishments that are legitimate forms of violence (the violation of freedom or of property through imprisonment, fines, and so on). Even taxation itself, Charles Tilly (1985: 181) has argued, is a form of violence: one of several potential forms that a state, enacting a dynamic of organized crime (albeit under the cloak of governmental legitimacy) exerts over its own citizens. Turning attention to how taxation is constitutive of a particular kind of state power, Jane Guyer (1992) describes how taxation influenced the development of state power in Europe. The fact that states took advantage of subjects' property to tax them eventually led to citizens making demands, on the grounds of property ownership, for participation. Democratic participation in Europe emerged over time, Guyer suggests, from the nexus of state power, property, and taxation.

It is not only in Euro-American thinking that taxation has been presumed to be constitutive of state power. The dominant model of state power in North Africa is the *makhzan* (see Chapter 1). *Makhzan* is used in North Africa to refer to zones in which a state power governs constituencies and extracts taxes from them. It is contrasted with *sībah*, zones in which it is perceived that state power fails to extract taxes. Derived from the Arabic root *kh-z-n*, meaning to "store," *makhzan* literally means "the place where things are stored, storehouse" (from which the English "magazine" is derived). Contemporary standard Arabic usage makes explicit the link between taxation and the role of state power in "storing" what has been extracted: the commonly used Arabic word for a treasury department is *makhzan*.

Construed as constitutive of state power in both Euro-American and North African ideas of state power, taxation is nevertheless only one of the forms of appropriation on which state power may draw. A contrasting model of state power to the tax-extracting state is the rentier state. A rentier state appropriates for itself the natural resources of its territory and extracts income from third parties who wish to access those resources. In its most extreme form, such as the oil-rich Gulf monarchies, the resources of rent are so plentiful that the state does not need to tax.

In each of these scenarios—the Weberian notion of the tax-extracting state, the *makhzan*, and the rentier state—state power is intrinsically concerned with appropriation. The state-movement appears singularly ill equipped to appropriate along such lines. The population it governs is—technically—composed of dispossessed refugees. The state-movement is furthermore displaced from Western Sahara's natural resources, which are instead exploited by Morocco. It might be argued that rations, which become available for the state-movement to distribute, act like rent from natural resources. But there is an important difference between the state-movement and a rentier state that, thanks to rent, does not need to tax. In a rentier state that can avoid raising taxes, the absence of the need to tax is associated with a reduced burden of legitimization or the maintenance of popular support (see Davis 1987; Ayubi 1995: 224–29). In contrast, in the case of the state-movement, the divorce from taxes, arising from the quite different circumstances of material dispossession in exile and the meeting of the needs for survival by international aid, is associated with an increase, not a reduction, in the state-movement's needs to generate and maintain legitimacy. The state-movement was obliged to maintain its legitimacy in the eyes of the refugees, who could leave the camps for other destinations if they so wished (see Wilson 2014b). It also had to maintain its legitimacy in the eyes of the international community on whose support for rations and, ultimately, the right to self-determination the liberation movement relied.

The state-movement seems far removed from the possibilities for appropriation found in either the tax-extracting state or the rentier state. Nevertheless, in its unusual situation, the state-movement proves an enriching case through which to rethink the prevailing tendency to link taxation, or its avoidance via rent, to state power. In his essay on the sociology of the fiscal state, Joseph Schumpeter (1954 [1918]) called for the study of taxation as a window onto state power. As the anthropology of the state has blossomed in the past two decades, anthropologists and other social scientists have turned attention—after surprisingly scant anthropological interest in taxation—to the relationship between taxation, state power, and sovereignty. Geographer Angus Cameron (2006) examines how the increasing centralization of fiscal control and the privatization of fiscal responsibility undermines the creation of a global fiscal domain, despite calls for such globalization. Janet Roitman (2005) traces taxation as a process of the conversion from private to public wealth. Attending to neoliberal forms of state power, Bill Maurer (2009) analyzes international responses to tax havens in order to assess the shift toward attempted governance through "soft law." Brenda Chalfin (2010) assesses neoliberal state power and sovereignty through the workings of customs agencies in Ghana.

The emerging anthropology of taxation has followed Schumpeter in stressing the historical specificity of a particular relationship between taxation and state power. At the same time, though, it has preserved the notion of the importance of the relationship between taxation and state power in particular. The very association between taxation and state power can, however, be conceived in broader terms. With reference to the rentier state, I have already discussed the need to conceptualize taxation as a specific form of a wider category of appropriation. We can also question whether appropriation tied to legitimate coercion is particular to state power or might also pertain to other projects of sovereignty. As I shall explore in the case of present-day Western Sahara, a precolonial *qabīlah* could appropriate resources in the form of tribute. Those refusing to pay were subject to the threat of raiding—a form, we might say, of legitimate coercion.

A revised notion of a relationship between appropriation and projects of sovereignty, rather than between taxation and state power, may be expanded even further. Despite the discursive focus that has been placed on appropriation, and especially taxation, the appropriation of both tax-extracting and rentier states is intimately linked to redistribution. Taxes are paid as part of a larger enterprise in which the political authority receiving taxes legitimizes their payment on the grounds of the (implied) provision of some kind of benefit to those paying them, whether in the form of material redistribution, protection from threats (see Tilly 1985), or some other form. This expectation may or may not be realized in practice, but the expectation is, nonetheless, necessary as a legitimization of the paying of taxes in the first place. In a rentier state, the lack of participation offered to subjects is legitimized on the grounds of the generous redistribution to citizens in subsidies and welfare services. The link between appropriation and redistribution is marked in the nuances of the North African notion of the tax-extracting state, the *makhzan*. In its broadest sense, the *makhzan* is not simply a place for storing things but a place for storing things that are taken temporarily out of circulation. They are thus stored there on the premise that they will go back into circulation of some kind at a future point.[2]

For the state-movement, rations were clearly a means of redistribution on a universal scale. Yet, as this chapter will explore, despite the tax-unfriendly circumstances of the state-movement, the redistribution of resources (rations) was related to the appropriation of other resources (refugees' labor). Bringing together means of appropriation and redistribution that, I shall argue, were related to the state-movement's claims to a monopoly on legitimate coercion, the state-movement operated an alternative to classic taxation that invites us to reconsider the relationship between sovereignty, appropriation, and redistribution.

## Studying "the Economy" in the Camps

When I began my fieldwork, I was drawn to studying both state power in exile and economic life at the intersection of two contrasting systems of circulation: long-standing rations and the markets that had developed in the camps from the late 1990s (see Chapter 6). When I tried to explain an interest in the camps' economy to interlocutors, however, I met with fervent retorts that there was "no economy" in the camps to be studied. Interlocutors remained skeptical despite my efforts to explain an interest in economic activities as all those activities pertaining to procuring resources, whether through production or other means, redistribution, all manner of exchanges that may occur along the way, and consumption.

Yet from such an anthropological point of view, the camps were rife with economic activity. On the one hand, the universal redistribution system directed by the state-movement ensured that food rations reached all citizens, in theory enabling them to subsist as refugees. These food rations were provided by a number of aid organizations, including the World Food Program (WFP), the UN High Commissioner for Refugees (UNHCR), and the UN Children's Fund (UNICEF). The contributions of these entities might, in turn, be funded by multilateral institutions such as the European Commission Humanitarian Aid and Civil Protection Department (ECHO). Roll out at the point of contact in the camps was typically subcontracted to a third party. For example, in the late 2000s Oxfam Belgium was contracted by ECHO to distribute food aid and tents to the refugees.

Despite the plethora of national and international aid agencies operating in the camps, any organization contracted to distribute rations to the refugees would work in situ through the structures of the Sahrawi Red Crescent (SRC).[3] This was also the organization that would deal with any charitable donations sourced from non-state philanthropic initiatives, such as Spanish solidarity groups. The SRC distributed rations to refugees via the Popular Committees (1980s) and then the councils (mid-1990s on) of the state-movement. As well as food ration distributions, which took place several times a month, refugees received on a monthly basis household items such as soap, sanitary towels, and gas bottles. Larger items, such as a gas ring and a tent, were distributed at much more infrequent intervals of every seven to ten years (tents) or on marriage (gas ring). Typical rations in the late 2000s are listed in Table 4.

All in all, then, there was a complex system of distribution combining rations per person (food) and rations per household/married woman (tents, gas bottles), sourced from a myriad of third-party aid agencies. This system was unified by the fact that all passed to the SRC, through which items were

Table 4

| *Item* | *Amount* | *Unit of distribution* | *Frequency of distribution* | *Funder (where known)* |
|---|---|---|---|---|
| Rice | 1 kg | Person | Month | WFP |
| Pulses | 1 kg | Person | Month | WFP |
| Oil | 1 liter | Person | Month | WFP |
| Flour | 5–10 kg | Person | Month | WFP |
| Sugar | Variable | Person | Irregular | |
| Tea | Variable | Family | Irregular | |
| Tuna | Variable | Person | Irregular | |
| Potatoes | 1 kg | Family | Month | UNHCR |
| Apples | 1 kg | Family | Month | UNHCR |
| Onions | 1 kg | Family | Month | UNHCR |
| Carrots | 1 kg | Family | Month | UNHCR |
| Sanitary towels | 1 pack | Woman | Month | UNHCR |
| Soap | A few bars | Family | Month | UNHCR |
| Camel meat | 500g | Person | twice a year (Eid Alfitr and Eid Aladha) | UNHCR |
| Camel milk | 500ml | Family | irregular (once to my knowledge in my fieldwork, and not all families received it) | |
| Tent | 1 | Family | in theory every seven years, but there was a backlog of about three years | Various |
| Gas bottle | 1 | Family | month (approximately) | |
| Gas ring | 1 | Family | upon marriage | |
| Dates | 1 kg | person | annual (Ramadan) | UNHCR |
| Second hand clothes | 2 | Person | twice a year | Swedish NGO |

distributed to all citizens, in principle on the basis of universal and equal entitlement.

It is tempting to see the local importance of rations in daily economic, and indeed, political life in the camps reflected in the proliferation among Sahrawi refugees of a vocabulary of rations. There were at least three common local terms for rations distributions, often extended to refer to rations items themselves: *tamwīn* ("provisioning," especially of food), *taqsīm*, and *tawzī'* (both meaning distribution, division).

By the 2000s, however, rations had acquired at least two shadows or parallel systems. Marketized trading activities grew up in the wake of the cease-fire in 1991, thanks to the resulting greater freedom of movement of goods and people from, to, and through the camps. In the late 2000s, each camp had a specialized area for market trading, known in Hassaniya as *marṣah* (see Chapter 6).

Alongside rations and the private sector, a third area of economic activities was the post-cease-fire influx of aid programs. In the form of either wages for local employees or programs for lending money and/or resources, what I shall call the "nonrations aid sector" saw transfers of resources to refugees from entities that were not properly in the realm of either the state-movement or the private sector—although aid programs might be influenced by both to a degree.

To the triangle of rations, markets, and the nonrations aid sector can also be added remittances from Sahrawi migrant laborers abroad, direct charitable gifts from European families to Sahrawi families (see Crivello, Fiddian, and Chatty 2005), pensions from the Spanish state to its former colonial employees, and clandestine commercial activities that are hidden from public view.[4] From an anthropological point of view, economic life in the camps was little short of frenetic. Within the rich possibilities for a study of economic relations in the camps, my focus here is on appropriation and redistribution linked to legitimate coercion, specifically the camps' innovated taxation. The most visible element in this innovated taxation was the rations that set the daily rhythm of life in exile.

## Universal Claims on State Power

At first sight, the refugees' dependence on rations seemingly distances the state-movement from state power that appropriates resources through tax or rent. Yet, as a process of governmentality, the redistribution undertaken by the state-movement can be seen as analogous to, and an innovation upon, classic taxation.

In classic taxation, a state power seeks to make as universal as possible the constituency it can tax. For this purpose (among others), a state power works hard to know, name, locate, and track its subjects (Foucault 1991; Scott 1998). Typically, the maximization of the taxable constituency is set against the restriction to a minimum of those to whom the state must redistribute material benefits.

We find exactly the reverse dynamic in the state-movement. The claims upon the state-movement for the redistribution of resources to those under its care were universal. The taxable constituency, on first examination, was null, since those in the camps came there in the role of dispossessed refugees.

The state-movement's inversion, whereby the activity envisaging a universal constituency was no longer extraction but (re)distribution, was nevertheless no less an operation of "seeing like a state" (Scott 1998) than taxation. The refugees had to be located, counted, and kept under the eye of the state-movement should they relocate. The state-movement achieved this in a number of ways. Registered with the state-movement in a specific neighborhood, refugees were entitled to receive rations in that particular place only. They needed permission to change registration to another location. Refugees might move their physical place of residence with relative ease and informality, apparently needing—at least in the late 2000s—no official authorization to do so. But authorization was needed for the place of registration for receiving rations to be changed, and the transferral of a rations entitlement might take place only some months after someone had moved to a new location. Each district (*dairah*) had an officer responsible for such registrations. At least once from 2007 to 2009, there was a camps-wide census in which each family had to send someone to the *dairah* administration to record family and professional details. On such an occasion in 2008, I asked Māghalāha's eldest daughter, Suelma, about her recent trip to the administration to provide census information. She explained that a young woman had asked questions and written down details about Suelma, her children, and their father. Electoral lists were also produced and updated at election times. There can be little doubt that the state-movement kept a close tab on the population in the camps.

Information about the size and distribution of the population remained private to the state-movement. There was (and still is) no publicly available census of the refugee population, which was the cause of ongoing disagreement between aid agencies and the state-movement as to the amount of rations that should be supplied for the exiled population.[5] The debate as conveyed to me in interviews with officers of both the state-movement and aid-funding agencies ran as follows. The aid agencies requested that a survey be carried out so that they could know how much food to provide. The state-movement resisted this, reportedly on the grounds that a survey to be carried out for the purposes of furthering a referendum on self-determination was welcome. A survey to be carried out with the view of reducing aid to be provided, however, was unwelcome.

The vicissitudes of the ongoing dispute about population figures are not of concern here from the point of view of seeking to know how many refugees were in the camps. It would be interesting for there to be a publicly available census of the exiled Sahrawi population (and, for that matter, the Sahrawi and Moroccan populations of the annexed areas). But it is not necessary to have a precise population figure for the camps either to study how that population is governed or to observe the construction of the debate surrounding the desire of various parties to know or conceal population figures for the camps. For the present purposes, of interest in this debate is a common experience shared by the state-movement and states that are the object of conditional aid packages: the subjection to intense international, politicized pressure for the methods of tracking a fiscal population to come under the scrutiny of internationalized standards defined by the donors rather than the recipients. The pressure on aid-recipient governments to adopt measures of good governance, such as transparency, anticorruption measures, and fiscal reform (e.g., Harper 2000), can be likened to the pressure on the state-movement to let the UNHCR and other donor agencies conduct a head count of the refugee population.

The fact that the state-movement counted and surveyed its population, and was under international pressure to share this information or to let others verify it, is an indication that it managed its population much as tax-extracting states do. The classic role for taxation, however, had been taken over in the state-movement by redistribution. One found not a ministry dedicated to the extraction of taxes, such as a treasury, but a "ministry" dedicated to the transfer of resources to which there was universal entitlement, the Sahrawi Red Crescent. This innovation on classic taxation may have had particular appeal for Sahrawis. The tax-extracting state in the form of the Moroccan *makhzan* was historically resisted by inhabitants of present-day Western Sahara (or at least this is the perception of many Sahrawis). The very absence in the camps of the extraction of taxes and its inversion

Figure 7. Rations distribution in Dakhla camp, 2008 (photo by Alice Wilson).

into the universal receipt of resources down the political hierarchy may have made the state-movement all the more appealing to Sahrawi refugees as a form of state power.

## The "Poor" Tax the "Rich"

Universal entitlements to refugee rations were a system of redistribution that was very much on display to the public of non-Sahrawi observers of the camps. Nonetheless, for a time the state-movement operated a secondary system of redistribution on a discretionary basis. It concerned transfers from the state-movement to refugees with costly social commitments. This system was far less on display to external gazes, if at all. It constituted a second element in the state-movement's innovated taxation. It allowed the state-movement to appear as a state power where the "poor" taxed the "rich."

For at least a few years, and until around 2005–2006, in times of costly social obligations (weddings, naming ceremonies for babies on the seventh day after birth), refugees were able to turn to the state-movement to seek help in meeting these obligations.[6] They might be given extra rations, such as 50kg flour, or 50kg rice, or 10l oil. In 2003, Māghalāha's family received help in their preparations for traveling by land to Mauritania to meet with relatives from the Moroccan-controlled areas of Western Sahara, as Suelma explained:

> Suelma: Our mother went to the *wilāyah* government office. She waited there until the governor agreed to see her. Some people have to go for days, but she only went once, and they told her they would help. They gave us a truck to share with another family. They also gave us one sack of rice, two bottles of oil, one sack of lentils and two sacks of flour. But they told us they couldn't give us any petrol.
>
> AW: Why not?
>
> Suelma: They saw our father was an old, weak man, and they didn't give us any petrol. So we had to find our own way to buy [a large vat of] petrol. It was very expensive, but, in the end, we went, and we met our father's family and our cousins [who had traveled from Moroccan-controlled Western Sahara to be] in Mauritania. We had never seen them before.
>
> AW: What did you do with the food?
>
> Suelma (surprised): We ate it. We took it with us in the truck, and it lasted us for about a month.

Such requests might be made to a local prominent figure, such as the head of the *wilāyah*, or to a government minister who lived in a family's *dairah*. While it is difficult to assess the extent of this practice, which by its very nature is undocumented, the numerous anecdotes I heard indicate that it was widespread, until around 2005, and that is was locally considered to be legitimate. After that time, refugees stressed to me, rations dropped. Indeed, in 2005 the UNHCR reduced the numbers of refugees for whom it was providing rations to 90,000, whereas it had provided for 155,000 in 2000 and 158,000 in 2004 (Zunes and Mundy 2010: 128).[7] Following the reduction, those who asked for help were given to understand that there was no extra help available. But it seemed that "asking" had been a legitimate way of increasing the resources one could access from the state-movement in times of exceptional need due to a social obligation.

The discretionary nature of this secondary form of redistribution might lead some to ask whether "corruption" was afoot. Talked of as *fisād* (rot, decay), corruption was indeed of concern to most Sahrawis in the camps in the late 2000s. It was one of the areas in which demands of the state-movement for reform were made. But to frame this secondary form of redistribution as "corruption" is to place it outside the context within which it was interpreted locally. It was quite another set of practices, such as nepotism in the distribution of resources and opportunities, that upset those Sahrawi refugees who voiced complaints about corruption (see Chapter 7 and the Conclusion). Rather, as Guyer (2004: 113) has explored, the rationed distribution of a scarce resource may need to be shaped according to local social and political hierarchies in order to be perceived locally as legitimate and fair.

Why might "asking" for extra resources have been considered legitimate in the camps? I was often surprised in the camps at the readiness with which people would ask for things or services that they needed. For instance, right at the moment in which someone was using a torch, another person might arrive and ask to use it. With time and growing linguistic awareness, I became equally intrigued at the readiness with which requests could be refused, with no offense being taken. The person using the torch might reply, laconically, "It's not free." Some kinds of "asking" were stigmatized in exile—especially the prerevolutionary practice of artisans "asking" for items from marriage prestations, several refugees (of non-artisan status) explained to me. But, given the many occasions when "asking" was taken for granted, the practice of going to the state-movement to ask for help might be understood as part of a wide-reaching "economy of asking."

Asking for help for costly social obligations from the state-movement was a particular kind of request, though. It concerned the obligation to provide appropriate hospitality. This, I was to learn, was a domain in which there should be no polite or appropriate way to say "no." Mbārak, a bureaucrat in his late twenties who worked at the Ministry of Information, explained the seriousness of requests for help with meeting hospitality obligations. If his friend came to him and said, "I have to slaughter a sheep for some guests. Give me some rice to serve them," then Mbārak in turn would go away and, if he had nothing to give to help his friend, find someone who could help him to provide for the first friend. "He has to do this," Mbārak explained, "otherwise he would bring shame [*'ār*] on himself." The term *'ār* is used across the Arab world with a range of meanings, including that of "disgrace" (Dresch 2006: 79–80). In this situation, the person from whom help was requested in order to meet hospitality obligations becomes liable to bringing disgrace on himself and his friend if he does not comply with the request, even if that means going on to third parties.[8] Bearing this in mind, it is interesting to observe that refugees' requests for help with providing honorable hospitality were not directed at rich individuals—even though by the early 2000s there were rich individuals, publicly known to be so. The legitimate form of asking for help for a costly social commitment, it seemed, was to go to the state-movement.

Why should the state-movement be targeted in such requests for help with hospitality? Plausibly, the state-movement sought to take over from those who, in a pre-exile context, would have been responsible for discretionary redistribution from the "rich" (themselves) to the "poor" (their dependents). One form that pre-exile discretionary redistribution took was *mnīḥah* (Hassaniya), a system of loaning livestock from one domestic group to another. The recipient group could drink the milk of the loaned female animals or use the male camels as pack animals. Recipients could keep the loaned animals until they were no longer required.[9] The system still operated among Sahrawi (and other hassanophone) mobile pastoralists. Interlocutors told me that these loans took place between "neighbors." But the specific contemporary case described to me by Jamāl, a young man who had spent several years as an adolescent in the pasturelands, involved groups whose prerevolutionary relationship would have been that of patron *qabīlah* lending to client *qabīlah*—a relationship Jamāl himself stressed. Indeed, Sophie Caratini (1989b: 57) writes that *mnīḥah* is far from an inexpensive way of herding surplus animals. More than just a means of helping the needy, *mnīḥah*, in her analysis, is a means of circulating animals while maintaining the hierarchical structure between powerful groups, who concentrate animal wealth through receiving gifts and tribute, and dependent groups, to whom animals are loaned (1989b: 57). In reading and asking about *mnīḥah*,

I never detected there being any shame in requesting it. Such openness about asking for *mnīḥah* fits a conception of material wealth evidenced in the redistribution expected of *shuyūkh* among Sahrawis and in other Bedouin settings (see Peters 1990; Shryock 2004): concentrated material wealth brought with it the responsibility to see (part of) those resources circulate.

While the practice of asking for help from the state-movement does not directly emulate *mnīḥah*, which was a loaning system, there are several points in common between them. In both cases, the "poor" can request resources with no shame. The transfer of resources also occurs in both scenarios down the political hierarchy. While the less powerful groups come to benefit from greater access to resources, the transfer only reaffirms the existence of a hierarchical relationship between the givers and the recipients. This is as true for *mnīḥah* as for the requests for help made to the officers of the state-movement in the camps. If the discretionary redistribution system, like *mnīḥah*, was a means of signaling hierarchical political relations through resource transfers, it becomes clear that it would have been inappropriate for a refugee to approach an affluent refugee to ask for help. Such a request might be interpreted as a suggestion of political hierarchy between the two parties, which, in the context of the camps, should only exist between refugee citizens and the state-movement.

The notion that, before the revolution, Sahrawis redistributed resources down the political hierarchy within the social relations of the *qabīlah* is supported by other studies of the hospitality obligations of Bedouin political elites. Among the Bedouin of Cyrenaica, the *shaykh* was expected to entertain dependents in their frequent visits, leading to the slaughtering of animals for the serving of meat (Peters 1990: 164). Tribesmen in contemporary Jordan retrospectively see their historical tribal leaders as "taxed" from the bottom up by dependents who would visit them, knowing that the leaders would be obliged to serve them meat (Shryock 2004: 50). Viewed in the context of practices in prerevolutionary Western Sahara and beyond, the discretionary redistribution of resources in the camps is far from an illegitimate transfer that would locally be seen as corruption. Rather, classic taxation had undergone a second inversion in the camps, whereby those who found themselves with exceptional needs "taxed" the "rich."

The "taxing" of the rich by the poor may acquire discursive dominance, but this does not preclude the parallel appropriation of resources by political elites from those whom they dominate. Andrew Shryock (2004) points out that his Jordanian Bedouin interlocutors' recollections of how the poor "taxed" the rich omit the historical extraction of tribute by the political elite for the Ottoman state. Similarly, Emrys Peters (1990: 165) describes that a competent *shaykh* in Cyrenaica would make sure that the wealth accrued through gifts from clients outweighed patronly obligations of hospitality and support. Its resistance to the *makhzan* notwithstanding, precolonial Western Sahara was not exempt from its own mechanisms of appropriation up the political scale within *qabīlah* relations. These mechanisms can be seen to inform alternative forms of appropriation up the political scale in the refugee camps.

## Old and New Forms of "Upward" Appropriation

The third element of the camps' innovated taxation was a form of appropriation up the political scale: the conscription of labor by the state-movement. Like the discourse of resistance toward a tax-extracting state and the conviction that political authorities should circulate the wealth that came with their dominance, appropriation up the political scale had local historical precedent. Prior to European colonialism in Western Sahara (and the hassanophone northwest Sahara more broadly), tribute had been extracted between *qabā'il*. This occurred in several forms, as noted by Caro Baroja (1955: 34–41).[10] *Ḥurmah* was paid directly from the tent of a protected family to the tent of a patron family; *ghāfar* was paid from the head of one (section of a) *qabīlah* to another. The failure to pay tribute exposed one to the threat of violence, that is, animal raiding on the part of one's rebuffed "protectors." Slaves, whose unfree status exempted them from paying tribute, were subject to the appropriation of their labor. Thus, even if Sahrawi refugees stressed a discourse of past resistance to a tax-extracting state power, there was precolonial precedent for appropriation up the political hierarchy within *qabīlah* relations. The appropriation of tribute and labor up the precolonial political and social hierarchy is represented in Figure 8.

In the context of the dispossession (at least initially) of Sahrawi refugees, the revolutionary form of appropriation up the political scale was the conscription of labor. In the early revolutionary period, the Popular Committees for women, and the army for men, conscripted the labor of anyone not already working for the state-movement in a ministry or in public services. As refugees liked to recall, the days of the war and the Popular

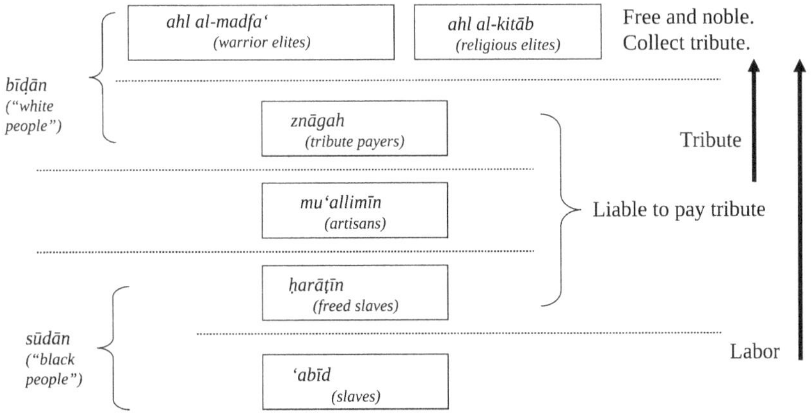


Figure 8. Extraction up the political scale in precolonial Western Sahara.

Committees saw every able-bodied adult working for the state-movement. "You could only see children and old people in the tents" was an oft-repeated image of the time. The level of coercion for this conscription is ambiguous. A report from the time suggests that work for a Popular Committee was not obligatory but that most people wished to engage in this work (Lippert 1985: 9). Until the early 2000s, everyone still working for the state-movement in the camps did so without remuneration. The schools, health care centers, textile workshops, and government offices of the state-movement were for a long time an experiment in unwaged labor on a scale that, outside prisons and detention centers, has rarely been seen.

Although there were prerevolutionary precedents for extraction up the political scale, the revolutionary form differed from them in a number of ways. The revolutionary system was universal, with no exemptions for the elite status groups that had previously collected tribute. Extracted labor was no longer linked with unfree labor either. The potential beneficiary of refugees' labor was furthermore conceived in the collective terms of the whole "people" (*sha'b*), rather than a particular status group—although this conceptualization necessarily mystified the gains of the vanguard of the liberation movement, who could direct refugees' labor.

The universal system of the redistribution of resources from the state-movement to its political subjects (rations distributions) therefore had its opposite: the universal system for the appropriation of resources from those political subjects to the state-movement (labor conscription). Was there "taxation" in the camps after all then, merely in the form of the state-movement "taxing" all for their labor?

From a number of angles, the state-movement's labor conscription resembles classic taxation. To clarify, however, these similarities are my own suggestion. Refugees themselves took the view that, with the exception of fees charged to traders in the private sector, such as owners of market stalls, taxi drivers, and traders bringing goods from Mauritania for resale in the camps, there were no taxes in the camps. The potential introduction of taxes for citizens outside the context of trade, proposed for the purpose of funding health and education services, was a topic of discussion in 2007–2008. For instance, the head of the SRC talked in an interview in October 2007 of the idea of a "national solidarity policy" whereby waged workers in the camps and abroad would contribute funds for schools and health services in the camps. But those refugees who discussed the idea of taxation with me rejected it as unsuitable on a number of grounds: fears (shared with other long-term refugee communities (e.g., Gabiam 2012) that exile might be made to resemble permanent resettlement,[11] and the irregular and precarious livelihoods of many refugees. One man also expressed concerns that corruption would prevent public sector workers from receiving their dues. Despite these objections to the principle of taxation, the state-movement was indeed appropriating resources from its citizens. The fact that those resources took the form of the transfer of labor, rather than material goods, not only fits the context of the refugees' (perceived) material dispossession but also finds some pre-exile precedent in the extraction of labor up the political scale there.

Another parallel to classic taxation is that, although the level of coercion for labor conscription to the Popular Committees and the army is, in retrospect, unclear, there was at least a moral expectation, in all likelihood so strong as to function coercively, that every able-bodied adult would work for the state-movement. Membership of this political community, therefore, entailed providing the state-movement with labor, just as membership in other political communities entails the payment of taxes.

A third similarity between labor conscription and taxation concerns the pairing of appropriation against redistribution. I have argued that the payment of tax is legitimized by a rationale that goods, services, or security are redistributed or provided in return. Similarly, in the refugee camps, the appropriation of labor in the form of national conscription was legitimized on the grounds that all refugees received in return rations, public services, and the collective efforts of all—political authorities and political subjects—toward the national liberation struggle.

The state-movement can, furthermore, be interpreted as operating a system of appropriation and redistribution that is linked to a claimed monopoly on legitimate coercion. Rather than imprisonment or fines for not paying taxes, the threat of the suspension of rations or the imposition of forced labor were deployed as a means of legitimate coercion. Refugees recalled that in the 1980s punishments for offenses such as using the vocabulary of tribalism might entail forced labor to make bricks. In the 2000s, it was believed by refugees that the state-movement would withhold rations from those who disobeyed its restrictions on marriage celebrations (see Chapter 5); one woman recalled that in the 1980s a man or woman found to be at fault by the Justice Committee for a marital dispute could have his or her rations cut off for a period.

Just at the point where the system in the camps begins to resemble a conventional tax system, in the form of the ceding of labor in return for public services, an important divergence from conventional taxation must, however, be stressed. Remarkable in the state-movement's appropriation and redistribution is how much the element of coercion managed to pass itself off as noncoerced consent. The refugees were *not* prisoners or detainees. They were revolutionaries. The image of "only children and old people in tents" was invoked with pride and nostalgia (and even regret that these were only memories). The (remembered) reason was that able-bodied men and women would all be at the battlefront or out working for the state-movement in weaving, building, cleaning, or staffing schools and hospitals. Refugees had been (morally) obliged to work for the state-movement, but at the same time they wanted to do so.

The coincidence of volition with the lines of legitimate coercion was such that it is not clear that there were punishments for failing to comply with labor conscription. When interlocutors recalled punishable offenses from the early revolutionary period, no one mentioned punishments for not working. There were doubtless people in the camps who resented the demands on their labor, many of whom may have left the camps for other destinations and consequently did not fall within the scope of this study.[12] But it remains that thousands of people did stay in the camps, and their giving of labor, unremunerated, to the state-movement was recalled with acquiescence. Dissent in the camps, when it came to a head in 1988, is reported to have voiced concern not at the coercive extraction of labor but at political repression (Zunes 1999). A curious aspect of the camps' appropriation and redistribution that, I have argued, was linked to a monopoly on legitimate coercion was that the moment of appropriation was enacted as voluntary rather than coerced. Such a blurring of the line between coercion and consent is not unusual in governing authorities (Gramsci 1971: 80n49)—but the state-movement perhaps took such a blurring to an extreme.

## "Volunteering" Taxes

While it might be argued that the acquiescence of refugees to labor conscription is equivalent to acquiescence elsewhere in paying taxes, there is a further aspect of the state-movement's appropriation and redistribution that once again distances the camps from conventional taxation. Even though, with the dissolution of the Popular Committees in 1995, the universal system of daily labor conscription no longer operated, refugees continued to volunteer their labor on a discretionary basis, as I was able to observe in the late 2000s. If the state-movement's extraction of labor operates as a pseudo-tax, then some people continued to "volunteer" tax labor in the camps, over and above the repealing of labor conscription that was (morally) mandatory.

The revolutionary mechanism for the conscription of labor on an ad hoc basis, which operated in both the early (Firebrace and Harding 1987: 16) and late revolutionary periods, was known as *ḥamlah*. *Ḥamlah* is an Arabic word meaning "campaign." It is used in arabophone contexts for campaigns run by governing authorities, such as public health campaigns for vaccination programs. In the context of the camps, it was used to mean a collective labor effort to perform a particular task. *Ḥamlah* activities usually concerned the provision of a public good and were carried out by teams of either men or women. For example, if a *ḥamlah* was held for the cleaning of the *dairah* school, then an announcement would be made by loud speaker from the administrative center in that *dairah* calling on all the women from a particular neighborhood to clean the school that day. The next day, women from another neighborhood would be called up, and so on until each neighborhood had been called. An alternative case of a national *ḥamlah* occurred when men were called up in teams to pick up trash from the *wilāyāt* and take it out into the desert to be burned. On such occasions, the national radio would broadcast a camps-wide schedule that assigned teams of men from their regular jobs in the army or in ministries to pick up trash across different locations for a week.

A simpler form of *ḥamlah* that did not necessarily even take that name occurred if a certain task needed to be completed for the state-movement: a team of women would volunteer to work together to do it. This was the case in preparations for the Sahrawi Cultural Festival of 2008. Across each *dairah*, teams of women worked voluntarily to assemble the furnishings of goat-hair tents that would go on display in the festival. Māghalāha joined such a group in her neighborhood. She worked long hours with other female neighbors of a similar age, weaving decorations for the tent and making rope to secure it. During the festival, Māghalāha and other women lived in the tent. They set up a rota for domestic labor—just as a mother and her adult daughters would in a family tent and just as the Sahrawi male students in Damascus did over the summer of 2007 when I knew them. The long hours of labor to prepare and run the tent were all unpaid. The only material rewards received were food stuffs handed over to the women during the festival to help feed them.

Food was in fact a prominent feature of a *ḥamlah*. During *ḥamlah* activities, someone or a group of people would usually be designated by the state-movement to provide refreshments and given extra resources for that purpose. Thus, one woman might make tea for the other women, or some women would make *zrīg* (a much-loved and refreshing drink that is a mix of milk, water, and sugar) for the men collecting trash. *Ḥamlah*, though hard work, was often associated with an atmosphere of fun, as people joked while they worked and relaxed together afterward enjoying tea.

The astonishing effectiveness of *ḥamlah*—which lasted even into the age of expectations of remuneration—and the remarkable former universal system for the conscription of unpaid labor, should be understood in the light of a prerevolutionary precedent for the recruitment of labor. In prerevolutionary times within a group of nomadic encampments, *firgān*, labor could be recruited for carrying out specific tasks in a system of reciprocal labor pooling known as *twīzah* (see Caro Baroja 1955: 124–25; Caratini 1989b: 132). This term is of Berber origin; labor pooling going by the same name has been discussed in a number of berberophone settings (Bourdieu 1962: 11–12; Boulay 2003: 407).

In the hassanophone context, *twīzah* activities were sex-segregated: for men, *twīzah* covered sheep shearing and well building or renovation; for women, it covered tent sewing and carding and spinning wool. The owner(s) of the tent, wool, or animals needing attention would also bear the responsibility of providing refreshments for those who had volunteered to share the work. Ideally, a sheep should be slaughtered for them. *Twīzah* was also associated with high spirits. In the case of women sewing a tent, they would throw stones at any man who happened to pass by, demanding that he give them something to help them before moving on.

Although there was no demand for *twīzah* for shearing or well repairs in the camps, it still operated for tent sewing (including throwing stones at male passersby). In 2006 the camps were hit by heavy rains, causing floods and damaging many homes, both tents and mud-brick rooms. In 2007, there were still families with tents to repair following the rains. While I was living with Sumaya in the early months of that year, she unfurled her damaged tent and called on female neighbors to help her restitch it. The *twīzah* lasted several days and was the occasion for finding that I had far to go in my own tent-sewing skills.

Once, when I was explaining my research interests to a judge I was going to interview about legal reforms in the camps, I mentioned that I was interested in understanding the relationship of past practices, such as *twīzah*, to current practices in the camps. The judge interrupted hastily to say, "We don't have *twīzah* anymore, but we do have *ḥamalāt*. The state has taken over this role." Thereafter, whenever I put the comparison to other refugees, they agreed that *ḥamlah* resembled *twīzah*. The similarities between the two go beyond the conscription of labor. The principle of sex-segregated tasks has remained, as has the association of donated labor necessitating acts of hospitality.

Yet there is an important point of distinction between *ḥamlah* and *twīzah*. Sébastien Boulay's discussion of *twīzah* among Hassanophones in Mauritania shows how the social relations of *qabīlah* membership are prominent in the context in which claims are typically made on others' labor contributions for *twīzah*. He first discusses *twīzah* as an example of egalitarian tendencies for collective cooperation, as opposed to hierarchical arrangements in other areas of life (Boulay 2003: 62–63). Interestingly, he writes of *twīzah* as a form of cooperation between families of the same social status (62–63). Going on later to discuss in more detail *twīzah* among women for spinning wool, Boulay explains that it is preferable that a woman will go to a *frīg* inhabited by "*parentes*" (French, female relatives) to recruit help (408). While the word for relative (*qarīb*) can in theory mean either an agnatic or a uterine relative, in Hassaniya, the first meaning that will be understood by the term *qarībatī* (my female relative) is a woman who belongs to the same *qabīlah*. Boulay (409) goes on to give an example of how a *twīzah* might proceed for a woman living in an isolated tent needing help to spin wool: she would go to the tent of her *parente* in order to be hosted there as a base, from where her *parente*'s neighbors would help her spin the wool.

It is not my suggestion that in the mobile pastoralist context *twīzah* took place exclusively within the context of the social relations of *qabīlah* membership. The recruitment of neighbors, even when many encampments would accommodate families from the same *qabīlah*, might well also include persons from a different *qabīlah*. But it seems that recruitment through the social relations of *qabīlah* membership was preferable (hence the request for help from a *parente*) and that labor pooling within *twīzah* took place within members of the same status group.

In *ḥamlah*, labor is claimed and shared in terms of membership in the state-movement. The teams of workers were formed because of their common citizenship rather than any links through a *qabīlah*. Often during my fieldwork, an interlocutor whom I had met in one area of my research would discover that we shared mutual acquaintances in another context. Such a discovery would occasion exclamations and inquiries as to the third parties' health. "How is *fulānah* [so-and-so]? How are her daughters? Are any of them married yet?" one chatty woman questioned me on discovering that I was living, at that time, with Māghalāha. Some months earlier, another man, more laconic, simply said, "You live with them? Then send my greetings to Khadīja, daughter of so-and-so." In both cases, it turned out that those exchanging greetings had been companions in a *ḥamlah* over a decade ago. The state-movement had linked people in *ḥamlah*, and the bond had survived the passing of years.

If *ḥamlah* differs from *twīzah* in the former claiming labor through the links within the state-movement, and the latter claiming labor through links within *qabīlah* relations, then this difference only reinforces *ḥamlah*'s success. Boulay (2003: 62–64) observed that *twīzah* was an egalitarian means of cooperation, with all persons involved working together on the same tasks. That this work took place within members of one status group, perhaps many of them members of the same *qabīlah*, made working together a means of showing that coworkers were equal to one another. The triumph of *ḥamlah* was to bring persons together from different *qabīlah* and status group backgrounds and, in the changed context of the revolution, make working together a means of showing that coworkers were equal to one another as citizens of the state-movement. The case of *ḥamlah* and *twīzah* also demonstrates how, once again (here, in the case of appropriation and redistribution linked to legitimate coercion), the state-movement drew on the social relations of the *qabīlah* to make state power.

## Deuniversalized Redistribution

I have argued that the state-movement engaged in appropriation and redistribution linked to a monopoly on legitimate coercion. Yet, to recapitulate, the state-movement's arrangements presented important contrasts with conventional taxation. The state-movement appropriated labor rather than property. It had to redistribute on a universal basis. The moment of coercion was experienced as voluntary to the extraordinary point that some people volunteered that which was being appropriated, over and above the required minimum. Significantly, as regards my wider argument that the state-movement's building of the social relations of state power entailed the recycling of the social relations of the *qabīlah*, at the point at which the extra voluntary labor was given, the state-movement relied on and redeployed a mechanism of the recruitment of labor pertaining to the social relations of the *qabīlah*, *twīzah*. The crowning moment in the state-movement's appropriation and redistribution linked to legitimate coercion was so effective not despite *qabīlah* relations, but in part because of them and their associated forms of appropriation and redistribution.

Unusual in its form, the state-movement's innovated taxation was also unusual in context. Before the 1991 cease-fire, money was hardly seen in the camps. There was only one shop per *dairah*, run by the state-movement. Thus, there were few forms of appropriation and redistribution other than those connected with the state-movement. In the late revolutionary period, however, that level of economic control and centralization no longer held. The market and the nonrations aid sector came to play a role in refugees' access to resources.

The emergence of new areas of economic activity allowed the state-movement to engage in practices of economic regulation that are familiar in the management of national economies. Although going market rates set the prices for most consumption goods, the state-movement imposed price controls in certain areas of consumption, such as the price of meat per kilo. It also intervened to regulate participation in the market and the nonrations aid sector. For example, the state-movement regulated a nongovernmental organization (NGO) that offered microcredit loans to refugees (see Elizondo et al. 2008). The state-movement required that loans only be made available to groups of two to six persons, half of whom must be workers in the state-movement's public sector. This measure sought to encourage public sector workers' participation in the market while retaining them in the public sector.

Another scheme aimed to allow the state-movement itself to benefit from the opportunities for profit available in the private sector. In summer 2007, the Ministry of Trade began a scheme in which it contracted workers in its own ministries to use resources, such as trucks, made available by the Ministry for their own private trade. Contracted workers paid a percentage of any profits made to the ministry.

The advent of the market and market-orientated nonrations aid sector, thus, extended the remit of the economic activities of the state-movement to include forms of market regulation deployed elsewhere in the management of national economies. At the same time, though, markets and the nonrations aid sector eroded the state-movement's appropriation and redistribution linked to legitimate coercion, in other words its innovated taxation.

By the late 2000s, universal material redistribution was shaken. Refugees could not survive on the levels of rations provided (see Table 4 above). Families relied on a myriad of means for making good the rations gap: donations from Spanish host families, remittances from relatives abroad, cash earnings in local labor markets, and the nonrations aid sector. But the camps also saw the emergence of a form of redistribution that was neither of the state-movement nor of the market or nonrations aid sector, but seemed to respond to the shortcomings of the former and the inequalities of the latter. *Qabīlah*-based collective funds for helping *qabīlah* members emerged, known as *ṣanādīq* (s. *ṣundūq*), meaning box or chest.

Similar funds exist in the contexts of arabophone tribes (Casciarri 2001; Dawod 2003) and village-based Palestinian refugee associations (Peteet 2005) and among Halpulaaren in Mauritania, where they are known by the French term *caisse* (Frésia 2009). The operation of such funds in the camps under the name *ṣundūq* deserves special attention. Each married Sahrawi woman had a physical *ṣundūq* (box, chest) in her home, in which she locked valued possessions. The *ṣundūq* in a home contain official documents such as old Spanish colonial identity papers, SADR or Algerian paperwork, photos of relatives living and dead, and even sweets, locked away from children. When I stayed in the pasturelands with Māghalāha's sister-in-law, Fatu, where the tent was the living space for her and her family, I observed that Fatu's *ṣundūq* was inaccessibly covered in household items such as blankets and clothing. This made it difficult to access for a thief (or, for that matter, any family member with a legitimate need to open it). In the camps, the tent living space was often supplemented with mud-brick rooms, where an equally inaccessible *ṣundūq* would lie under a stack of suitcases or similar items. I once opened Khadīja's *ṣundūq* to remove some money that, at her invitation, I kept there. At that time, a guest was visiting and was in the same room as the *ṣundūq*, watching television. When he had left, Khadīja and her daughter reprimanded me for opening the *ṣundūq* while a guest had been in the room: one should never, I was told, indicate the location of the *ṣundūq* in front of anyone foreign to the household. (Khadīja's daughter then advised me to bury my money in the sand, just like everyone else.) The *ṣundūq*, then, was an essential part of any household and should remain inviolable.

In the late 2000s, some *qabā'il* in the camps began to set up *ṣanādīq* in their own names, serving their own members. The practice was not common to all *qabā'il*, nor was it limited to the camps. I heard reports of *ṣanādīq* in Mauritania and, intriguingly, in Spain among Sahrawi migrants living and working there. The *ṣundūq* of a *qabīlah* in the camps, I was told, might take the form of an investment, such as a herd of camels, or a truck that engaged in trade between the camps and Mauritania. A *qabīlah*, or a section thereof, that organized itself to set up a *ṣundūq* would send a person from home to home of relevant families, asking them to make an ad hoc monetary contribution per male of fasting age in the family. The idea was that tribe members could draw on the funds made available by this investment in times of need—such as hosting and feeding mourners, supporting a relative who was attending an invalid receiving medical treatment outside the camps, or a compensation payment following an accident (see Chapter 3)—but not for celebrations such as wedding parties.

*Ṣanādīq* initiatives seemed fragile. In 2008, the section of the *qabīlah* to which Māghlāha's husband Tawwālu belonged tried but failed to set up a *ṣundūq*. Returning to the camps in 2011, I found that in the intervening years this *qabīlah* section had gone on to collect payments regularly. But by September 2011 Māghlāha's husband was left asking what news there was of the *ṣundūq*, because the family had not been asked to contribute for some months.

*Ṣanādīq* were also controversial. In the camps at least, it was not the case that all *qabā'il*, or sections of *qabā'il*, had *ṣanādīq*. Some interlocutors whom I questioned about *ṣanādīq* did not know of any such initiative in their own *qabīlah* and were opposed to the idea of it being instated. In the words of one young man, whom I had gotten to know as a student in Syria and who later returned to work in a family shop in the camps, "It's not right" for people to prefer their tribes. Some of those who had contributed to *ṣanādīq* were also skeptical that any proceeds were ever really used for those in need. They feared that the proceeds might merely benefit those persons whom the *qabīlah* had appointed to manage the funds. One young man at the Ministry of Information offered his view of someone who had taken advantage of a *ṣundūq* to amass personal wealth: "You see that man who always changes money at the market? He was in charge of a *ṣundūq*, and see how rich he is now."

Whereas in the context of the camps *ṣanādīq* served specific *qabā'il*, in the context of Sahrawi migrants in Spain, reportedly any Sahrawi could register to join a *ṣundūq*. Members would draw on a *ṣundūq* mainly for the costs of repatriating to the camps the bodies of those who died. Ironically, it may be that in the diaspora the *ṣundūq* had gone beyond the context of *qabā'il* to "any Sahrawi," whereas in the camps—a supposed center of Sahrawi nationalism—it was attached to the idea of the *qabīlah*.

It is not clear which prerevolutionary forms of redistribution the *ṣundūq* most resembles. While it seems that the need to pay a specific compensation payment might in the past have led to funds being collected within a *qabīlah*, I was not able to find any prerevolutionary accounts of funds being collected "preemptively," as was the case for the late revolutionary *ṣanādīq*. The emergence of the *qabīlah*-based *ṣundūq*, while not particular to the camps, is all the more intriguing there because of the state-movement's antitribalist outlook and its innovated taxation. However fragile and controversial, the existence of *ṣanādīq* bespoke a need and desire to supplement the increasing shortcomings of the help that refugees could obtain from the state-movement and to do so outside the context of relations formed through the state-movement. Help between relatives and neighbors was always important in exile, but it was particularly important to the state-movement that extra-household networks of welfare were formed in the context of the state-movement (e.g. the Popular Committees, *ḥamlah*), and certainly not through the *qabīlah*. The *ṣundūq* indicated the extent to which the state-movement had lost ground in its former quasi-monopoly over redistributing resources through its own structures for welfare provision and organizing help and support networks. The state-movement's system of universal material redistribution, once a lynchpin of appropriation and redistribution linked to legitimate coercion, had been severely undermined.

## Discretionary Distribution and Conscription Eroded

The other lynchpins of innovated taxation fared little better than universal redistribution. By 2007, the camps' system of secondary redistribution on a discretionary basis had ceased. As we saw, the discretionary redistribution of resources to refugees who had costly social obligations was not seen locally as illegitimate, but rather as a legitimate way of dealing with those costs. Two factors, nevertheless, came to impede the state-movement's capacity to pursue such discretionary redistribution. The drop in rations in 2005 meant there were fewer rations to go round. But a second factor was that discretionary redistributions came to be perceived by the state-movement as liable to attract charges against the state-movement from donors—but not from refugees—of corruption.

Abba, a bureaucrat in his fifties, explained to me that, when he went to ask for help with a naming ceremony for his son in 2008, he was told the time was over when such extra help could be given. If such help were given at all, Abba had been told, the food had to be transferred out of the aid donations' packaging. This, he explained to me, was to ensure that no such sacks of food found their way to being sold in Mauritania, raising the possibility of corruption charges against the state-movement. Accusations of the illegitimate resale of rations have indeed been leveled at the state-movement (e.g., Cozza 2004, 2010). When I interviewed officers from the World Food Program in Algiers, they explained that an audit of rations aid in the camps had found no conclusive evidence of the systematic misuse of aid. Yet undoubtedly the state-movement feared accusations of the misuse of aid. Increased pressure from multilateral funders of rations hampered the state-movement in its desire to redistribute resources according to criteria that had been legitimate in both its eyes and those of the refugees themselves. The second lynchpin of the state-movement's innovated taxation had been broken.

As for the appropriation of labor by the state-movement, it virtually collapsed altogether. Universal labor conscription for women in Popular Committees ended with their dissolution in 1995. The decommissioning of prolonged military service for men also followed the cease-fire (I was not able to ascertain the exact date for this). Public services remained a sector in which thousands of Sahrawi refugees worked, from the early 2000s, in return for (low and often irregular) wages. But the state-movement struggled to retain its workers. The possibility of greater cash-in-hand earnings in private and nonrations aid sectors contributed to the attrition rate from the public sector (see Chapter 6). Many refugees who obtained the necessary international travel documents (see Chapter 7) migrated to Spain and other international migration destinations to seek work.

All that remained of the once universal appropriation of labor was *ḥamlah*. It was a reminder not only of the revolutionary élan that once was but also of appropriation and redistribution linked to a monopoly on legitimate coercion that had been eroded on all frontiers.

## Beyond Taxation

The state-movement has a strange story as regards taxation—one that invites us to see taxation in a new light. Against the notion of the *makhzan* and the assumptions of a Weberian approach to state power, the state-movement's innovated taxation suggests that it is not taxation itself that helps constitute a sovereign state. Rather, appropriation and redistribution linked to a monopoly on legitimate coercion—which, in practice, might take a form radically contrary to conventional taxation—would help constitute the social relations of sovereignty. Ironically, when sweeping economic change brought the state-movement closer to the economic activities of other state authorities as regards regulation and intervention, the basis of the very activities that comprised the alternative to taxation in the camps was eroded. Bereft of effective appropriation and redistribution linked to a claimed monopoly on legitimate coercion, the state-movement was increasingly forced to encounter perhaps the most challenging alternative to taxation of all: to extract that most precious political commodity, consent, while offering in return only the intangible promise of a collective endeavor toward a desired, yet ever elusive, future.

The state-movement's innovated taxation reconfigured the appropriation and redistribution associated with the social relations of the *qabīlah*. This recycling reiterates the potential for compatibilities between the social relations of *qabīlah* and state-movement in the constitution of projects of sovereignty. Yet, as in the case of the deciding of laws (Chapter 3), over time the state-movement's attempted displacement of the *qabīlah* was modified. The *qabīlah* emerged as an ambiguous yet apparently tolerated actor in the work of redistribution; *qabīlah* relations reappeared in the palimpsest of the state-movement's original attempt to overwrite them. Willing to compromise on its initial antitribalist outlook, the late revolutionary state-movement shifted toward including the social relations of the *qabīlah* in its governance—to the extent that this inclusion was construed to be compatible with the continuation of the state-movement's broader social and political agendas. The next chapter examines how the state-movement made a similar compromise in its attempts to manage social inequalities.

Deeply undermined though the camps' innovated taxation has become, it stands as an invitation to reassess the theoretical preoccupation with state power and taxation. If the economic vocation of a project of sovereignty is to pursue appropriation and redistribution linked to a claimed monopoly on legitimate coercion, it seems that it is not ethnographically necessary that this take the form of "taxation" in a "state." Even the most familiar monopoly may merit a closer look.

CHAPTER 5

# Managing Inequalities: Organizing Social Stratification, or Marriage Reinvented

All states involve the reflexive monitoring . . . of the reproduction of . . . social systems.

—Anthony Giddens, *The Nation-State and Violence*

It only took a few days after my arrival in the camps in January 2007 for me to be invited to a wedding. A few days before the approaching celebration, Sumaya's neighbor had pointed out to me the large party tent that had been set up, squeezed in amid the tents and mud-brick rooms of the crowded neighborhood of February 27 camp where Sumaya lived. When the day came and the celebrations took off, amplified music blared out from the party tent, interspersed with high-pitched ululation. That afternoon, Sumaya, her daughter, the neighbors, and I went to watch and applaud the dancing at the wedding. To my surprise at the time, in a sense some of the wedding also came to us. That evening, the bride's father came to have dinner with us at Sumaya's home, a few households away from the party tent where the wedding camel was being served. I later understood that the hassanophone modesty code, *ḥishmah*, required the bride's father to give a wide berth to markers of the bride's impending sexual activity, hence his steering clear of the party tent. This was the first of many refugee weddings I was to attend. As well as being good parties, they provided insights into governance in the refugee camps.

Whereas, in Chapters 3 and 4, I considered well-known tropes of sovereignty, law, and taxation, in this chapter, I consider how the social relations of sovereignty also concern themselves with the organization, legitimization, and reproduction of social (in)equalities. I call these connected processes the management of social (in)equalities. To explore the state-movement's management of social (in)equalities, I analyze marriage practices such as wedding celebrations. I begin by exploring the relationship between sovereignty and the management of social (in)equalities, and the relevance to these of refugee marriage practices. I then consider how Sahrawi marriage practices have transformed from the days of the pasturelands to changing revolutionary practices.

## Sovereignty and (In)Equalities

In proposing to explore the management of social (in)equalities as an aspect of the social relations of sovereignty, I take inspiration from scholars who have studied how social revolutions seek to restructure social (in)equalities. Theda Skocpol (1979) has argued that social revolutions are distinctive in bringing about both social and political change—as opposed to a political revolution, which she understands to bring about political change, and to processes such as industrialization, which she understands to bring about social change. Taking up Skocpol's ideas, Donald Donham expands on them: "According to Theda Skocpol, the defining feature of social revolutions, what makes revolutions, is the coincidence of two basic changes: in the way the state is organized, on the one hand, and *in the means by which social inequality is structured and legitimated*, on the other" (1999: 34, emphasis added). Donham (35) thus highlights how, although a revolutionary regime may ostensibly adopt a rhetoric of promoting social equality, in practice (and as he explores ethnographically in the case of the Ethiopian revolution), what is at stake is an altered structuring and legitimation of social inequality that plays out through "microprocesses": "a countlessly repeated uprooting of social relations, in thousands of local communities."

The notion that social revolution in particular seeks to *change* the structure and legitimization of social (in)equalities, nevertheless, implies that the structuring, legitimization, and reproduction—or, more concisely, the management—of social (in)equalities among a governed population is of interest to governing authorities more broadly. This is not to say that the management of social (in)equalities is of concern *exclusively* to governing authorities that take the form of projects of sovereignty. Clearly, the governing authorities of a household, city, business, charity, or university inter alia may be concerned with the management of internal social (in)equalities. But I venture that it may be a necessary—though not exclusive—aspect of the social relations of sovereignty to organize, legitimize, and reproduce social (in) equalities in a governed population (whether in the form of class distinction or some other form). Just as a sovereign authority is concerned with deciding which laws will hold in its sphere of governance, or how it will appropriate resources to sustain itself, it is also concerned with defining the forms of social (in)equalities it wishes to be reproduced among the governed population.

The connections between sovereignty and the management of social (in) equalities have not been as widely discussed as presumed connections between sovereignty and law and appropriation, respectively. But the mutual implications linking sovereignty and the management of (in)equalities have not gone unnoticed. Anthony Giddens notes that "*All states involve the reflexive monitoring of aspects of the reproduction of the social systems subject to their rule*" (1985: 17, emphasis in original). Reflecting on how taxation helps constitute particular forms of governance, Jane Guyer (1992: 57) observes that one useful aspect of taxation for governing authorities is that tax gradation offers state power an official theory of social inequality. Drawing on the overlap between these insights and those of Donham and Skocpol into social revolution as a project to restructure and legitimize social inequalities, in this chapter I examine, through the case of the state-movement, how the social relations of sovereignty manage the acceptable limits of social (in) equalities in a governed population. To understand sovereignty, we must attend not only to the deciding of laws and the appropriation of resources but also to how governing authorities make, mask, and legitimize social (in) equalities.

My means of exploring the state-movement's management of social (in) equalities is an analysis of marriage practices, which I take to comprise marriage ceremonies and marriage prestations. I consider these practices in the context of marriage strategies (see Bourdieu 1977), by which I mean the selection of marriage partners. Among Sahrawis and other Hassanophones—as well as in the Middle East and North Africa (MENA) and beyond—marriage has long been a means of marking social (in)equalities. Consequently, marriage became an arena in which the state-movement intervened as part of its revolutionary attempt to change the way social (in)equalities were organized, legitimized, and reproduced. In doing so, the state-movement joined other liberation movements in MENA and beyond that have intervened in marriage strategies and practices in the context of seeking revolutionary change.[1]

Marriage in the state-movement not only was relevant for a study of the management of social (in)equalities but also proved amenable as a research topic. The general principles of marriage strategies in the state-movement were accessible to a foreign researcher through the observation of existing marriages among interlocutors. Some marriage practices, especially parts of marriage ceremonies, took place in public. Even though local sensitivities around the mention of *qabā'il* and status groups made a detailed study of marriage partner choices unfeasible, marriage practices could at times serve as a proxy for assessing underlying marriage strategies. In addition, the state-movement's treatment of marriage can be compared and contrasted to historical accounts of prerevolutionary marriage strategies and practices among Hassanophones, and, within them, Sahrawis. Finally, marriage practices altered considerably over the course of the revolutionary period to the late 2000s and even during my fieldwork in 2007–2008. Studying these changes proves to be a means of appraising changes not only in the management of social (in)equalities but also in how the state-movement approached this management, especially in its relationship to the *qabīlah*.

## Marriage Sahrawi Style: Building a Tent

In Hassaniya, Sahrawis talk of marriage through the idiom of having or building a tent. Women would eagerly ask if I was *mutakhayyamah*, or *bi khaymatik*—literally "endowed with a tent" or "[had] a tent," but meaning here "married." If someone was getting married, refugees talked of this in terms such as "we're going over to join some people who are building a tent" or "I heard that so-and-so is building a tent." When I began to follow marriages more closely for my research, if I told interlocutors that I was interested in marriage, *al-zawāj* in Arabic, they would exclaim "Oh, [you mean] *al-khaymah*," meaning, literally "tent," but in this context "marriage."

In many respects, Sahrawi ways of "building a tent" in the prerevolutionary period fit broader patterns of marriage in MENA. Research on marriage strategies (the selection of marriage partners) in MENA has focused on the preference for "close" marriage, or marriage with a close relative, especially, but not exclusively, between a father's brother's daughter (FBD) and a father's brother's son (FBS).[2] This preference, even if only practiced to varying degrees and, often, in a minority of actually contracted marriages,[3] has fascinated anthropologists. In contrast to rules requiring exogamy in various societies elsewhere, preference for FBD-FBS marriage entails marrying the closest person to ego in kinship terms who is not prohibited as a sexual partner by incest taboos (Lévi-Strauss 1959).

Hassanophones, and Sahrawis more specifically, have historically shown a (varying) preference for FBD-FBS marriage and other types of marriage with a close relative. Of fifty-one marriages contracted by males from the Ahel Meiara subfraction (Caro Baroja's term) of the Ahel Taleb Ali fraction of the Awlād Tidrārīn tribe, studied by Caro Baroja (1955: 164–65), thirty were contracted within the subfraction, ten within the fraction, nine within the tribe, and two with women from outside the tribe. Caro Baroja (1955: 167–68) reports similar tendencies among the Arosien and Rgaybāt tribes. Pierre Bonte (2008: 81), though, finds the incidence of cousin marriage in the Awlād ʻAmmonni tribe of the Adrar emirate in Mauritania to be just 10 percent.

For Bonte, the variation in the incidence of cousin marriage, and indeed of marriage within the patrilineal group, indicates that attention should be paid not so much to a preference for "close" marriage fulfilled only to varying degrees in practice but to "Arab" marriage. He understands the latter as the only actual rule followed in marriage strategies in MENA: the prohibition of female hypogamy, that is, it being forbidden that a woman marry a man from a lower-ranking status group (Bonte 2008: 89). Hassanophones generally adhered to "Arab" marriage; that is, a man of noble *ḥassan* status could marry a woman of *znāgah* status but not vice versa (on status groups, see Chapter 1). The exception to "Arab" marriage among Hassanophones occurred when a dominant group would allow its women to marry men of lower status but count the resulting children as belonging to the status of their mothers. Interpreted as a strategy for demographic increase, this is reported of the Rgaybāt (Caro Baroja 1955: 20) and of the Awlād Quaylān in Mauritania (Bonte 2008: 161). This apparent exception can be seen to maintain the rule: the practice preserves the result that a woman's fertility may not be put to the benefit of a social status inferior to her own.

Ultimately, "Arab" marriage and, contained already as a possibility within it, "close" marriage signaled the presence of social (in)equalities. Pierre Bonte explains that "close" marriage marked the claimed equality between intermarrying agnates (Bonte 2008: 100). Furthermore, marriage with a partner from outside the group reproduced and reinforced potential relations of hierarchy (100). Potential (in)equalities between marriage partners and the groups from which they hailed manifested themselves in tangible form through marriage practices, such as marriage prestations and marriage ceremonies. Prerevolutionary marriage practices necessarily varied among Hassanophones and indeed among those who came to be known as Sahrawis (see Fortier 2001; Tauzin 2001; Boulay 2003; Bonte 2008). Somewhat ironically, the state-movement sought to reconstruct a "traditional Sahrawi wedding" in the Sahrawi Cultural Festival, held in Auserd refugee camp, in December 2008. Such a reenactment might arouse skepticism, perhaps especially among anthropologists wary of its "creation" of a standardized wedding. Yet older Sahrawi refugee women with whom I watched the reconstruction later commented on how impressed they were by the careful recapturing of the layout and events of a wedding such as they had seen—in some cases as a bride—in their youth. Important to draw from the reconstructed "traditional" Sahrawi wedding, then, is the notion of a corpus of material and social marriage practices that were recognizable to refugees who had become adults before exile. This corpus, of which I offer a brief and necessarily selective account, informed refugees' experience of change during the revolution.

Like other North Africans (see Mir-Hosseini 1993), Sahrawis called the marriage prestation from groom to bride, required in Islam to make the marriage licit, by the Arabic term *ṣadāq* (rather than the alternative term *mahr*).[4] Hereafter, I shall use *ṣadāq* specifically to refer to the groom-to-bride prestation of that name practiced by Sahrawis and other Hassanophones. Historically, *ṣadāq* was given from the groom's family to the bride's. *Ṣadāq* took the form of camels, drawn from the groom's father's herd, and other precious objects, such as pieces of cloth or bracelets, and might include a slave-woman (Caro Baroja 1955: 266–67; Caratini 1989b: 224). There are different accounts of how the amount of *ṣadāq* varied among Hassanophones: according to status group (Du Puigaudeau 2009: 226–27); according to tribe, with the bride's family accepting to bargain the prestation down to a standardized amount (Caro Baroja 1955: 266–67); and according to the social distance between spouses (Bonte 2008: 102–4). In Bonte's historical ethnographic account of *ṣadāq* in the Adrar region of Mauritania, the prestation would be lower for a marriage between patrilateral parallel cousins, symbolizing the equal status of the marriage partners. It would increase as the social distance between marriage partners increased. If the marriage were taking place between persons of the same status group but not genealogically related (e.g., from two different *qabā'il* both of warrior status), the *ṣadāq* would be high to symbolize the parity of the intermarrying groups. If the spouses were unrelated but of unequal status (he of a superior group to her), then the *ṣadāq* would be low. Analogous dynamics of *ṣadāq* variation have been reported for late twentieth-century Mauritania (Boulay 2003: 362–67). We do not have such a detailed reconstruction of variations in *ṣadāq* for Western Sahara. But Caro Baroja (1955: 268) refers to the possibility of *ṣadāq* not having been paid—without explaining under which circumstances nonpayment might occur.

In the refugees' remembered accounts, the wedding celebrations, which took place at the *frīg* of the bride's family, lasted seven days.[5] Afterward, the couple took up temporary residence in the bride's natal *frīg*, living in a canvas tent, *banyah*, that the bride's mother set up every night and took down every day. Their conjugal life was conducted with great discretion for reasons of the modesty code *ḥishmah*. The latter is very similar to the modesty code studied by Lila Abu Lughod (1986) among the Awlād 'Ali Bedouin in Egypt's western desert. As observed by Hassanophones, this modesty code prohibits reference to sexual relations within sight or earshot of certain kin, affines, and older men in general.[6] Khadīja recalled of her first marriage, conducted a few years before going into exile, how *ḥishmah* required her sexual activity to be disguised from view:

> When I first married, my mother would go every night to set up the *banyah* far away. The groom would sit there with his friends, laughing and talking, until I came. First, I would go to sleep in my family's tent, and wait for everyone to be asleep. Then I would creep out in the middle of the night, to join my husband, and stay until just before dawn. Then I would get up and creep back into my family's tent, so that my father would not be able to see me.

The bride and groom usually remained living in the *banyah* until after the birth of the first child. During that time, the women in the bride's natal *frīg* would make her a goat-hair tent. Finally, the bride would be dispatched, with her tent, all its domestic furnishings as provided by her family, as well as camels of her own given by her own family (distinct from any given in the *ṣadāq*), to live with the groom's *frīg*. A Sahrawi proverb presents this marital home as the bride's true place of belonging: "the woman's place/home is where she brought up her children, not the place/home where she was brought up." Her arrival to live, finally, with her husband's kin was called *rḥīl*, from the Arabic root *r-ḥ-l*, "to go away, depart." In Hassaniya, *r-ḥ-l* is also used with the more specific meaning "to move away to a new place." The event of *rḥīl* was also accompanied by a marital prestation of gifts from the bride's to groom's family, known as *faskhah*. These gifts, separate from the bride's endowment by her natal family (her *rḥīl* goods), consisted of a sheep or goat for slaughtering; expensive clothes for the groom's mother and father; ritualized gifts for the groom's family, such as a set number (e.g., twenty) of hospitality items (blankets, cushions, drinking bowls, and so on); and cloves to perfume hair, mirrors, and combs. The ritualized gifts would be distributed to members of the groom's kin's *frīg* and their neighbors and connections. After the *rḥīl*, the bride normally resided in her husband's *frīg* for the duration of the marriage, although she might make long visits to her natal *frīg* for childbirth or during a husband's absence. If the couple's wedding was quantifiable in a finite number of days, the process of becoming a married couple, for Sahrawis and other Hassanophones, was, in a sense, literally a process of building a tent, typically taking months or years.

## Changing the Tent

As Sahrawis's exile stretched to years, refugee marriages took place. Marriage practices were certainly altered by the circumstances of exile. Yet refugees' representations of early revolutionary marriage practices convey that the transformations went beyond the effects of displacement and dispossession, to reflect the state-movement's revolutionary agenda to alter the organization, legitimization and reproduction of social (in)equalities.

It was not hard for me to encounter refugees' representations of early revolutionary marriage practices. This was not only because marriage practices were, during my fieldwork, the subject of heated controversy. In addition, whether they had lived through such marriages as protagonists, workers, children of the 1980s, or not at all, refugee men and women of different ages would speak, often without my prompting, with fascination about early revolutionary marriages. Zaynabu, who had been widowed in exile and remarried, recalled how, as a member of the Popular Committee for Social Affairs and Justice (see Chapters 2 and 3), she had worked at many weddings in her *dairah* throughout the early revolutionary period. At that time it was this Popular Committee's responsibility to host weddings. Without revealing any emotion, she continued to tell me that any wedding guest at that time was "not allowed" to stay anywhere except in the homes of the designated Popular Committee members. I gained further insight into representations of the weddings of the 1980s when, in the summer of 2007, the handful of Sahrawi refugee young men studying in Damascus proudly showed me (at their own initiative) a video of a wedding from "the early days" in the camps. Over tea, we saw the wedding take place to hand-beaten drums and with just one sheep for slaughter. "See," they told me, "we didn't have anything then." In the 2000s, the early revolutionary wedding was remembered as a symbol of revolutionary values and past material hardships.

A recurring reminiscence of the early revolutionary marriage, among refugees who had experienced it both directly and only indirectly, was that "in those days you could marry a woman with a copy of the Polisario magazine, or a bunch of sticks to light a fire." Most often, refugees laughed as they conjured up this image—unthinkable by the late 2000s. Such a token prestation occurred in the context of what refugees recalled as the state-movement having "banned" *ṣadāq*. As one man recalled of the 1980s, "giving money or things [of value] to marry a woman was forbidden." Because the state-movement did not favor written bureaucracy in its governance, it is hard to find a written record of its policies, such as this ban (if such records exist). Only *ṣadāq*, as opposed to *faskhah* or *rḥīl*, was popularly remembered as having been "banned" by the state-movement; only *ṣadāq* is mentioned elsewhere as having disappeared or having been reduced, by decision of the state-movement, to a symbolic level (Lippert 1985: 19; Perregaux 1990: 74; Caratini 2000). Religious and practical reasons may explain the focus of the ban falling on *ṣadāq* rather than marriage prestations more widely. Only *mahr*, fulfilled locally through *ṣadāq*, is required in Islam, so the latter's suppression may have required the intervention of the state-movement in ways the suppression of *faskhah* and *rḥīl* (not required in Islam) did not. In practice, material dispossession made all three kinds of transfer difficult to carry out anyway. Certainly, in refugees' memories, *faskhah* and *rḥīl* were not normally practiced in the early revolutionary period. *Rḥīl* for marriages contracted after exile was further undermined by the fact that the prolonged absence of men at the military front was little suited to women moving to live near their in-laws. Also, if *faskhah* and *rḥīl* may be understood at least in part as reciprocal prestations in response to *ṣadāq*, then the suppression of *ṣadāq* may have undermined potential acts of reciprocity, making a wider ban on all three marriage prestations unnecessary.

The falling of the ban on *ṣadāq* in particular, rather than on the other two prestations, merits attention beyond religious and practical reasons, however. There were also ideological odds at stake. The state-movement was proud to publicize the banning of *ṣadāq* in its official materials directed at a foreign audience, couching this in terms of its rejection of the practice of "buying" women (Polisario front 1988: 55). While the state-movement is undoubtedly interested in garnering the support of an imagined or actual liberal Euro-American audience at whom such a declaration was likely aimed, this does not preclude that it may also have been interested in the ban for questions of internal governance. It is doubtful, though, that *ṣadāq* was ever experienced by Sahrawis as "buying" women. There may be another ideological motivation for the prohibition.

As discussed earlier, in the prerevolutionary negotiation of *ṣadāq*, *qabīlah* relations exerted considerable influence, such as in prescribing a standardized amount or determining its level according to the spouses' intra- or inter-*qabīlah* relations. *Ṣadāq* created not only material barriers to marriage in a context of dispossession, then, but also social barriers to marriage in a context of a revolutionary aspiration to promote social egalitarianism. It was in the interests of the revolutionary project to seek to overcome both kinds of barriers and certainly not to neglect the latter. The urgent ideological motivation in banning *ṣadāq* was surely, as was the case for other Arab revolutionary movements, the desire to eliminate a means of reproducing the intra- and inter-*qabīlah* hierarchies to which the revolutionary regime, in its aspirations to egalitarianism and its rejection of tribalism, was opposed.

There might be even further reason for the state-movement to manipulate *ṣadāq*. As Ladislav Holy (1989: 86–87) has noted, in a context where marriage between agnatic relatives is preferred, intermarriage not only results from agnatic relations but can also be constitutive of them. Not all kin ties can be activated by the members of a particular group, so the groups with which one does intermarry *become* close agnatic kin (86–87). In the hassanophone region, as we have seen, some groups actively encouraged the creation of agnatic ties through intermarriage with nonagnates. If agnation and related *qabīlah* solidarities can be constituted through intermarriage, then in the context of explicit nation formation, feelings of membership in that nation might also be constituted through members' intermarriage. The suppression of *ṣadāq*, functioning as an invitation to widen intermarriage, may thereby have encouraged the very notion of membership in a Sahrawi nation.

*Ṣadāq* did not disappear, though. Indeed, since a groom-to-bride prestation is required in Islam to make a marriage legal, the state-movement could not impose that no prestation be made at all. If it had done so, the resulting marriages would not be licit in the eyes of Islam (*ḥalāl*). *Ṣadāq* was replaced, and Islamic requirements respected, by the state-movement giving a statutory symbolic prestation on behalf of the man for each new marriage (Caratini 2000). Reports I collected indicated, without being precise about the time scale, that the symbolic *ṣadāq* began at an almost insignificant amount and gradually rose to around one thousand Algerian dinars (in the late 2000s the equivalent of about ten euros).

But what of the symbolic personal prestations, such as a handful of sticks or a sheet of paper? If *ṣadāq* was banned, why not just one, but two symbolic prestations? Only one of either the official, mandatory, symbolic prestation sponsored by the state-movement or the personal symbolic prestation would have sufficed to comply with Islamic prescriptions. The existence of both prestations suggests how revolutionary marriage practices aimed at more than merely accommodating Islamic requirements in a context of acute material shortages. A standardized prestation for all, rather than an informal personal ad hoc prestation, was essential for the goal of promoting social egalitarianism. Through the standardized prestation, the state-movement ousted the *qabīlah* as a provider of *ṣadāq* and as the locus of the (potential) hierarchies that influenced the amount to be transferred. The state-movement "[made] public the equal treatment of the government for all" (Caratini 2000: 449). It also undermined refugees' participation in the stratified social relations of the *qabīlah*. Nevertheless, the doubling of the symbolic prestation through the personal offering shows that, even when the state-movement ousted the *qabīlah* as the social context of *ṣadāq*, the notion of a man's personal association with *ṣadāq* never fully disappeared.

In addition to standardizing *ṣadāq*, the state-movement adopted other roles previously undertaken by the *qabīlah*. As Zaynabu recalled, the state-movement provided spouses with a sheep or goat for slaughtering; the wedding celebrations were organized by members of the Popular Committee for Justice and Social Affairs; Popular Committee members prepared the goat, fed guests, and hosted them in their tents, with the *dairah* musical group providing entertainment.

After the wedding celebrations of one day, the state-movement would provide the new couple with household items received from humanitarian aid provisions: a canvas emergency relief tent (rather than a goat-hair *khaymah*), cooking utensils (as available), and blankets. The previous role of the bride's natal group in equipping her (*rḥīl*) was thus now taken over by the state-movement. Nonetheless, the idea that the bride's natal kin would equip her new homestead did not fully disappear. Khadīja told me that, when her eldest daughter married, around 1986, she gave her daughter the cushions from her own tent for the bride's new home. While women already married at the time of their arrival in the camps lived in exile near their affines, new brides in the early revolutionary period did not usually progress to moving to live near their affines. Since at this time husbands were often away for long periods at the front, it made sense, given the prerevolutionary precedent for wives to live near their own families in the early stages after marriage and when husbands were absent, for refugee brides to stay near their mothers.

At a certain point, the state-movement challenged the authority of the *qabīlah* to legitimize a marriage. The Malikite school of Islamic law, followed by Hassanophones, requires the consent of the bride's male guardian (*wālī*) for a marriage. The *wālī* would usually be the bride's father or another member of her agnatic kin, that is, from her *qabīlah*. The groom, absent among Sahrawis from his own marriage contract because *ḥishmah* prevents him from interacting with his father-in-law, would also be represented by a member of his agnatic kin, that is, from his *qabīlah*. Anne Lippert (1985: 19) and Christine Perregaux (1990: 73) both report that, in the 1980s, the state-movement placed great emphasis on each spouse having to consent to a marriage, with one of Lippert's interlocutors going so far as to say that a young girl did not need her family's permission to get married. Caratini (2000), however, questions that the attempt to take the authorization of marriage out of the hands of a woman's parents was effective. I found that refugees held differing opinions as to whether in the 1980s the authorization of marriages had been taken out of the hands of the *qabīlah*. At least in Khadīja's experience, the authorization of the *qabīlah* was for a time skirted. After her divorce from the father of her first nine children, Khadīja remarried in the late 1980s, when, she explained, the marriage contract was no longer carried out between representatives of each spouse's *qabīlah*. Instead, she told me, the groom would attend the local government office and register his name. Then the bride would visit the same office and register her name, and they would be married. Zaynabu and Brahim similarly registered separately for their wedding, although Zaynabu also recalled that they afterward conducted a contract "at the tent."[7]

In a number of areas—the state-movement's symbolic *ṣadāq*, the recruitment of labor for the celebration of the wedding, the equipping of the new household, and even, at one point, marriage contracts—the early revolutionary period saw the state-movement oust the *qabīlah* as the sphere of social relations through which marriage was forged and legitimized. Marriage became one of the frontiers for advancing both the unmaking of the social relations of tribes, with their associated stratification, and the making of the social relations of state power, with aspirations toward egalitarian relations among citizens. The transformed early revolutionary marriage practices became symbolic of the new revolutionary society—a symbol whose potency, remembered with laughter, nostalgia, pride, and reticence, long outlived those days when one could marry with a bunch of sticks.

## Rivals in Marriage

While my interlocutors could not agree on a date for the state-movement ceasing to provide symbolic *ṣadāq*, at some point after the cease-fire of 1991, the state-movement's mandatory provision came to be no longer shadowed by an equally symbolic personal payment but overshadowed by materially significant personal prestations. The latter dwarfed the state-movement's and eventually led to the official symbolic prestation disappearing altogether. After the cease-fire, the refugee camps themselves were changing. The political and economic relaxation of the 1990s allowed for greater movement of people and goods in, through, and from the camps. As Popular Committees were reformed into councils, the Committee for Justice and Social Affairs was dissolved altogether (see Chapter 3). In this dramatically altered context, marriage practices changed too. Where the early revolutionary changes were desired by the state-movement, this was not the case for the late revolutionary changes. They were at the heart of demographic, economic, and political tensions affecting the refugees in the 2000s. I grew familiar with refugees' complaints of how expensive weddings had become. Some refugees referred specifically to a "crisis" (*azmah*) of prohibitively costly celebrations. I heard members of both older and younger generations bemoan that, in exile, "we have returned" (*rajāʿnā*) to the customs of the past.

I attended weddings throughout 2007 and 2008 (and in subsequent visits). Sometimes I knew one of the families well enough either to work with the bride's party or to be part of the groom's party. In the early days, on such occasions I would work with the wedding party, struggling through sixteen-hour days or longer, to emerge exhausted and amazed at the stamina of the women who did not seem to need rest, sleep, or even food. On one occasion, the guests had eaten every last bit of food the women themselves had prepared and served, which they stoically brushed off saying, "We filled up on the smell." With time and the experience of such days of exhaustion, I became less valiant in my commitment to sharing in the work responsibilities of those closest to the bride or groom and a little more willing to creep into the tent where the old women had gathered. In one capacity or another, I was able to work, attend, and discuss weddings throughout 2007 and 2008—a period when marriage practices changed.

By 2007, the marriage practices in vogue in the camps expressed several years of the cumulative intensification of the material aspects of a wedding celebration. This included a significant groom-to-bride prestation incumbent on the groom. In her discussion of the resurgence of a groom-to-bride prestation after the early revolutionary period, Caratini (2000) suggests that a reason for this shift may be that a significant groom-to-bride prestation proved an effective means of a woman seeking protection from a husband divorcing her too easily. With it having become prohibitively expensive for a man to seek a new wife, men might be discouraged from leaving an existing marriage.

This may explain some, but perhaps not all aspects of the resurgence of a groom-to-bride prestation. By the late 2000s, the groom-to-bride prestation was seen as so costly as to be prohibitively expensive for a man to marry at all. The prestation was perceived, then, as a cause of delayed marriages for young refugees more broadly. Also significant is the fact that when a groom-to-bride prestation reestablished itself, it did so in a new form—for which reason I do not refer to it as "*ṣadāq*." As we have seen, a marital home was previously equipped by the bride's family (before the revolution) and, later, by the state-movement (in the early revolutionary period). Once the camps opened up in the late revolutionary period to a growing informal market economy (see Chapter 6), there were more goods available for homes to ease the material strains of exile. Yet these goods were unavailable through rations distributions from the state-movement. There being prerevolutionary precedent for the groom to provide material goods at the time of the contracting of a marriage (in the form of *ṣadāq*), it is plausible that it became established practice in the late revolutionary period that the groom, aided by his kin, should provide material goods at the time of the contracting of the wedding. The form of the new prestation was household equipment for the bride that the state-movement could not provide (see below).[8] In the context of most brides staying in exile to live near their own families, the new prestation revived, even as it inverted, the pattern of prerevolutionary prestations whereby the party moving to live with the spouse's kin provided and equipped the marital home.

As new consumer goods became available, these were added to the list of things that a groom was expected to provide, much as a tendency toward escalation in groom-to-bride prestations has been noted elsewhere (e.g., Masquelier 2005). A strong impulse to "keep up with the neighbors," by no means particular to Sahrawis but epitomized for them in one of their interpretations of the proverb "Do what your neighbor does, or move away from him," would only have increased escalating expectations of the goods that grooms were expected to provide. By 2007, preparations to buy the necessary goods would begin months or even years in advance on the groom's side of the family. The (aspiring) groom himself would work especially hard to save up money, as I noted from various young male interlocutors. Mbārak, who worked in the Ministry of Information, had saved some money by bringing perfumes and other goods back from his previous studies in Libya, to sell in the camps. A friend of his had set up a shop selling groceries in his home *dairah*, and another colleague in the Ministry had a second job driving a shared taxi between Smara camp, Rabouni, and Tindouf. Zaynabu's sister's son, who was engaged to one of Zaynabu's younger daughters, saved up from his work building houses. Māghalāha's daughters pointed out, though, that for some young women the most desirable groom was one who had a work permit and a job in Europe (see Chapter 7).

Caratini (2000: 450) writes of the "reappearance" of the marriage prestation after the early revolutionary period. Yet I never heard refugees refer to this prestation as *ṣadāq*. Instead, these goods were known collectively as *dabash* ("things") or *majīb* ("things that are brought"). *Dabash* is also the word used to mean things carried on a camel, which is how household items would have been carried in the days of camel transportation during mobile pastoralism. The *dabash* items typical of a 2007 wedding are listed in Table 5.

Women who had married in the early 2000s explained to me that each year the *dabash* would improve as new items became available. "When I married, you just got a black and white TV set with your *dabash*. Nowadays, the brides get a color TV and a satellite dish," one young woman explained to me, who had married in 2003.[9] The *dabash* items, ranging from carpets,

Table 5. Typical Wedding Gifts from Groom's to Bride's Party (*dabash*) in 2007

| *Item* | *Quantity* |
|---|---|
| **Items for the bride** | |
| Tent | 1 |
| Blankets | 12–20 |
| Cushions | 8–16 |
| Carpets | 4–6 |
| Television | 1 |
| Satellite dish and receiver | 1 |
| Solar panel | 1 |
| Light bulb | 1–2 |
| Box with jewelry for bride | 1–2 |
| Full clothing sets for bride (inc. shoes) | 10–15 |
| Wash stand | 2 |
| Drinking bowl (*jīrah*) | 4–6 |
| Chest for bride to store items | 1 |
| Suitcase for bride to store items | 3–4 |
| Cooking pots | 1–2 |
| Dishes for serving food | 3–4 |
| Wardrobe | 1 |
| Cabinet for storing television | 1 |
| "Arab" style sofa set | 1 |
| **Items for the wedding feast** | |
| *Inḥīrah* (camel for slaughtering) | 1 |
| Sugar | 20kg |
| Flour | 50kg |
| Rice | 20kg |
| Tea leaves | 2kg |
| **Items to distribute to the bride's kin and their neighbors** | |
| *Milḥafah* (women's clothing) | 80–100 |
| Comb | 100 |
| Hand mirror | 100 |
| Cloves | 2kg |
| Henna | 5kg |

blankets, plates, solar panels, clothes, and often even a tent, would be collected and stored at the house of the groom's family until the wedding day.

As the appointed wedding day approached, the bride's family would hire a large "party" tent, called a *qā'ah*, to be set up near the bride's home, wherever it fitted between the neighbors' tents. The groom's family might set up something similar, on a slightly smaller scale, near his family's home. Each of the parties would purchase a camel destined to be slaughtered, an *inḥīrah*. In the days leading up to the wedding, relatives, neighbors, and friends would be informed of the wedding and invited. On the day, relatives and friends of the groom would gather at the groom's house, where a sheep would be slaughtered for them. At the same time, at the bride's family's house relatives and friends would gather and prepare their camel. In the afternoon, before sunset, the groom's party would load all the people, the *dabash*, and their camel into cars and make a procession, called a *défilé* (from the French *défilé*, "procession, parade"), over to the bride's, honking horns, waving streamers, and singing.

On arrival at the party tent, the groom's party would be received with ululation and a musical party with singers, *nishāṭ*, at which female guests would take it in turns to dance in the center of the tent, surrounded by rows of women and children seated on the floor (see Figure 9). Older men, for reasons of *ḥishmah*, would be safely out of hearing range or would not attend at all, while young men would hover around the outskirts of the party tent, looking in. After the party, guests from both sides would mill around; then, at sunset in a side tent with the "old men" (*kūlah*), the marriage contract would be performed between the guardians of each of the bride and groom in front of a judge. When I was once taken to see a contract taking place, the tent side cloths were raised up, so that older women sitting outside the tent could see and hear the contract progress. They shouted out at various points suggesting clauses for the bride, such as that the groom would be unable to take a second wife. At night, the camel meat, prepared by the bride's family, would be served to all the guests and sent out to neighbors. A camel can readily feed two hundred people, and the guests (mostly women) might number this, a good proportion of whom would bed down in the party tent for the night. In most cases—I heard of only one exception, discussed by refugees as unusual—the bride and groom would not appear in public together at any point during the wedding. Each spouse would be attended by a close group of relatives and friends in different locations. The location of the bride might be kept secret, so her husband would have to "search" for her. In some cases, the bride would be brought to him that first night. In other cases, it might take several nights for the bride to be "handed over" to her husband.

The next day, the groom's family would sacrifice their camel, and there would be more singing and dancing. In some cases reported to me, if the

Figure 9. Women dance in a party tent, 2007 (photo by Alice Wilson).

marriage had been consummated the night before, the bloodstain proving the bride's honor might be displayed in the party tent on the second day. The slaughtering of the second camel concluded the formal wedding celebrations and saw most guests leave. After a few days, each of the bride and groom might slaughter a sheep to which they would invite their friends and relatives. This "afterevent" was ambiguous in its relationship to the wedding: it was not part of the wedding, but it often followed it. After the wedding, the bride and groom would take up temporary residence in a spare room or tent near the bride's family. Over the next months or even years, the groom would pay to have a mud-brick room or rooms built for him and his wife to live in, still near her family. Until a new room was ready, the groom would live in a semipermanent state of "*ḥishmah* alert." Even if he was a close relative of his parents-in-law, once married, a husband avoided contact with his parents-in-law because *ḥishmah* made him embarrassed to interact with those to whom he was now also related by his sexual relationship with their daughter. Since he was often living in a spare room at the bride's family's, he was, therefore, potentially in danger of meeting his mother-in-law or father-in-law when crossing the courtyard between the tent and other rooms forming the domestic complex.

Because most new couples remained living with the bride's kin, in the late 2000s *rḥīl* was not usually made. *Faskhah* as a freestanding event in its own right had, by 2007, made a comeback. The items taken could amount to as much as "half of what was brought for the wedding," as one interlocutor estimated. Interlocutors agreed that *faskhah* was not obligatory and often not possible in the context of exile. Yet by 2007 there was an expectation that some kind of initial formal visit should occur, even if it were delayed for years on the grounds that there was not enough money for it. In 2008, when her eldest child was five years old, one of Khadīja's daughters was finally preparing to make a *faskhah* visit to her mother-in-law in the distant camp of Dakhla.

In 2007, refugees suggested that a man needed about four thousand euros to marry. This was a formidable amount in a refugee setting where many families' cash incomes were insecure and there were only limited chances to obtain the documentation to go to work in Europe. To put this sum in context, in February 2007, the figure given by the president in a speech to Spanish journalists as an estimate of the amount of money a family needed to survive for a month was a hundred euros. My guess is that, in addition to their food rations, a family of four or five could manage at that time basic living costs on about a hundred euros a month—but not "extra" items such as hospitality obligations. It is therefore unsurprising that some young men spent two or three years, or more, trying to amass their *dabash*.[10]

A groom could expect help from close family and a wider circle with the costs of getting married. Wedding guests would help by bringing items such as blankets or cushions. Indeed, Māghalāha's youngest daughter, Alma'lūma, explained one day that women from her family were unlikely to attend a wedding on her mother's side about which we had heard because "it's not right to go without taking something." Closer relatives might take a ram for slaughtering; one woman I knew who could not attend a colleague's wedding herself sent money. The pressure to help with contributions was in itself a cause for complaint. Abba, from the Ministry of Information and the mature father of a large family, once grumbled: "80% of my money is frittered away, for a goat for so-and-so who is getting married or naming a new baby. I just had to spend 200 euros on furnishings [*salón*] for my brother in law's wedding." On the other hand, he himself had received help from his family in Moroccan-controlled Western Sahara for the costs of his own remarriage in 2006.

While the groom could expect help, he was still expected to pull his own weight. On one occasion, when I was attending a wedding with the groom's party, some guests I did not know asked me whether the groom had acquired the *dabash* himself or with help. I sensed that the question worked in at least two ways—a test of my knowledge of Sahrawi practices and an inquiry into the groom's circumstances. Māghalāha's family, close relatives of the groom, later asked what the other guests had said to me. They were furious and offended when they learned what had happened. The question was offensive, they explained, because it suggested the groom had not put his own *dabash* together. But anyway, Suelma continued, it did not matter how it was put together: "The important thing is that [the bride] receives her *dabash* ready for her."

## Marriage Reinvented

The marriage practices I observed in 2007 were not only expensive, but they also bore a curious relationship of difference and similarity to both prerevolutionary and early revolutionary marriage practices. Some practices had precedent, such as the idea that the bride hid from the groom; older women recalled how they too had "hidden" from the groom. Various changes had also been introduced, though, sometimes seeing alteration and restoration combined in complex ways.

One form of change was new elements that contrasted sharply with both early revolutionary and prerevolutionary practices. Alma'lūma recalled a wedding at which evidence of the bride's virginity was displayed at the celebrations: "They held up her stained sheet, and we waved it around as we danced." Such a display was new. Older women told me that they had never heard of this when they were younger. Such display contradicts the principles of *ḥishmah*, which avoids mention or evidence in the public domain of sexual activity. The discretion stipulated by *ḥishmah* is even to the point that a married woman will not inform her own mother or sisters of her pregnancy. Khadīja's daughter, Minetou, told no one of her pregnancy until, finally, her belly becoming visible even under the capacious folds of the *milḥafah*, her family discovered it for themselves. Older women believed displaying evidence of virginity was a custom from Tindouf. The postmarital celebrations that were separate for bride's and groom's sides of the families were also, according to some interlocutors, a new custom taken from

Tindouf. The influence of Tindouf—all too easily blamed, due to its proximity, for perceived "non-Sahrawi behavior"—is uncertain. Strikingly, the separate celebrations for bride's and groom's families held a few days after the wedding were at odds with the remembered prerevolutionary practices, when the wedding took place at the *frīg* of the bride's family and involved both sides gathering together.

A second kind of change entailed rupture with early revolutionary marriage practices, namely, the disappearance of the state-movement's role in equipping the marital home and in disbursing a symbolic *ṣadāq*. The increasingly common provision of a tent by the groom was symptomatic of the new, absent role of the state-movement. Not only did the state-movement no longer intervene in the endowment of new couples, but it was unable to do so in the same way it had done in the past. There was a shortage of tents supplied by humanitarian organizations and, therefore, a waiting list of up to several years for new couples to receive a tent from the state-movement. The new market mechanisms (see Chapter 6) filled the gap. The tents grooms provided were purchased second-hand, typically put together from cuttings of tents refugee families had reduced in size. Such families literally sold off parts of their homes to increase their possibilities for participating in the new cash economy. The absence of intervention from the state-movement was notable in other ways too. The people who came to work at the wedding were no longer members of the Committee of Social Affairs and Justice, which had been disbanded. Rather, they were family members and neighbors (and perhaps an anthropologist). Entertainment, such as singing, was put on at the expense of family members, rather than thanks to the *dairah* musical group.[11]

Another form of change concerns a reinforcement of an early revolutionary tendency that was simultaneously a further shift away from prerevolutionary practices. Postmarital residence is one such case. The early revolutionary period had expanded the circumstances in which brides remained living near their own families, while still maintaining the link between this residential pattern and a husband's absence. The late revolutionary period broke the association between uxorilocal residence and a husband's absence. In exile in the 2000s, if a groom wanted to insist on the marital home being near the wife's kin, this could cause the marriage to be called off altogether. Such a cancelation proved significant for a young woman in Auserd camp. She had decorated her hands with henna, the last stage of beautification, to attend a wedding as a guest. At the last minute, the wedding fell through precisely because the bride's kin refused the groom's request that she move to live near his family. The young woman, whose natal home was a mere twenty-minute walk from the groom's, ended up marrying the man herself. Caratini (2000) attributes women's reluctance, after the cease-fire and men's return from the front, to move to live near affines to practical and affective reasons. Once refugees supplemented tents with mud-brick rooms, women were more likely to wish to build their rooms near their own family, so that they could keep them even if the marriage dissolved. Hassanophone women also retained strong emotional ties to their natal families, as observed by Rebecca Popenoe (2004) of Hassanophones in Mali. Such ties are not distinctive to Hassanophones: Lila Abu-Lughod's (1993: 173) Bedouin companions told her that "the Arabs want their daughters to stay with them." Refugee families were perhaps unusual in being able to exploit altered social circumstances in the late revolutionary period to indulge that connection, with mothers and daughters refusing to separate on the latter's marriage. In addition to practical and affective concerns, the liminality of exile may have facilitated refugees' tolerance for expanding uxorilocal postmarital residence in exile; uxorilocality was originally itself a liminal phase of postmarital residence.

A further kind of change built on prerevolutionary practices, while simultaneously altering them. The most prominent example is that the groom-to-bride prestation, absent except symbolically in the early revolutionary period, reemerged changed in name and content. *Dabash* covered the items encompassed in *rḥīl* (prerevolutionary period) or the state-movement's endowment of a new couple with available household items (early revolutionary period). The fact that the *dabash* was composed primarily of commodities for the bride's home, rather than of camels to be consumed or herded with the bride's kin's camels, may have contributed to the increased pressure on the groom himself to bear greatest responsibility for amassing the *dabash*. In the prerevolutionary mobile pastoralist context, when the camels for *ṣadāq* were sourced from the groom's father's herd (Caratini 1989b: 54), the prerevolutionary groom hardly had the opportunity to amass his *ṣadāq* personally. The procurement of commodities for *dabash*, however, was more amenable to personal accumulation on the part of the groom. A second example of the modified revival of prerevolutionary practices is the return of *faskhah*. Its reappearance restored some of the potential for reciprocity between the spouses' parties that had been ousted by the state-movement in the early revolutionary period. Notably, though, it did not restore the full scope of the prerevolutionary potential for reciprocity, where the bride's family responded to *ṣadāq* through both *faskhah* and *rḥīl*.

Finally, some prerevolutionary practices that had disappeared in the early revolutionary period were restored. The reemergence of a groom-to-bride prestation with real, as opposed to symbolic, value, facilitated the return of divorce compensation prestations made by a wife to a husband reluctant to grant her a divorce.[12] In the early revolutionary period, when divorce negotiations were dealt with through the Committee for Social Affairs and Justice (see Chapter 3), such divorce compensation fell out of practice. In the late revolutionary exile period, however, a few controversial cases of a husband refusing to grant his wife a divorce unless such a prestation was forthcoming were much discussed among refugees. In one case of which I heard, the man had demanded a cash payment from his estranged wife's family, who had raised the money by resorting to fellow tribesmen. In another case, the most scandalous of which I learned, a wife demanded a divorce just weeks after the marriage. The man had insisted on full repayment of his *dabash*, including "the zinc on the roof of the rooms he had had built."

Taking stock of the relationship between late revolutionary marriage practices and early revolutionary and prerevolutionary precedents, had there been, as some refugees maintained, a "return" to the old marriage practices that the revolution had initially set out to reform? Figure 10 summarizes schematically three stages of marriage payments: pre-, early, and late revolutionary. In the prerevolutionary prestations, potentially reciprocal transfers occurred between both the contracting parties, with shared responsibility for the amassing of material goods to be exchanged. In early revolutionary prestations, the state-movement was responsible for most of the transfers of goods. In late revolutionary prestations, the material prestations from the state-movement disappeared, and the state-movement retreated from performing key roles in the marriage ceremony. The bulk of the material prestations were from groom's side to bride's. The retreat of the state-movement did not coincide with the recreation of the full range of reciprocal transfers of the pre-exile period.

Late revolutionary prestations differed from both prerevolutionary and early revolutionary practices. The excessive expense of wedding ceremonies, which some refugees experienced and described as an economic "crisis," therefore arose at least in part not so much from a "return" of previous practices but from their "reinvention" (West 2009). In Harry West's (2009: 33–34) elaboration of Eric Hobsbawm's (1983) notion of the invention of tradition, the reinvention of tradition is "a process that simultaneously

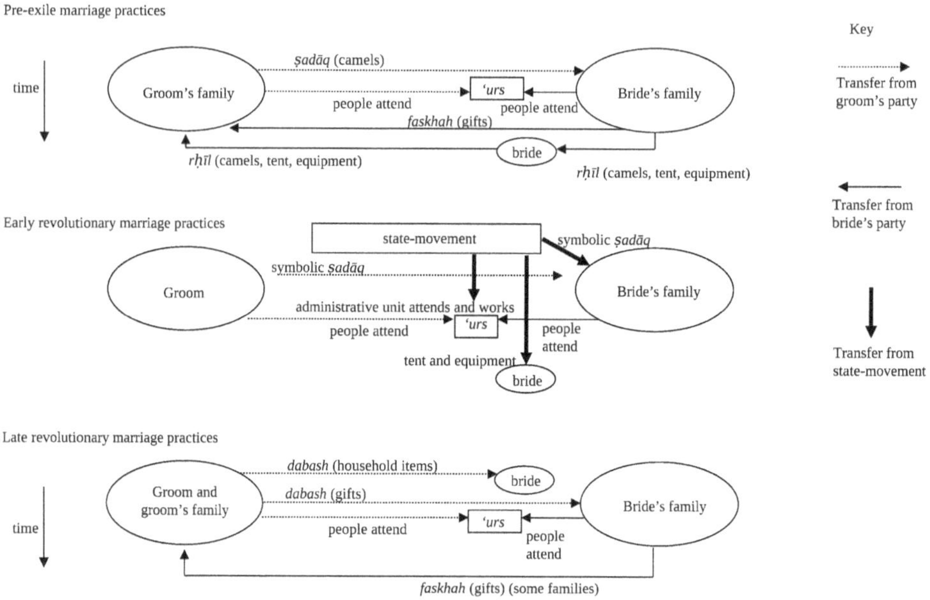


Figure 10. Changing marriage practices.

makes reference to the past while remaking the past in the present." That late revolutionary weddings had come to be experienced as excessively expensive, and therefore the cause of delay for grooms to marry, was not merely because the state-movement had withdrawn from undertaking the range of responsibilities it managed in the 1980s. Rather, the terms of the "reinvention" of Sahrawi marriage prestations exacerbated, beyond prerevolutionary precedents, the excessive expense of wedding celebrations for grooms. The reinvention concentrated on the shoulders of the groom the responsibility for providing an ever-escalating set of demands for equipping the marital home—a stage in marital life that, before the revolution, could come months or years after marriage and procreation had begun. Simultaneously, the reinvented marriage practices reduced the prerevolutionary balancing of responsibilities between the groom's and bride's parties. The memory of shared responsibilities characteristic of the prerevolutionary marriage practices had not disappeared in the early revolutionary period, as we saw in Khadīja's giving her own cushions to her recently married daughter. In the late 2000s, though, when I questioned young people about *dabash* and the way things used to be done before exile, I did not find any of them who knew that the equipment of the household had previously been the responsibility of the bride's family. Rather, they would complain of the pernicious effects of their "traditions" that a groom had to pay so much to be able to marry a bride.[13] The refugees with whom I talked who had grown up in exile were aware that the late revolutionary practices were different from the early revolutionary practices and that the latter in turn were different from the prerevolutionary practices. But there seemed to be little awareness that the 2007 marriage practices were significantly different in their own right from the prerevolutionary practices and in ways that only exacerbated their perceived contentious character as "too expensive" for young men.

The state-movement's retreat from intervention in marriage practices by no means signified that the state-movement had lost interest in marriage, as events in 2008 confirmed.

## Crisis Point?

In December 2007, the twelfth Popular General Congress of Polisario was held in Tifariti, Polisario-controlled Western Sahara. Along with some 150 foreigners, I made the trip out to Tifariti to attend the opening ceremony of the PGC, at which inaugural speeches were made by Sahrawi and foreign dignitaries. This was the only part of the business of the more than one thousand congress delegates foreigners were invited to attend. On December 14, PGC delegates, foreign guests, and journalists gathered in the main hall to hear the various opening speeches. These included the report of the president of the Sahrawi Arab Democratic Republic and secretary general of the Polisario Front, Mohamad 'Abd al'Azīz. The report addressed a number of areas of political and social life, both in the period since the previous PGC and in the months and years ahead. In the discussion of goals and concerns looking ahead, one section in particular caused a reaction from the Sahrawi delegates:

> In socioeconomic questions, one of the most significant concerns and that could have catastrophic consequences is without a doubt the fall in the birth rate and migration, as both threaten the existence of the Sahrawi people. In this respect, it must not be forgotten that wasteful spending in social events and the rising

> price of bridewealth are serious obstacles for young people who wish to get married. Nor are [these practices] suitable to our religious principles or our social reality.[14]

The Sahrawi part of the hall gasped, erupted even, and it was a few seconds before the president could continue. Had the Sahrawi delegates let out their irrepressible consternation that the state-movement should disapprove of their manner of conducting a wedding? Or had they spontaneously approved the unapologetic reminder of the harsh realities of a liberation struggle? At the time, I felt unable to gauge the nature of the response from the Sahrawi delegates. These lines, the only part of the speech that aroused a reaction of this kind from the Sahrawi listeners, are telling with regard to the state-movement's concerns about late revolutionary marriage practices. If in daily life I had heard refugees refer to expensive weddings as a "crisis," the speech made clear that, for the state-movement, the economic crisis of expensive weddings was intimately related to a perceived and feared crisis of demographics and, ultimately, the very survival of the liberation movement.

In the months following the drama of the president's discussion of marriages in his speech at the PGC, I noticed that wedding ceremonies were changing. Soon after the PGC of December 2007, the procession, camel slaughtering, party tent, and live music were rumored among the refugees to be "banned." It was not clear from refugees' discussions which organ within the state-movement was responsible for the "ban" (nor was this question of interest to most refugees). During the period after a PGC, the Sahrawi National Council was dissolved pending reelection. In the absence of a sitting SNC, presidential decrees could be passed directly, defining policy, without the need to go through PGC or the SNC. In general in the state-movement, policy decisions, whether arising from a PGC decision, new law, or presidential decree, were disseminated among the refugees not through the state-movement's official print media or other written sources but through face-to-face meetings arranged between state-movement officials and the "grassroots." News of policies reached refugees orally, then, and usually in second-hand accounts passed on from someone who had attended one of these meetings. News of the "ban" on certain marriage practices spread among refugees through such face-to-face routes. In March 2008, I came to experience the effects of the "ban," as did Zaynabu's family as they prepared for a wedding to be hosted by Zaynabu's first husband's daughter from his first marriage.

A few days before the forthcoming wedding, I was present when one of Zaynabu's younger daughters, in her mid-twenties, suggested that we should take a sheep with us when we attended the wedding. The eldest sister, in her late thirties, objected: "They banned it," she said. I asked, "Who banned that?" to which she replied, "The state." She went on to explain that there was to be no camel slaughtering at a wedding and a limit to the number of sheep slaughterings. The younger sister replied that she did not think anyone could be told off for taking a sheep when such a close relative was getting married. Silence followed, in which I could feel unspoken tension that seemed to be a spectral echo of the gasp of the PGC delegates a few months earlier. Even within one family, people did not agree on the right way to celebrate a marriage.

The wedding day came. The sister who had lobbied for slaughtering a sheep piled into a car with a group of relatives and a car-sick ram (she had had her way in the end). The driver of the car wanted to avoid the open desert tracks and take the tarmac road via Tindouf, where the Algerian authorities allowed Sahrawis, but not foreigners, to circulate. So I had to watch the car drive off, leaving me behind and feeling somewhat put out that the progress I had made in trying not to get special treatment as a foreigner now meant that I was well integrated enough to be overlooked when this was deemed convenient. Yet, a few hours later, a third sister rushed in telling me we had to "go now" to join the wedding. She explained that the first car had gone off to join the bride's party in Elayoune camp. There was still time for us to join the groom's party, gathering in our refugee camp, Smara. "What about our older sisters?" I asked, for the eldest two did not seem to be included in either group. "No, they aren't coming," she told me, as we headed east toward the tent where the groom's family had gathered his bride's *dabash*. We arrived in plenty of time to see the goods loaded for the hour's drive to the bride's camp. In groups of two or three cars, we traveled across open desert. We could not enter Elayoune as one group, since a *défilé* was now banned. When we arrived at the bride's family's tent, we found that two small tents had been put together to make a reception space, where, at its most crowded, I estimated there were about forty-five women. Music was being played from a cassette player. There was no party tent, no live music, and that evening there was mutton but no camel meat. We stayed a night for the wedding, and the next day guests returned home. I went to see the two eldest sisters to ask them why they had not come: the bride was their half-sister's daughter, so a very close relative to them. "There was no camel meat, no live music. . . . There's nothing to go for," they told me.

This scenario was not untypical of weddings in 2008. Most of the weddings I attended that year were significantly simpler than they had been a year before. Rumors continued that various elements of the marriage ceremony had been banned following the PGC. Yet I noticed that the changes were not consistent. I would see a camel go past in a groom's party, or I would join other women for live music in a party tent. I heard, but was unable to verify through official sources, that the punishment for those who continued to arrange for *inḥīrah*, *qāʿah*, and *nishāṭ* at weddings was that rations aid would be cut off from the new couple for two years. For months, I puzzled over why some people complied and others did not and kept asking about it. One day, as we rested on the floor of the tent, chatting, I raised this with Māghalāha's daughter, Suelma. She leaned in, assuming the position of one about to confide, and explained to me that the adherence to the ban depended on the *qabīlah*. I was stunned. At the time, it was the first inkling I had that the *qabīlah* might wield such influence over state-movement policy. The clouded explanations I had gathered until then, I surmised, might reflect not only variation in refugees' access to information but also, perhaps especially, people's wariness about discussing *qabīlah* affairs with a foreigner. With those interlocutors with whom I enjoyed the necessary confidence, I was able to inquire about the influence of the *qabīlah* on marriage practices. From host family members and ministerial employees, I learned that, in seeking to implement the prohibitions relating to marriage practices, the state-movement had turned to *shuyūkh*, asking them to request the members of their *qabāʾil* to reduce the costs of their marriages. In the versions recounted to me, the *qabāʾil* had each gathered their elders to discuss the matter, and each had come to a decision about what to ban. *Qabīlah* X had banned *nishāṭ* and the *qāʿah*.[15] *Qabīlah* Y had banned *nishāṭ*, *qāʿah*, and *inḥīrah*. Part of *Qabīlah* Z had come to a particular decision, and part of it had come to another. The elders of *Qabīlah* X were then rumored to be banning *inḥīrah* as well and the wardrobe from the *dabash*. The latter turned out to be a false alarm: only the *inḥīrah* was added to their list of prohibitions. *Défilé* seemed to be banned across the board by the state-movement for "safety," since accidents, some of them fatal, had occurred between the vehicles as they raced to the bride's kin.

Before the cease-fire, the state-movement had intervened directly in the control of marriage practices, setting and providing a symbolic *ṣadāq*, staging the wedding through its own administrative unit, and equipping the new household. Now, in contrast, the state-movement was working through *shuyūkh* in order to influence marriage practices as a response to the crisis of marriages being too expensive for young men. The relationship between the state-movement and the *qabīlah* had undergone a major shift—from the state-movement seeking to replace the *qabīlah* as a means of undermining it to the state-movement seeking to work through the *qabīlah* as a means of better achieving the state-movement's interests.

Several possible reasons might explain this change. The state-movement might have accepted turning to *shuyūkh* on this matter because marriage was seen as a sphere in which family, and through that the *qabīlah*, continued to hold influence. A senior state-movement official put the following argument to me: whenever a marriage took place, it occurred between two persons who were members of *qabā'il*, and it was inevitable that many of their relatives would like to attend. Such an explanation may not go far enough, though. The social relations of the *qabīlah* are not reducible to those of family but include stratified political relations, as borne out by the fact that the state-movement had banned tribalism in the first place. Moreover, it transpires that, when put to the test by a perceived crisis of both economic and demographic dimensions, the state-movement found its own capacity to prescribe desired behavior to be wanting and resorted to seeking to work through the capacities of the *qabīlah*. In doing so, the state-movement exposed a political crisis—in addition to the economic and demographic crises of which refugees spoke explicitly—in its own capacity for governance. Not only had the state-movement been unable to impose restrictions directly, but even the *shuyūkh* did not merely "take orders" from the state-movement. Rather, they held meetings with the relevant elders to discuss the state-movement's requests and arrived at their own independent decision (or were at least believed to have done so by my interlocutors). Abba, the bureaucrat weighed down by contributions to the weddings of family members, explained his view that the state-movement was not able to apply all its measures and so was turning to *qabā'il* to use their influence where the state-movement's had failed.[16]

## Marriage Matters

Changing marriage practices in the Sahrawi refugee camps are an illuminating window onto the state-movement's attempts to manage social (in)equalities, and its relationship with the *qabīlah* in attempting this management. Where prerevolutionary variations in *ṣadāq* had expressed possibilities for social (in)equality, the early revolutionary standardized *ṣadāq* and marriage ceremonies reconfigured marriage as a means of reproducing only the notion of social equality.

The extent to which this policy, and its moral legacy in the late revolutionary period, may have allowed marriages to form that contravened the former marriage prohibitions is intriguing. Caratini (2000: 447–48) holds that unions in exile that contravened "Arab marriage" were rare, typically opposed by a bride's parents, and, when they did occur, ended quickly in divorce under pressure from the bride's family. In my own fieldwork, because of the sensitivity of inquiring about *qabīlah* and status group membership, it was not feasible to attempt a study of the incidence of "close," and indeed, "Arab" marriage in either the early or the late revolutionary periods. In my observations, marriage with a close relative, including between FBD and FBS, did occur in both the early and late revolutionary periods—as well as marriages not contracted between close relatives or even fellow members of a *qabīlah*. Marriages that contravened the prohibition of a woman marrying below her own status group were rare and attributed by refugees to a new dynamic of marrying "up" a scale of material wealth. In Abba's words: "If a tribesman comes to ask for a woman in marriage and another person comes too who is not a tribesman, but richer, then the family will choose the latter, even if it is a black man. I can point out cases to you."

If few cases of women "marrying down" occurred in exile, we might, nevertheless, still say that, in both early and late revolutionary periods, the state-movement continued to intervene in marriage to seek to organize, legitimize, and reproduce a certain notion of social (in)equalities in its governed population. Moving from a standardized prestation to prohibition of expensive parts of the prestation, the state-movement updated, but still maintained, a definition of the limits of acceptable social inequalities for its governed population.

The acceptable limits of social inequalities were of concern not only to the state-movement but also to the refugees more broadly (see Chapter 6). By highlighting here the state-movement's enduring efforts to define those limits, even to the point of resorting to the manipulation of the social relations of the *qabīlah*, my broader aim has been to show how the management of social (in)equalities is a concern for the social relations of sovereignty. The remaking of sovereignty in the case of Sahrawi refugees brings to the fore how governing authorities make, mask, and manage social (in)equalities.

As was the case for deciding when laws hold (Chapter 3) and appropriating resources (Chapter 4), in the task of managing social (in)equalities, the state-movement switched from overwriting *qabīlah* relations to seeking to work through them or letting them show through in the palimpsest, where the state-movement had been unable in and of itself to achieve its desired goals. This reversal is not necessarily paradoxical; it suggests the compatibility of the social relations of both *qabīlah* and state-movement as constitutive of projects of sovereignty. Because the social relations of the *qabīlah* were implicated in the management of social (in)equalities through marriage practices and, ultimately, marriage strategies, the state-movement's own attempted management of social (in)equalities entailed, in differing circumstances, both ousting and manipulating the social relations of the *qabīlah*.

Looking beyond the relationship between the state-movement and the *qabīlah* in the management of social (in)equalities, the changes in marriage practices among Sahrawi refugees shed light on the question of the growing strength of *qabīlah* membership in the late revolutionary period. That the state-movement resorted to the *qabīlah* to manage marriage practices, and, ultimately, social (in)equalities, suggests that *qabīlah* relations were indeed stronger in the late revolutionary period than before the cease-fire. But it was no foregone conclusion that the *qabīlah* was always able to succeed where the state-movement had failed. The inconsistent application that I observed of the rumored prohibitions could not always be explained by the parties' *qabā'il*: continuing instances of *inḥīrah*, *qā'ah*, *nishāṭ*, and even *défilé* after the 2007 PGC might indicate disregard for both a *qabīlah*'s and the state-movement's instructions. As the pressure to reduce wedding celebrations increased, I also observed that the postmarital celebrations increased in opulence. This perhaps indicates that, where there might be formal compliance with a ban, its spirit would still be contravened by an even more luxurious feast that was merely displaced from the formal wedding celebration.

Another possible impact of changing marriage practices on the dynamics of *qabīlah* relations is that, with *dabash* becoming so expensive, and there being scope for help for the groom from kin as well as friends and neighbors, some *qabīlah* ties might be deliberately intensified in order to increase the circle on which a groom could draw for help. Sedentarization in the camps may indeed have facilitated the extension of the sphere of *qabīlah* contacts, in that a nuclear family was now likely to come into contact with a larger absolute number of fellow *qabīlah* members than in the days of mobile pastoralism. (There was also more contact with non-fellow tribe members, though). These factors—the pressure to seek help for preparing *dabash*, along with access to a wider pool of fellow *qabīlah* members—might indeed mean that late revolutionary marriage practices were a factor encouraging the strengthening of *qabīlah* membership. Any such tendency surely only intensified the conditions of the political crisis whereby the state-movement found potential for more effective governance in the *qabīlah* than in its own institutions. Yet there is also a counter-argument to the idea that *dabash* reinforced *qabīlah* solidarities. A major erstwhile point of *qabīlah* solidarity, reduction of *ṣadāq* in "close" marriage, was actually undermined by *dabash*. There was no longer any reduction in the case of marrying one's FBD or classificatory equivalent. The different elements of the *dabash* were just as necessary for a wife who was closely related as for a wife who was not. Late revolutionary marriage shows not only that the *qabīlah* had assumed a role and importance not seen in the early revolutionary period but also that the *qabīlah* as known before the revolution was undermined.

Finally, how might marriage practices in the Sahrawi refugee camps inform approaches to "Arab" marriage? Did revolutionary marriage practices at any point question the "rule" prohibiting female hypogamy? If there is little evidence of marriages that contravened "Arab marriage" taking place in exile, there are nevertheless still grounds for seeing early Sahrawis' revolutionary marriage practices as distinctive. Groom-to-bride prestations in MENA may express in material form *either* social equality *or* social hierarchy. In the early revolutionary period, the time of standardized *ṣadāq*, marriage prestations among Sahrawi refugees came to stand exclusively for the equality of all, without the potential to express hierarchy. Marriage to mark hierarchy/equality and marriage to mark equality (only) are not interchangeable. While the first includes that, at times, marriage marks the lack of hierarchy (an alliance between equals), the project to make marriage the mark of equality excludes the possibility of marriage to mark hierarchy. The revolutionary project, then, took on not only the preference for "close" marriage but a practice that held even more widely than that preference: the "only rule" in "Arab" marriage. It is perhaps not surprising that this aspect of the revolutionary project met formidable hurdles, not least a counter-reinvention of marriage practices that reasserted marriage as a means by which hierarchies (of wealth) could be implied. What is surprising is that, for some fifteen years in the early revolutionary period, marriage ostensibly became a means of marking equality between citizens. During that period, it was socially accepted that the absence or presence of any hierarchies (that might have been tacitly felt) could not be made explicit in the public domain through marriage practices. Men and women accepted that the state-movement (and perhaps the groom too) would make merely a symbolic *ṣadāq*, a symbol of all citizens being equal.

By the late 2000s, acceptance for marriage practices as an expression of the revolutionary equalizing project had diminished. In December 2008, in the Sahrawi Cultural Festival organized by the state-movement, in which, among other "Sahrawi traditions," a "traditional Sahrawi wedding" was staged, a rumor flew around that the state-movement was offering to pay for the marriage of a couple who were willing to volunteer to marry—for real—in the Cultural Festival. The nature of the rumored sponsorship was unclear, but the possibility that the state-movement would intervene in such a way was believed. The rights and wrongs of the proposition were discussed seriously by refugees. Mbārak, the young bureaucrat who had saved up some money by selling goods brought back from Libya, opined, "It's not right." "What isn't right?" I asked him. I anticipated that perhaps his answer might entail reservations about contracting marriage in a staged wedding at a cultural festival. "It's not right for the state (*al-dawlah*) to do that for the man. He has to bring his own things to marry her." Perhaps the window of marriage as a means of marking equality was closing or had closed.

Although I have argued that late revolutionary marriage prestations were different from preceding prestations, the refugees who told me they had "returned" to the marriage practices of the past were perhaps right, in a sense, after all. The practices had not returned in their material forms—*dabash* was not the same as *ṣadāq*: it was less susceptible to being reduced for a close relative, and there was less room for reciprocity between the groom's and bride's parties. But the social meaning of the pre-exile marriage practices as a means of signaling within the public domain the presence or absence of social hierarchy—in short, the social meaning of "Arab" marriage—had indeed returned. The next chapter, which turns to the dilemmas of undesired irruptions of *qabīlah* relations, explores refugees' concerns at how the growth of private markets in the refugee camps exacerbated socioeconomic distinctions among refugee families.

# PART III

## Dilemmas

CHAPTER 6

# Troubling Markets: Tribes, Gender, and Ambivalent Commodification

I'm Sahrawi! I'm not interested in wealth. It is enough for me that I am Sahrawi.

—Lines from song "Sahrawi, Sahrawīya" by Nājam 'Allāl

One afternoon in the summer of 2008, Māghalāha's son 'Abdi accompanied me on foot to a nearby large marketplace, known in Hassaniya as *marṣah*, in Auserd refugee camp. The sights of a *marṣah*, by now familiar to me, contrasted sharply with the image of refugees' memories from the 1980s of a single shop per *dairah*, run by the state-movement and barely stocked. Now a *marṣah* came to life in the early hours of the morning at the butchers' stores. At dawn or shortly after, men and women would arrive by foot or by car to jostle to the counter in the hope of arriving in time to buy the more expensive and preferred cut of camel meat, liver. Customers continued to stand in line at the butchers as long as the supply of the meat lasted.

As the day progressed, the full array of *marṣah* stalls would open. Never far from butchers were grocery stores open from the earliest to the latest hours. They offered both basic items such as tea, sugar, and rice, and luxuries such as fruit (brought via Tindouf and often in desert-weary condition), yoghurt, and frozen whole chicken kept in gas-powered freezers. Clothes stalls selling Western style clothing (*spor*) as well as male and female local garments, including the latest designs of women's clothing (*milḥafah*) brought from Mauritania, abounded. Cosmetics and lotions likewise turned a considerable trade. Specialist shops selling baby clothes or shoes, usually brought from Spain, could be found in a large *marṣah*, as could hardware stores selling floor tiles, wash basins, concrete blocks, and wardrobes for building and equipping a home. The *marṣah* was also the place where you could pay for shoes to be mended, clothes to be sewn, hair to be cut, euros to be changed for Algerian dinars, and worn-out cars to be resuscitated against the odds. As 'Abdi and I walked past these scenes, he pointed out a row of shops to me: "See all these shops? They all belong to the Awlād Tidrārīn [tribe]." I looked and saw not only shops and their wares but also, as refugees (in possession of the right kind of knowledge) could see, a space that was associated with a particular tribe.

In Part III, "Dilemmas," I consider how *qabīlah* social relations resurfaced in the refugee camps as unruly irruptions in the palimpsest through which the state-movement had originally sought to overwrite and obscure *qabīlah* social relations. These irruptions challenged the aspirations (Part I) of the state-movement to build a state authority and undo the social relations associated with the *qabīlah* as an alternative project of sovereignty. The irruptions also contravened the compromises (Part II) whereby the state-movement modified its policies over time to tolerate and even invite the reemergence of *qabīlah* relations in ways that putatively advanced the state-movement's own agenda. In contrast, the rise of markets, the focus of this chapter, and the possibility that tribal allegiances would motivate voters, the subject of the next chapter, can be understood as dilemmas: these irruptions of *qabīlah* relations were experienced as disconcerting not only by officers of the state-movement, but also by refugees who did not hold formal office in the state-movement.

By the rise of markets in the Sahrawi refugee camps, I mean the growth there of markets for commodified goods and labor.[1] This growth was inextricably linked to refugees' access through migration to such markets abroad.[2] In the early revolutionary period, refugees had extremely limited access to markets, either in the refugee camps or elsewhere. The rise of markets in exile from the late 1990s, which was part of broader political and economic openings that burgeoned at that time (see Chapter 2), has been perceived as locally controversial. Often discussed is the degree to which refugees found it problematic that the advent of markets had led, in their view, to increasing socioeconomic differences between refugee families (Shelley 2004; San Martín 2010). Refugees' complaints about these growing distinctions were endorsed (and encouraged?) by the state-movement, which

I have argued was committed to a wider project to manage social (in)equalities by seeking to reduce or eliminate social inequalities, and at least curb their expression in material form in the public domain (Chapter 5).

The emergence of markets in exile has also been explicitly linked with the resurgence of *qabīlah* relations (Gimeno 2007: 34; San Martín 2010: 155). The opening vignette illustrated one form of the link between markets and *qabīlah* relations. The state-movement had overseen the layout of the residential refugee camps with a mind to disguising from view the possibility of the physical manifestation of a particular tribe (Chapter 2). Markets, which had developed more or less spontaneously from the late 1990s without the state-movement directing whose shop should be placed where, had created spaces where the dominance of a particular tribe could be literally seen (by those with appropriate local knowledge).

With both rising socioeconomic differentiation and the resurgence of *qabīlah* relations contravening—materially and socially—the revolutionary orthodoxy of social egalitarianism, the advent of markets in the refugee camps has been seen as a challenge to the state-movement itself (San Martín 2010). Such an approach resonates with wider observations of how the advent or extension of markets may both disrupt social relations and challenge governing authorities (e.g., Polanyi 1944; Humphrey 2002; Verdery 1996; Elyachar 2005; Li 2010).

This chapter explores multiple grounds on which refugees and officers of the state-movement found markets in exile troubling. After first tracing the advent of markets in exile, I consider how markets created opportunities for new manifestations of *qabīlah* relations, gendered inequalities, and challenges to the influence of the state-movement. Yet, by looking more widely at trends toward commodification in both the public and private sectors of the camps, I also show how, in each of its troubling dimensions, the rise of markets, nevertheless, also presented opportunities for contrasting tendencies: the undermining of *qabīlah* relations, the reinforcement of the state-movement's claimed role as emancipator for women, and the expansion in some areas of the influence of the state-movement. I advocate sensitivity toward the ambivalence of marketization: for the state-movement and for *qabīlah* relations, and more broadly for governing authorities and social relations. For Sahrawi refugees in particular, the rise of markets presented a dilemma that highlighted the stakes of revolutionary commitment in the late 2000s: should priority be given to the interests of an individual refugee, a family, a *qabīlah*, the state-movement, or indeed, the notion of the revolution itself?

## For Sale in Exile

The ubiquity in the late 2000s of refugees' consumption of goods bought on local markets disguised the relative novelty of marketized trade in the refugee camps.[3] Markets took off in the camps from the late 1990s. In the early revolutionary period, money was rare in exile. Refugees, living off rations, worked for the state-movement in the absence of traditional wages. There was only one simple shop per *dairah*, and few refugees had any money. The post-cease-fire late revolutionary period, with its greater freedom of movement of people and goods through the camps, saw trade take off.[4] Pioneer shopkeepers found the capital to set up a store from various sources. One possibility was the disbursement of Spanish pensions to refugees who had worked in the Spanish colonial administration. Over the course of the 2000s, other sources of capital for setting up a store, or indeed income with which to become a consumer, were remittances from relatives who had migrated to Europe, gifts of money from European families who hosted Sahrawi refugee children for summer holidays, wages from aid agencies for local employees, and, increasingly, wages in the expanding private sector labor market. Under the pressure of refugees' increasing interest in access to markets for commodified labor, after over two decades of directing unwaged labor on a mass scale the state-movement introduced wages for its own employees from the early 2000s. Refugees' demand for participation in markets for commodified goods and labor was driven not only by a desire to attenuate the severe material shortages of the early revolutionary period. Also, with rations levels dropping below subsistence levels (see Chapter 4), families needed to participate in markets as workers and consumers to survive.

A refugee family in the late 2000s typically sought to have at least one member of the family working in the private sector. In 2007–2008, Māghalāha's son 'Abdi, worked as a construction laborer for cash. Khadīja ran her own business, a "Turkish bath." Zaynabu's eldest son ran a hardware store in the *marṣah*, while her younger son ran a grocery store next to the family home. Nevertheless, unlike access to basic rations, access to the resources to participate as a trader or consumer in markets was not equally distributed among refugee families. For instance, it was commonly the case in the late 2000s that refugee families had a relative, such as an aunt, uncle, father, sister or close cousin, in Spain. But presuming this person was in work, it made a big difference to the likely access to remittances whether this relative was a daughter or father, sending remittances to parents or direct dependents, or an uncle or aunt, sending remittances in the first instance to the nuclear family and only more rarely to a sibling's family. Sumaya's husband, Fadili, had a resident's permit for Spain, and was able to support Sumaya and her children from money earned during periods of work in that country. Zaynabu's and Māghalāha's relatives in Spain included siblings but, at that time, none of their own children. Since each of these siblings had dependents of his or her own, Zaynabu and Māghalāha benefited more rarely from remittances than Sumaya. Chance played a role, too, in one's access to resources through fictive kinship. Some European families who hosted Sahrawi refugee children as part of a summer holiday program sent gifts in the hundreds of euros, while others sent ten, twenty, or nothing at all. The vicissitudes of access to cash meant that many families bought basic foodstuffs on credit. In grocery stores, the storekeeper usually kept a notebook in which debts were recorded as customers came and went. If a debtor arrived with money to clear some debts, the book was brought out, arrangements made, and money handed over in hushed tones.

The unequal distribution among refugees of access to markets was one of the reasons for which refugees were troubled by the advent of markets, perceiving them to exacerbate a trend toward socioeconomic differentiation among refugee families. Māghalāha's neighbor, Tumanna, whom I had seen supervise her children's homework (Chapter 1), explained on another occasion that it was "not right" for one family to eat meat every day while the family next door had none. The image of camel meat not being jointly enjoyed by close neighbors was particularly evocative for refugees. Outside the context of the *marṣah* (where camel meat was available only to those who could afford to buy it), the meat of a slaughtered camel would be shared between the people within range. I observed the wide distribution of meat from noncommercial camel slaughterings not only in refugee camp weddings in 2007 but also in the pasturelands when neighbors of the *frīg* where I was staying sent out camel meat from their slaughtering to neighbors several kilometers away. Tumanna went on to reflect that such differences had not existed in the early days of exile.

Socioeconomic differentiation among refugee families certainly contravened the revolutionary goal of social egalitarianism. The dispossession of the early revolutionary period had encouraged material egalitarianism among refugee families. All had lived in equal hardship, or at least this was how the 1980s were remembered. By the 2000s, when some families could eat meat every day, expand and beautify their homes, and rent accommodation outside the refugee camps during the summer to escape the heat, while other families patently could not, markets were criticized by refugees for contributing to and exaggerating unwelcome differentiation among refugees.

From the point of view of the state-movement, markets materially disturbed the rhetoric of egalitarianism. For a state-movement that had sought to control almost all aspects of political, economic, and social life in the early revolutionary period, the advent of markets was an area of economic life that did not lend itself to such control by the state-movement. Like other state authorities, the state-movement pursued various strategies to regulate markets and refugees' participation therein. For instance, the state-movement required NGO microloan projects to favor state-movement employees (Chapter 4). It sought to pass sumptuary laws curbing what it construed to be excessive consumption (Chapter 5). More distinctive to the circumstances of the state-movement than concern with the social and political ramifications of burgeoning markets was the possibility that markets provided new opportunities for the foregrounding of *qabīlah* relations, to which I now turn.

## *Qabīlah* Relations on the Market

The refugee camps and their constituent parts created by the state-movement—neighborhoods, districts and provinces, schools and hospitals, administrative centers and ministries—were conceived as spaces that could not, or at least should not, be associated with a particular tribe. Individual homes could be associated (discreetly) with the tribe(s) and status group of its members, for instance, when neighbors were talked about in the third person by naming their tribe or (more controversially) a stigmatized status group such as (former) slaves or artisans. But, although certain residential areas might be reputed to host a population dominated by a particular tribe, no residential area was exclusive to a particular tribe (Chapter 2). Similarly, when one entered an administrative building, or a hospital, a refugee knew that it was a space in which refugees of all backgrounds might meet. Marketplaces, however, were different. As 'Abdi pointed out to me, rows of shops had developed that might be owned by members of a particular tribe. This was not necessarily the case with all rows of *marṣah* shops. But where such an association could be made, marketplaces created a physical space associated with a particular tribe, whereas previously this had been avoided or disguised.

A similar effect might also arise from a single shop. This was not merely because refugees—not unusually for consumers—liked to spend their money where they already had connections, which might lead them as a first point of call to the store of a fellow tribesperson. Stores were also gathering places where fellow tribespersons might drop by, knowing that they would meet each other and catch up on relevant news. This was a sociable, desirable, and comfortable prospect.

I especially experienced this effect at the *marṣah* in Rabouni. As the administrative capital of the refugee camps, Rabouni was a "cosmopolitan" place. It brought together refugees not only of different social backgrounds but also from all the different refugee camps who passed through for work, administrative formalities, and shopping at the extensive *marṣah*. The latter offered specialist goods usually unavailable in the refugee camps, such as second hand clothes (*juṭīyah* in Hassaniya).

Strategically placed near both Rabouni's waiting area for shared taxi cars to each of the refugee camps and several of the ministries was a row of grocery stores. I got to know these stores and storekeepers over a period of several months from late 2007 to 2008 in which I made weekly trips to Rabouni to teach English at the Ministry of Information. On one occasion, I found a senior official of the state-movement, whom I had been seeking for an interview, enjoying tea in one of these stores. I was pleased at my luck to have found him. In fact, I later learned, in the experience of his colleagues in Rabouni it was well known that this was a store where he might likely be found, for it was run by members of his *qabīlah*. A store could become a pseudo-tent in which one might consistently meet members of the same tribe as the owner. I noticed that, when a refugee bumped into an acquaintance unexpectedly in a store known not to be his or her usual stall, this might elicit the friendly question "What are you doing here?" Meetings in stores of mutual fellow tribesmen would not cause such reactions of surprise.

It seems that *marṣah* stalls functioned as zones of comfort for members of the same tribe as the owner. In describing his fieldwork among tribes in Jordan, Andrew Shryock (1997: 151–52) explains that, as he moved from the domestic group of one poet to another, he traveled between different spheres of protection. Shryock likens this to a border crossing for which he needed a guide. His informants were not comfortable about accompanying him to complete these crossings, and he would feel "handed over" from one social sphere to another. Shryock (156–60) even goes so far as to say that he was like a person seeking refuge or sanctuary from another tribe. I sensed a similar dynamic in others, and even in myself, as I began to understand the refugees' social map of the *marṣah*, which very much included tribal identities. Moving from one shop to another could feel like moving from one zone, if not of protection then of comfort, to another.

Markets also provided the opportunity for the resurgence of another aspect of *qabīlah* relations. *Qabīlah* relations assign a person not only to a named *qabīlah* but also to a status group (see Chapter 1). As refugees' labor increasingly became a commodity to be sold in a market spanning both a private and public sector, the division of labor began to reflect *qabīlah* relations in the form of status group affiliations.

Prior to the revolution, status groups had also influenced the division of labor, with different status groups being associated with the performance of different tasks. Some status groups were indeed defined by the work for which they were known: artisans were associated with metal and leather work and slaves with domestic labor. Members of upper-status groups were associated with skill in particular tasks, too. For instance, the sewing for some forms of tent repair was formerly reserved for women of *bīḍān* status (Boulay 2003: 451).

In the early revolutionary period the state-movement pooled the labor of both women and men through Popular Committees (see Chapter 2) and the army respectively. As an effect of this pooling, persons from divergent status groups found themselves working together. The significance of the mixing of status groups in labor pooling was not lost on the refugees. Sophie Caratini (2003: 40) recounts that early revolutionary pooling of labor, with its disruption of old hierarchies between status groups, caused controversy among refugees.

The subsequent advent of a market for commodified labor in the refugee camps constituted a means of labor recruitment in which the state-movement could not intervene directly, as it had for Popular Committees and the army. The market for commodified labor, thus, created the opportunity for the division of labor to "re-ethnicize," with certain status groups being associated with particular areas of expertise.

One form of the "re-ethnicization" of labor concerned artisans. The oldest generation of *mu'allimīn* in the camps had once worked on leather and metal goods in the pasturelands. In the late revolutionary period, their children emerged as a group distinguished by their labor. They ran *marṣah* stores where they repaired radios, televisions, refrigerators, and other electrical domestic appliances. Women from *mu'allimīn* families were in demand on the occasion of weddings, religious festivals, and other celebrations among women of all status groups as henna decorators. As the state-movement's recruitment of labor for public service moved increasingly from conscription to paid labor, an ethnicized division of labor even emerged in work for the state-movement. Refugees of *bīḍān* status often claimed to me that the "only difference" between them and refugees of former slave or freed status was the willingness of the latter to work in "anything." Sectors of work for the state-movement that were shunned by refugees of *bīḍān* status, such as rubbish collection, were widely perceived to be dominated by refugees of former slave or freed status. In a market for commodified labor, the division of labor partially reverted to polarization along the lines of *qabīlah* relations in ways that the state-movement had originally set out to avoid.

## Gendered Values

The resurgence through markets of social relations that the revolution had sought to change can also be observed in the gendering of the division of labor. From as early as 1974, the liberation movement espoused the emancipation of women (Lippert 1992). Over the years, a lasting feature of refugees' self-image has been their pride in the perceived extent to which women refugees have successfully taken on political and administrative roles in the state-movement and its revolution.[5] Refugees and some observers (Perregaux 1990; Lippert 1992; Juliano 1998) have claimed women's role in the revolution as both the continuation of and transcendence of women's existing roles in the pasturelands. As in other mobile pastoralist communities (e.g., see Chatty 1980), Sahrawi women played a prominent economic, social, and (through marriage) political role in the context of the pasturelands (Caratini 1989b). Alongside its claims to support the emancipation of women, the state-movement nevertheless also endorsed a gendered division of labor: initially women were assigned to Popular Committees and men to the army. The advent of markets in the refugee camps created new possibilities for gendered inequalities in the division of labor among refugees—both the division of labor as endorsed by the state-movement and that which played out more widely. Labor markets thereby amplified the limits to the emancipation of women that the state-movement officially sought to promote.

In exile, women's circulation and work outside the circle of natal and marital spheres had become legitimate. But notably women's circulation outside domestic spheres was concentrated initially on work for the state-movement, especially via the Popular Committees. To the extent that the state-movement extracted activities from the *frīg* and transferred them to the early revolutionary public domain (Chapter 2), in their work for the revolution, women often performed similar roles to those that they had long undertaken. The difference was that, in exile, they performed them not merely for their families but also for the state-movement.

The advent of markets in the refugee camps challenged the state-movement's claimed emancipation of women. Work that had previously been performed by women, unpaid and for the state-movement, now began to be undertaken by men, paid and either for private demand or for the state-movement. An example is the preparation of the mud-bricks with which many buildings in the refugee camps, both homes and government offices, were made. Making mud-bricks was grueling work. The top stony layer of the desert had to be dug away and the red earth beneath extracted, mixed with water, shaped into bricks, and laid out in the sun until baked. During the war years, when men were at the front, women made both these bricks and buildings. In the late 2000s, this was unheard of. Indeed, in September 2011 when SADR television played a clip from the early revolutionary period showing women making mud-bricks, Māghalāha's niece called out to her cousins and to me in excitement at such an unusual sight: "Look at the women making bricks!" "Māghalāha used to make them," her daughter added for my benefit, chuckling at what now seemed incongruous. By the time the construction industry became one of the thriving areas of waged labor in the refugee camps, it had become exclusively male.[6]

The transformation of the production of mud-bricks reflected a wider trend whereby the unpaid economy of male and female labor in the early revolutionary period had diversified by the late 2000s into spheres of unpaid or scarcely paid female labor and better paid (in the context of exile) male labor. Many of the tasks that women performed for the state-movement—such as cleaning schools, providing home-stay accommodation to visiting Sahrawi or foreign delegates, and preparing for special events such as the Cultural Festival—entailed long, often arduous hours of work. Yet such tasks, common means through which women were expected to demonstrate their commitment as citizens (*muwāṭināt*) and fighters (*munāḍilāt*) to the liberation movement, went unpaid. In contrast, the main ways through which men were called upon to fulfill their duties as citizens and fighters, such as service in the army or in ministries, were waged (even if these wages were low). The advent of markets saw women's contributions receive lower pay as compared to men's.

A further gendered dynamic in the rise of markets was the creation of new roles: for capitalists investing in trade and stores, for workers selling their labor, and for consumers aspiring to or actually purchasing commodities. Each of these roles acquired gendered distinctions. Female entrepreneurs are by no means unknown in the western and central Sahara, historically (Lydon 2009) or in contemporary settings (Scheele 2012). I met a few female entrepreneurs in the refugee camps who had invested in businesses. Khadīja ran her baths and a small store for dry foodstuffs. Mona, a mother in her forties in February 27 camp, placed an order with a male trader for a large number of women's robes from Mauritania and sold them to friends at gatherings in their homes. The majority of refugee traders and investors, though, were male.

Notably, both Khadīja and Mona and, with few exceptions, the other women traders I came across ran their businesses from their homes, not from the *marṣah*. While the *marṣah* had created a new space in the refugee camps within which women regularly circulated, their presence there was overwhelmingly in the role of consumer. For a woman to work outside her home in the *marṣah* was extremely rare in the refugee camps. The seamstress Fanna (Chapter 2) was one of the exceptions in the late 2000s. As I learned in my visit to Moroccan-controlled Western Sahara in 2012, such avoidance on the part of Sahrawi women for manning *marṣah* stores was by no means the case there. In the refugee camps, though, such work was (with some exceptions) generally not deemed suitable for a woman. Refugees who voiced objections did so on the grounds that a woman working in the *marṣah* might be exposed to meetings with all kinds of unknown people there. Such an objection was less commonly raised about women's work

Figure 11. Women shop for clothes in a market in Auserd, 2011 (photo by Alice Wilson).

outside the home for the state-movement (to which I return below). With the advent of the *marṣah* as a working environment that was beyond the domestic sphere but not legitimized by the state-movement, the promotion of equality between men and women ostensibly espoused by the revolution faltered.

## Contested Political Influence

Alongside questions of *qabīlah* relations and gendered distinctions, the rise of markets also challenged the influence of the state-movement as a governing authority. Refugees' participation in labor markets in the camps and abroad undermined the state-movement's erstwhile voluntary public sector of teachers, administrators, legal specialists, and health workers. Once refugees could access waged labor, this eventually pressurized the state-movement into introducing, from the early 2000s, "wages" in its public sector. These wages might be as low as thirty euros a month for primary school teachers—at a time when the president, in a press conference in 2007, estimated that a refugee family needed a hundred euros a month to survive. Ministries' budgets might also dry up, with the result that public sector wages for some might not be paid at all. Suelma's husband spent months in 2007 and 2008 without being paid by the ministry for which he worked. Low and unreliable wages in the public sector were unable to compete with more lucrative avenues in the private sector for those lucky enough to pin down work there. In 2007, the monthly wage for a worker paid to work at a *marṣah* stall was around a hundred euros. In the construction industry, payment was made in proportion to the size of the commissioned buildings rather than the time spent. When in work, interlocutors who worked in construction talked of making two hundred euros per person in three weeks.

Unable to compete with the reputed wages of the private sector, the public sector suffered from a "brain drain" effect as trained personnel took up more materially rewarding opportunities elsewhere. The husband of Zaynabu's niece, a judge, had left the refugee camps to look for work in France. Zaynabu's eldest son, who had been a teacher for ten years in the refugee camps, had left teaching to set up his hardware store in the hope of better supporting a growing family of children and ailing elderly relatives, all his dependents. The daughter of Zaynabu's neighbor, a doctor trained in Cuba, left to work in Spain—although, by 2014, she had returned to the camps to work in Smara camp hospital, telling me, "I want my children to grow up in their culture, not as a minority. And I have more status here than I have in Spain." Her decision to return to the camps seems to be an exception, though: an employee in the Ministry of Health told Gómez Martín, who conducted research in the mid-2000s, that of three hundred Sahrawi doctors trained in Cuba, forty were in the camps and only eleven were working in the public system (Gómez Martín 2011: 39 n62).

The lack of accurate population figures for the refugee camps makes it hard to estimate the scale of attrition from the public sector. The reactions of the state-movement and refugees suggest a large scale. In conversation with some health workers based in Rabouni, one of them explained: "We were told that there will be no more training abroad for health workers, because too many of those who go don't come back to the camps." The uncertain circumstances surrounding the support offered by the state-movement for refugees requesting Algerian passports (see Chapter 7) suggests the state-movement's interest in curbing refugees' access to labor markets abroad. The state-movement also sought to make it desirable for families to keep members in the public sector, for instance, by requiring the participation of public sector workers for access to microloans.

As for the reactions of refugees to the brain drain, by the late 2000s the schools and health care centers that had once been the pride of the refugee camps had become a topic of national consternation. In the words of one bureaucrat who spoke with passion and to widespread approval from the floor at a pre-election meeting in November 2007, the refugee camps were experiencing a "crisis" (*azmah*) of understaffing in public services. Refugees in a position to do so found means of making up for gaps in public provision in the refugee camps. One senior official from the Ministry of Justice sent his children, at the cost of fees, to school in Tindouf. He explained his decision to me with resignation: "Here the teachers' pay is very low, and sometimes they don't get paid for months, so they don't come [to teach]."

The fact that many refugees had ceased to work in the public sector, turning instead to the private sector either in the camps or abroad, had administrative implications. Refugees were integrated into the state-movement on the premise of a dual affiliation to both political and administrative organizations (Chapter 2). Refugees who did not work at all for the state-movement might therefore lack an affiliation to an administrative organization altogether. This could create obstacles for these refugees' participation in elections since membership in an electoral constituency was determined though one's affiliation to the administrative organization. This problem presented itself more often for men than for women. Khadīja, who ran her own business and did not actively work for the state-movement, could be registered to vote, along with women like her who resided in the refugee camps, as fighters (*munāḍilāt*) on the home front. Many men who worked in the private sector retained an affiliation to the administrative organization by being registered with the army, which required only sporadic attendance at army events. Thus, Zaynabu's son-in-law ran a taxi for most of the year but retained an army affiliation that occasionally took him out of the refugee camps for army service for a few days. But other refugees retained no formal connection with the state-movement. A young shop owner near Māghalāha's home, in response to my asking him in which constituency he voted in elections, replied, "My affiliation is to me." The pull of markets was, for some refugees, a pull away from involvement and engagement with the state-movement.

## Opportunities Against the Odds?

The rise of markets in the refugee camps presented so many challenges for refugees and the state-movement that it is tempting to see markets as a threat to the goals of national liberation and social revolution for which the refugee community claimed to stand. Nevertheless, for each challenge posed, the rise of markets also created contrasting opportunities: for undermining *qabīlah* relations, for reinforcing the role of the state-movement as emancipator for refugee women, and for strengthening the position of the state-movement as a governing authority.

One afternoon in June 2008, Bassiri, a bureaucrat at the Ministry of Information in his early fifties, offered to take me to visit shops in the *marṣah* near his home in Auserd camp. He knew that I was interested in learning more about markets in the refugee camps and took me for a tour of several shops where he knew the owners well: a food store, a shop selling building and decorating materials, and another selling handicrafts aimed at foreign visitors to the camps. Afterward, we returned to his home to rest and drink tea. I asked him there whether he felt that the markets reinforced *qabīlah* loyalties among refugees. He reflected that, while this was possible, sometimes people avoided trading partnerships with fellow tribesmen, apparently because tribesmen felt entitled to take from the profits. He gave the example of a well-established businessman who, allegedly for that reason, had set up in business with his colleague from the army. For Bassiri, markets reinforced, at least for some traders, ties beyond tribes.

As noted previously, the commodification of labor had undermined the state-movement's early preference for intervening in the division of labor so as to mix up status groups. Yet, at the same time, markets continued to disrupt prerevolutionary differentiation between status groups. Opportunities to prosper through trade were, in the late revolutionary period, open to former upper-status groups just as much as to former lower-status groups. This confusion of old hierarchies was, again, not lost on refugees. When I asked Zaynabu if she thought that markets had seen formerly stigmatized groups such as black people take on roles that other refugees shunned, she disagreed.

She pointed out a neighboring black family: "You know the blacks' shop we went to? You saw them, they're doing well . . . better than us. Their houses are better, their furnishings are better." Her elderly husband, Brahim, who was often silent during family conversation, chipped in to agree. The reactions of Zaynabu and her husband indicate that refugees did not always experience markets as a means of reinforcing status group hierarchies, but also might experience them as a means of bringing them into question. In this sense, markets partly continued the trend, propagated earlier through the state-movement's orchestration of the division of labor, whereby former status group hierarchies were contravened.

The rise of a waged labor economy in the refugee camps had created new gender inequalities. These included the refugees' low tolerance for the social acceptability of women working in a *marṣah*, which pointed to the limits of women's emancipation under the aegis of the state-movement. But at the same time this limitation reinforced the achievement of the state-movement in having overseen an emancipation of women that had at least extended the socially acceptable scope of women's work to include work for the state-movement outside the domestic sphere. Married and unmarried women moved within and between refugee camps every day in the business of the state-movement (as well as for personal visits and errands). Such travel for the state-movement could include overnight stays away from home, for special events such as attendance at a congress, training opportunities offered by delegations visiting from abroad, or regular work in a SADR ministry.

At the Ministry of Information, married and unmarried women broadcasters stayed overnight in women's quarters so as to be able to make early and late broadcasting schedules. I often stayed with these women overnight when combining teaching English at the Ministry of Information with interviews in other ministries. I came to see the ministry personnel as their own pseudo-*khaymah* or household. The women shared a rota in which each took it in turns to cook meals, as fitted around broadcasting schedules. (Male broadcasters staying overnight more frequently ate at a restaurant in Rabouni market but were sometimes invited by the women to share a meal. Later in 2008, the ministry opened a canteen for all the employees.) At the end of the evening, either in one of the small rooms (during the winter months) or outside on the sand in a closed courtyard (during the summer months), the women laid out blankets for each other, as sisters would for each other at home. In the morning, the first round of tea would begin. By the second or third cup, as the Ministry came to life again, women might go to join men for tea or vice versa. Ministry personnel whose schedule or distance of commute did not require them to stay overnight joined in these teas as they arrived.

The fact that some women, both married and unmarried, could stay away from home under the justification of performing work for the state-movement did not mean that all women and families chose to do so. Some families had different levels of tolerance. Māghalāha's youngest daughter, Alma'lūma, who was unmarried and in her early twenties, regularly stayed away from Auserd camp in February 27 camp when she had the opportunity to take a training course there with a visiting foreign delegation. Typically, she might spend only one or two nights a week at home with her family. Yet, when the opportunity to study in Cuba was discussed, she explained to me that her father Tawwālu would not give permission for her to go so far away for her studies.

A more conservative woman lived a short walk away from Māghalāha's home. 'Aishetou was in her mid- to late twenties and divorced. She worked in the Ministry of Information, which at the time could only be reached from Auserd camp after about an hour of travel across the open desert. To avoid this journey, other women employees at the Ministry from Auserd camp (and even from closer refugee camps) stayed overnight, as described above. These women included unmarried, married and divorced women. Nonetheless, 'Aishetou explained to me that she would not stay in Rabouni overnight because of "the men." The tolerance among particular families and individuals for women staying away from home under the protective cloak of the state-movement therefore varied. When women (and their families) were willing for women to work outside the home, such work could be legitimized by the state-movement, but hardly by the *marṣah*. This distinction reinforced the notion of the state-movement as emancipator for women.

What of the notion that the rise of markets in the refugee camps undermined the state-movement as a governing authority? In several ways, markets also presented new opportunities for the state-movement to extend its sphere of influence. The private sector was a source of potential new profits for the state-movement. The latter developed profit-sharing schemes with workers from the Ministry of Trade. It made capital such as trucks available to workers for long-distance trading, on condition that these employees would hand over a percentage of profits made to the Ministry (Chapter 4). As several *marṣah* traders explained to me, the state-movement also introduced customs on the route from Mauritania to the refugee camps and charged traders a proportion of the value of the goods being brought in. (On refugees' reaction to proposed further taxes on *marṣah* traders, see Chapter 4.)

While families aimed for at least one member to earn wages in the private sector, either in the refugee camps or abroad (or both), this did not necessarily indicate disregard for labor force participation in the public sector or even for the authority of the state-movement. Refugee families typically kept a foot in both the private and public sector labor markets, much as elsewhere families may keep members working in both formal and informal labor markets (González de la Rocha 1994). Thus, in Māghalāha's family, while 'Abdi worked in construction, his elder brother Mal'ainīn worked in the Ministry of Information. Zaynabu's two sons worked in 2007–2008 in shops, while one married and one unmarried daughter both worked for the state-movement—the first in the local administration in their *dairah* and the second in the Cultural Center in February 27 camp. Sumaya's husband Fadili worked in Spain, and Sumaya herself and her son both worked for the state-movement, she in her local administration and he in the Ministry of Information. Khadīja ran her own business and had two daughters and a son working (in 2007) in Spain, while two of her married daughters in the refugee camps worked as secretaries in the Criminal Court.

Sometimes a single refugee kept a foot in both sectors, as was the case for Zaynabu's son-in-law, who ran a taxi and served in the army. Similarly, when looking for a ride from Rabouni to one of my host families, I benefited from the fact that various employees ran their car as a taxi on the way home. This diversification of a family's labor force participation offered some security against the vicissitudes of pay in each sector. Yet there were also advantages to keeping connected to the state-movement through one's work. These advantages were formalized in schemes such as the aforementioned microloans that required the participation of public sector workers. Yet informal advantages were also rumored to exist. The coveted visa and ticket to Spain, Italy, or France for an adult refugee supervisor accompanying a group of refugee children for the summer holiday program was typically awarded to a refugee who had accumulated a number of years working for the state-movement.

Even when refugees migrated abroad to look for paid work, this did not necessarily mean that they abandoned their political engagement with the state-movement. Economic and political aspirations could intersect. Sahrawis living abroad, including in Spain, were mobilized for the SPLA by the state-movement in January 2001 in response to the perceived threat of the failure of the organizers of the Paris-Dakar rally to seek permission from Polisario for the rally to cross Western Sahara (Bhatia 2001: 293). In her study of Sahrawi migration, Gómez Martín (2011: 52) explains that the first generation of educated Sahrawi refugees who migrated to Spain in the late 1990s saw themselves as "fighting for the cause" from Spain, even though at the time the wider refugee community and Polisario representatives in Spain perceived their migration as closer to a form of betrayal. By the 2000s, Gómez Martín observes, the growing numbers of Sahrawi migrants in Spain established themselves as vocal activists for Western Sahara, as well as a source of economic support for the refugee camps. Not only did the state-movement change its stance vis-à-vis migrants to seek to incorporate them politically, for instance, by giving them the opportunity to participate in the Popular General Congress (see Chapter 7), but, in addition, in the eyes of the refugee community, migrants in Spain had become a perceived center of political activism. One young female broadcaster, who had helped look after me in my stays in the Ministry of Information in 2007–8, told me when I visited her in 2014, "I'd like to go to Spain. That's where the most activism is happening now."

## Ambivalent Markets

Studies of transitions to and the expansion of markets for commodified goods and labor have stressed the extent to which markets may constitute and reconfigure political and economic relations, to the advantage of some and to the disadvantage of others. Sahrawi refugees felt acutely aware of how the rise of markets had brought troubles to their community in exile and their liberation movement. This feeling was captured by the bureaucrat who spoke out in the November 2007 participatory meeting against the crisis of understaffing in the refugee camps' public services. His criticism left implicit the widespread discomfort in the camps that markets had helped reignite *qabīlah* relations. In markets, refugees and the state-movement confronted a dilemma, an unruly reemergence in the palimpsest of the very *qabīlah* relations that were supposed to be overwritten.

Recognizing the dilemma posed by the rise of markets for refugees and the state-movement, I have sought to highlight in addition the ambivalence that characterized the advent of markets in the Sahrawi refugee camps.

Access to markets provided refugees with much-needed relief from extreme material shortages; at the same time, because the access to resources through participation in markets was unequally distributed among refugees, markets saw increasing differentiation between refugee families' levels of material consumption, which caused controversy among refugees. Markets provided new forums for *qabīlah* relations to flourish, yet they also presented new reasons to avoid them. In the market for commodified labor, "ethnicized" distinctions along the lines of status groups (re)emerged; on the other hand, old status group hierarchies were undermined, as persons from historically marginalized status groups reaped in profits from trade. The rise of commodified labor introduced gendered inequalities, yet the suspicion with which women's work in the *marṣah* was regarded reinforced the notion of the state-movement as emancipator of women, whose work outside the home for the state-movement was considered legitimate. Here, as elsewhere, markets were ambivalent in their effects. If refugees spontaneously criticized markets for their perceived negative effects, they also, in responding to specific questions about markets, recognized this ambivalence.

Laden with both challenges and ambivalence, the rise of markets in the refugee camps brings into focus a broader dilemma faced by the refugees. Caratini (2003: 42) has suggested that with the refugee camps' post-ceasefire economic and social transitions came new possibilities for the pursuit of individual and family interests to take priority over the pursuit of those of the refugee camps' leadership. Perhaps the pursuit of private interests was not so much new in the late revolutionary period—for there is little reason to think that there had not been refugees who pursued individual interests through the structures of the state-movement in the early revolutionary period. But new to the late revolutionary period was surely the *context* for the pursuit of private interests: if in the early revolutionary period any pursuit of private interests would have had to be tacit, in the late revolutionary period, when, for the first time in exile, a public and private sector were juxtaposed, markets for commodified goods and labor provided the means for the pursuit of private interests to become explicit. Markets brought into sharp focus the question of which interests, in a situation of potential conflict, should be given priority: the interests of a person's individual welfare, that of his or her family, the interests of the refugee community, the state-movement (or indeed a current within it), or revolutionary values that claimed to transcend any of these? Should a doctor trained in Cuba and returned to the refugee camps stay to work there, for very little material reward, or go to Spain and earn a regular wage? Should a mother who had worked long, tiring years for the state-movement continue to do so still for virtually nothing or try her chance at setting up a store from her home in the hope of buying a few home comforts?

Refugees might sometimes be disappointed with their peers' answers. Zaynabu's eldest son shared with me his concern at his younger brother's attitudes to working in the small store by the family home: "He is always looking for his own money. It's because he was in Cuba. When they come back from Cuba, the students don't understand the way things are here." On the other hand, refugees who had made choices—such as to pursue economic opportunities abroad—might, as in 2001, come back to the camps to take action against a perceived national threat. As voiced by the man who spoke out about crisis in the public sector to applause from the floor, at least some refugees turned to the state-movement expecting it to intervene, manage, and redirect a terrain of ambiguous and shifting inequalities in order to inject new stamina into the revolution.

Ambivalent markets illustrate the ongoing dilemma of which interests should take priority. I pursue this question further in the Conclusion, where I reflect on how a moral contract, according to which refugees and the state-movement expected of each other that, ultimately, priority would be given to the interests of national liberation, underpinned the Sahrawi refugees' revolution. Before, though, I examine in the next chapter how in elections, as when facing the rise of markets, refugees and the state-movement confronted the dilemma of a troubling potential irruption of *qabīlah* relations.

CHAPTER 7

# Party-less Democrats: Electing the Best Candidate or the Biggest Tribe

> Democracy has a skin, and then there is what is underneath it.
>
> —Sahrawi journalist

After the close of the Popular General Congress in December 2007, in early 2008 preparations began for the February 2008 elections for the Sahrawi National Council (SNC). In the weeks before the elections, I set out from Māghālaha's home in Auserd camp to visit Fatma, the SNC member for the neighboring district (*dairah*). I worked out which was Fatma's home from Māghālaha's description: working my way along the edge of the district, I should look for the home that had a tent, a mud-brick room, and a corrugated iron hut. Upon my arrival, Fatma invited me into the mud-brick room, which was sparsely and neatly decorated with simple floor cushions to receive guests. With the help of her son, who was about ten years old, she replenished the charcoal on the furnace and set about making us tea. As we settled in, I began to ask about how she had come to represent her *dairah* at the SNC.

Before her marriage and during its early years, Fatma explained, she had been a teacher in the local primary school. Following her mother's death, she was obliged to stand down from teaching to look after her children, who were still young. With time, as they grew older, she became involved in her neighborhood's administration, helping with the branch known as "media and culture." Encouraged by peers, in 2003 she was the first woman to stand for election as MP (member of parliament) for her *dairah*, competing against three male candidates. Fatma won. She went on to be reelected for a second term in 2006. In 2008, she was standing for the third time in the SNC elections. But reforms had been introduced that would widen both the sphere of candidates against whom she competed and the scope of the electorate to whose votes she must appeal. As we progressed through the three rounds of tea, I asked her about the reforms. She shared her views about how the reforms might contribute to political life in exile, which echoed the official explanations that had been offered to me by electoral officials in the administrative capital of the camps, Rabouni. As I walked home, I wondered how Fatma's story would translate in the new rules of the game. What kind of judgments would the redefined electorate be making in deciding whether to vote for Fatma? And would the reforms make political relations in the camps "more democratic"?

This chapter addresses these questions by attempting to "get under the skin"—to use the words of the Sahrawi journalist cited at the opening—of the camps' political relations. The camps' governing authorities, as well as not a few refugees, eagerly and proudly claimed that these relations were democratic. As explored previously (Chapter 2), claims that the camps were "democratic" rested on a complex attitude toward *qabīlah* relations. The state-movement partially premised its claims to engage in democratic practice on the alleged inclusion of some aspects of *qabīlah* relations, in particular, its interpretation of the legacy of the *jamāʿah* or tribal council. Nevertheless, this celebration of a specific tribal democratic pedigree was the exception within a broader panorama, whereby the state-movement and refugees feared that tribal loyalties were an obstacle to democratic practice.

In pre-electoral meetings, as well as in conversation with me, officials and voters made clear that the 2008 electoral reforms belonged to the second thrust, namely, the promotion of democracy via the rejection of *qabīlah* relations. The reforms redrew some electoral constituencies, widening both the number of candidates per constituency and the number of voters to whom they were to appeal. As one official explained in an interview after the elections, constituencies had been widened "so that the person with more family [a common euphemism for tribe] does not win . . . . You need to give more choice so that you are not left with *les candidats de famille*," he continued (switching to French). The potential for *qabīlah* relations to exert influence over voters was probably the biggest point of tension in elections for the refugees and state-movement alike. In the palimpsest traced in this book, through which the state-movement attempted to overwrite *qabīlah* relations, any influence of the latter over electoral decisions was a dilemma: an unruly irruption of *qabīlah* relations.

Refugees' and their leaders' claims that the promotion of democratic relations in the camps relied (with the above exception of the "capturing" of the legacy of *jamā'ah*) on the suppression of *qabīlah* relations rest on two assumptions of interest to scholars of democratic relations and democratization. The first assumption is that *qabīlah* relations—and, implicitly, tribes more broadly—are bad for democracy. Many beyond the camps have concurred in such an assumption. The second assumption is that the refugees may engage in democratic relations in the context of the camps. Many observers of political life, however, would disagree that there can be democratic relations in a state of exception (which is also the view of some Sahrawi refugees).

This chapter probes both assumptions. By addressing whether the 2008 reforms were successful on their own terms (to decrease the potential influence of *qabīlah* loyalties and to deepen the state-movement's democratic mandate), I ask whether tribes are "bad" for democracy, and whether there can be democratic relations in a state of exception. I argue for a broadened understanding of democratic relations and possibilities and for recognition of what I call "democratic casualties" as perhaps an inherent feature of democracy as a project.

## The 2008 Legislative Electoral Reforms

The context through which I shall explore the above issues is the 2008 electoral reforms. Following the Popular General Congress (PGC) of December 2007, reforms were introduced to the electoral system for the SNC. They followed a range of reforms over the course of the camps' existence that sought to introduce or deepen existing democratic institutions (see Chapter 2).

The SNC was founded at the third PGC in 1976 and replaced an earlier temporary body, the Provisional Sahrawi National Council (Pazzanita 2006: 378). In this early form, consisting of the twenty-one members of the Political Bureau (see Chapter 2) and the twenty heads of the *dawāir* (who were directly elected), the SNC had little power. But its mandate was invigorated in the 1990s. From 1995, in addition to its power to approve laws, the SNC acquired powers to draft laws, assess government policy proposals, and pass a motion of no confidence against the government or a minister. From 1999, when the SNC's numbers were set at fifty-one, the majority of its members came to be elected directly by the people. Voters were assigned to a constituency according to the institution through which they were "active" within the state-movement (see Chapter 2).

The SNC—often called "Parliament" by the refugees—was thus the legislative power of SADR that debated and passed laws. A number of SNC members, or MPs, explained to me that in practice SADR laws tended to be suggested by the Council of Ministers, rather than by MPs. Government by presidential and prime ministerial decree, without SNC approval, was also of not infrequent recourse in the late revolutionary period. Such decrees were reported by some MPs to have been the staple of early revolutionary legislation. Because written records of such decrees were not made available to me (nor, to my knowledge, to refugees), the extent of rule by decree in the late revolutionary period is hard to assess—although I shall discuss one instance below.

If the SNC was not the only source of regulations that came to affect refugees' lives, it did have a unique role in its mandate to hold the government to account. Periodically, the SNC conducted a wide-ranging evaluation of ministerial policies. If it found ministers, or the whole government, wanting, it could vote to demand the dismissal of individual ministers or the whole government. It exercised this right in 1999, passing a vote of no confidence on the whole government. The president, faced with the constitutional choice of dissolving the SNC or dismissing the government, opted for the latter. Because the SNC members were empowered to hold ministers to account, they were constitutionally prohibited from serving as ministers, in order to avoid a conflict of interest between government and those empowered to evaluate it.

The 2008 reforms arose, then, in a context of a longer trajectory of reforms. Indeed, this trajectory was envisaged to stretch not only back in time but also forward to independence, when, according to the SADR constitution, further rights, including a universal suffrage Parliament to replace the SNC, would be granted. The 2008 reforms saw fit to tackle three areas: to broaden the representativeness of MPs, to increase the qualifications and competence of those elected to that office, and to discourage voting along the lines of *qabīlah* affiliations. These aims were "evangelized" by officials in pre-electoral discussion meetings. The reforms were read aloud, followed by explanations such as an injunction to choose a candidate on the basis of competence rather than being a fellow tribesman (*wuld ʿamm*). Audience members could be receptive: in one *dairah*, the headmaster of the local school stood up to make an impassioned speech against tribalism in voting, to widespread applause.

In practical terms, the reforms revised the electoral constituencies in the provinces (*wilāyāt*), introduced a quota for women in the *wilāyāt*, increased the number of MPs representing the Women's Union, established new criteria for standing as a candidate (across all electoral constituencies), and instigated new opportunities for candidates in all constituencies to disseminate information about themselves to the electorate.

The increase in the number of seats in the SNC was from fifty-one to fifty-three, distributed along the lines in Table 6. Given voters' incorporation into constituencies on the "activist" grounds of the area in which they were officially affiliated to the state-movement (see Chapter 2), the mode of representation operative in the SNC was not that whereby one member represented a proportion of the electorate similar in size to that fraction represented by other members. Rather, each seat represented a type of "activist" sector. Thus, the seats for the *dawāir* and February 27 school represented voters who were "fighters" (*munāḍilīn*) on the "home front." In practice, then, they were predominantly female "fighters" (*munāḍilāt*), since, in the ideal structure of the liberation movement, men usually had an activist role through a ministry or the army, rather than on the "home front." The ministries and the army had their own MPs, four and ten respectively. The ministries were arranged into four sectors—economics, politics, media and defense—each electing their own representative. The military seats were likewise divided into four sectors based on the military zones into which the Sahrawi People's Liberation Army divided Western Sahara. The three mass organizations, the Workers', Women's, and Young People's Unions, also had their own representation: one seat for each of the Workers' and Young People's Unions and four for the Women's, three of which were new with the 2008 reforms.[1] Finally, the Consultative Council (composed of *shuyūkh*) operated as its own SNC constituency, electing five MPs. This total of fifty-two MPs, once elected, voted whether to accept the member of the Polisario National Secretariat whom the president nominated to be the head of the SNC. Thus, with the head of the SNC, there were a total of fifty-three SNC members.

As regards increasing the "representativeness" of MPs, the reforms pushed to increase women's representation in the SNC. As we saw, the number of seats in the all-female constituency of the Women's Union was raised

Table 6. Distribution of Seats in Saharawi National Council, 2008

| *Electoral constituency* | *Number of seats* |
|---|---|
| *Dawāir* | 26 |
| February 27 school | 1 |
| Ministries | 4 |
| Women's Union | 4 |
| Workers' Union | 1 |
| Youth Union | 1 |
| Army | 10 |
| Consultative Council | 5 |
| Head of SNC | 1 |

from one to four, increasing the number of guaranteed seats for women. In addition, the number of seats in the female-dominated *wilāyāt* was increased. An additional seat was awarded to the largest two *dawāir*, Smara and Dakhla, bringing the total number of seats for all the *dawāir* to twenty-six: Smara (seven), Dakhla (seven), Auserd (six), and Elayoune (six). Furthermore, the *dawāir* constituencies were restructured. Whereas prior to 2008 each *dairah* had formed its own electoral constituency electing its own MP, in 2008 all the *dawāir* in one *wilāyah* were merged to form one electoral constituency that would elect six (Auserd and Elayoune) or seven (Smara and Dakhla) MPs from a *wilāyah*-wide list.

In the *wilāyāt*, a quota system was also applied intended to favor the election of female MPs. There are three common kinds of gender quotas. They typically target the potential pool of candidates, the candidates standing for election, and those elected (see Dahlerup 2006: 19). The state-movement's electoral design in 2008 combined reserved seats for women (the Women's Union's four seats) with the relatively unusual means of a quota targeting in the first instance not the candidates but the voters. Each ballot paper in the *wilāyāt*, in order to be valid, had to include the names of at least two female candidates.

The widening of the electoral constituency in the *wilāyāt* was described by electoral officials as an attempt to strengthen the mandate of the SNC; those elected from the *wilāyāt* would have the backing of not just one *dairah* but of the whole *wilāyah*.

As regards the introduction of criteria for candidacy for the SNC ostensibly aimed at increasing the qualifications and competence of MPs, to an extent these also had the effect of broadening representation—but, I shall argue, at a price. As of 2008, candidates standing for the SNC had to be at least twenty-five years old and of sound mind, and, in addition, needed:

- *either* to hold a certificate of higher education and have five years of work experience in a state-movement institution
- *or* to have five years of experience working in a named position of responsibility in the state-movement administration at *wilāyah* level or above.

A generalized principle of criteria for candidacy had longstanding precedents in the state-movement. As prescribed by the Polisario statutes (see Es-Sweyih 2001: 92–94), candidates for certain positions (e.g., the National Secretariat) needed to meet criteria such as a minimum number of years of previous experience. Whereas, in the early revolutionary period, SNC members were either members of the Political Bureau or heads of *dawāir*, after the reforms to the SNC in the 1990s, there were apparently no particular criteria to stand for the SNC other than to be an adult of sound mind. At least some Sahrawis felt that some elected officials lacked "competence" (Es-Sweyih 2001: 79). The 2008 criteria addressed this issue by forcing potential MPs to have passed through fields of professional or political experience that, in the eyes of electoral officials, would "raise" the caliber of members of the SNC.

The introduction of new electoral criteria also tackled the question of MPs' representativeness. In legitimizing the candidacy of anyone who met the requirements, the criteria created the notion of a level playing field for all those who did meet them—above and beyond factors such as age, gender, and *qabīlah* background. This attempt to create a level playing field is not insignificant, given the backdrop of prerevolutionary exclusions from certain political roles for women, younger men, and those of stigmatized status groups, not to mention a tendency in exile for a small elite to dominate senior positions (Mundy 2007: 279, 284). The new criteria offered the opportunity to legitimize the candidacy of otherwise disadvantaged candidates, increasing their chances of election and, therefore, potentially broadening the scope of representation among MPs. Nevertheless, this came at the cost of creating a separation between those who did and did not meet the criteria—an issue I take up below.

The introduction of new criteria for candidacy, and, in the case of the *wilāyāt*, the broadening of electoral constituencies, intersected with the introduction of new forms of dissemination of information about candidates. As mentioned earlier, electoral officials believed that the broadening of electoral constituencies in the *wilāyāt* could diminish the influence of *qabīlah* loyalties on voting. With voters now putting forward the names of six or seven candidates, rather than one, this breadth of choice meant that each voter could hardly accommodate all his or her votes on the grounds of *qabīlah* affiliation.[2] Arguably, the introduction of criteria allowed voters to conceive of candidates in terms of professional experience, independently of a candidate's *qabīlah*.

At the same time, the dissemination of information about candidates through new channels increased the chances that voters would actually find something out about candidates' qualifications. Each candidate had to submit a résumé (*biṭāqah fannīyyah*), which stated the experience that enabled the candidate to meet the criteria for standing. The résumé was to be read out at the discussion meetings preceding the elections, and the candidate was to have five minutes in which to address directly those gathered at the discussion meeting. In addition, in the *wilāyāt*, the candidates could each speak on the local radio for fifteen minutes. In *wilāyāt* with local television services (at the time only Auserd and Dakhla), each candidate could speak for five minutes on television.

In some candidates' and officials' accounts of the new media platforms, the résumé could be displayed at the *dairah* administrative building (*al-idārah*). In practice, in the elections that I observed in Auserd, few candidates did have the résumé displayed outside the administrative building of each *dairah*. I was unable to determine whether this was due to the choice of an individual candidate or to the workings of the *dairah* in question. All of these channels of dissemination—the résumé, media, and speeches in front of the electorate—were new to elections in the state-movement.

## Tribes and Democracy: An Awkward Relationship

The above reforms went to considerable lengths to minimize the likely effect of *qabīlah* loyalties on election results. In line with the state-movement's mandate, explored throughout this book, to undermine tribes, the state-movement and many refugees assumed that—with the exception of the alleged *jamā'ah* legacy—tribes were "bad" for democracy. The presumption was that tribes undermined nationalism and egalitarianism and that *qabīlah* relations were the wrong sorts of loyalties on which to decide votes.

In making assumptions that tribes were bad for democracy and elections, Sahrawi refugees and their leaders were far from alone. Many in and commenting on the Middle East and North Africa (MENA) (and beyond) are convinced of the unsuitable nature of tribal affiliations to democratic politics—and this concern can be situated within a wider debate about the persistence in MENA of undemocratic regimes.[3] MENA's governments, political parties, and tribal elites have at times been shown to have used tribal affiliations as a means of directing political support in ways perceived to undermine a democratic process (Davis 1987; Casciarri 2006; Parizot 2006; Bonte and Ben Hounet 2009). Close to the case in question, Mauritanian post-independence political parties have sought to obtain votes from *qabā'il* as a block, with *qabā'il* themselves seeking to capture the attention and favors of political parties through the promise of awarding blocks of votes (Villasante de Beauvais 1998; Abdoul 2004). This feeds into a system of political patronage in which those who have benefited from this system are obliged to return the favor of support received by distributing appointments to fellow members of their *qabīlah* (sometimes attracting comparisons with Bayart's (1993) notion of the "politics of the belly"). For pessimistic commentators, the presence of tribes impedes democratic political relations in Mauritania (Abdoul 2004).

The use of tribes in the pursuit of power is not particular to multipartyism; in the single-party elections in Gaddafi's Libya John Davis (1987) studies, the lack of political grounds on which to distinguish between candidates for elections (since all candidates are standing with the same party) leaves voters from the Zuwaya Bedouin tribes with little option other than to queue up to cast their vote for a fellow tribesman. Elsewhere in the Arab world, ruling or aspiring parties have sought to manipulate the support of tribes (Dawod 2003; Casciarri 2006; Ababsa 2009; Ben Hounet 2009).

If the relationship between tribes and democracy may be fraught, it does not, however, follow that tribes are in and of themselves bad for elections. In the case of the multiparty elections in Mauritania, while there is no doubt that clientelism feeds on, and is fed by, *qabā'il*, there is debate as to whether this arises from the presence of *qabā'il* or, rather, from the shortcomings of the Mauritanian state. For Antil (2004) and Villasante Cervello (2006), the weaknesses of the Mauritanian state, rather than the presence of *qabā'il* themselves, underpin the cycles of tribal clientelism.

In a rare insight into local and national elections in a tribal region of Algeria, a country in which the political importance of tribes has been lost from national political culture, Ben Hounet (2009: 275) finds that, in the age of multipartyism, the importance of tribes for voters in tribal areas is greater in local elections than in national elections. Even in local elections, however, multipartyism has reduced the importance of tribes as a factor explaining the casting of votes. Each of the contesting parties usually places candidates from the most important local tribe at the top of their list at a given election. Ben Hounet (2009) explains that this means that any member of that tribe can vote for a fellow tribesperson and still has a choice to make about party affiliation (252). Voters take into account candidates' party affiliation, educational background, and professional experience (276).

Ben Hounet's study suggests that the political importance that tribal membership assumes in the casting of votes depends on a range of contextual factors beyond tribal membership itself. It may be in the absence of political choices to be made along policy lines that tribes become key targets for political mobilization, either at the instigation of political parties hungry for votes or tribal elites hungry for political achievement. Where there are choices about policies or qualifications, then tribal membership may well be reduced to only one of a range of factors taken into account in voting. Tribalism is not necessarily the deciding factor—and indeed sometimes electoral designs prevent it from becoming so. As we shall see, the SADR 2008 elections further destabilized the assumption that tribes are poor bedfellows for democracy.

## Democratic Relations in a State of Exception?

The SADR 2008 reforms assumed that Sahrawi refugees, by taking part in these elections, were engaging in democratic political relations. This begs the question of whether there can be democratic relations in a state of exception where conventions of democratic practice, such as freedom of association, are restricted. Sahrawi refugees were divided on this question.

On the one hand, it was not uncommon for refugees and officers of the state-movement to assert, when questioned about their political system, that they enjoyed "true democracy." For instance, in 2007 a member of the Human Rights Watch (HRW) delegation accompanied me in some of my observation of a discussion meeting in preparation for the PGC. The HRW delegate left after the morning session, and I returned in the afternoon to rejoin the women for their reading and discussion of the papers the state-movement had circulated to stimulate debate. In reply to the women's eager questions as to what the HRW delegate was doing in the camps, I explained that he was there to see if human rights were being protected. The women nodded their understanding and yet were confused; they voiced both their convictions that his time in the camps would let him see "the true democracy" that the refugees enjoyed and their confusion that he was examining human rights questions in the camps when they felt it was imperative that he visit Moroccan-controlled Western Sahara. "Poor people [*masākīn*]," they sighed over their compatriots in the annexed areas, "They don't have any democracy."[4]

On the other hand, the idea that the camps, with their particular interpretation of direct democracy (see Chapter 2), offered refugee citizens the opportunity to engage in democratic political relations had its skeptics among the refugees. In conversations with civil servants in the shade of the Ministry of Information's courtyard, over tea in a chilly office on a winter's morning, or in a follow-up interview in someone's home, some refugees were dismissive of democratic possibilities in the camps. "Where democracy is concerned, we are like babies. We haven't taken our first steps yet," one man told me. Another said, "There is no real democracy here, and not anywhere in the Arab world." The enthusiasm that I encountered was, thus, not shared by all.

The skepticism of some refugees can be seen as part of a wider, increasingly visible "culture of dissent" among Sahrawi refugees and members of the Sahrawi diaspora. The reforms of the 1990s paved the way for internal criticism of the state-movement to flourish openly. From the early to late 2000s, a movement named *khaṭṭ al-shahīd* (the movement of martyrs, literally "the line of the martyr"), while claiming to be part of Polisario, criticized the Polisario mainstream for corruption and nepotism and demanded a return to war against Morocco (Campbell 2010).[5] Since 2011, criticism, demonstrations, and calls for the reform of Polisario have been voiced by a group going by the name of the March 5 movement (Human Rights Watch 2014: 42–44).

As Carmen Gómez Martín and Cédric Omet (2009) point out, what is curious about these Sahrawi critics of Polisario, who are, nevertheless, not pro-Moroccan, is the extent to which, operating within a framework of support for self-determination (a framework thus shared with the state-movement), these dissidents hold back from demanding the fall of Polisario per se. They simultaneously support and criticize Polisario. Recognizing this, Gómez Martín and Omet see these activists in terms of "non-dissident dissidence"—an interesting concept through which to question whether political opposition must take the form of opposing political parties, as is favored in contemporary Euro-American interpretations of democracy.

If Sahrawis, both in the camps and beyond, voiced demands for greater checks on officers of the state-movement, external observers might easily further criticize political conditions in exile. Freedom of press was curtailed in the camps. At least in the late 2000s, political publications about the camps and the Western Sahara issue in circulation in the camps had to be approved with a stamp by the Ministry of Information. As the main political machinations in the camps occurred orally in face-to-face meetings (Chapter 2), the controls on official print, audio, and televisual media were not necessarily a sign that the refugees lacked freedom of expression across the board. Indeed, in the discussion meetings that I attended, criticisms of the state-movement were expressed with freedom and without fear; broadcasting those criticisms through media outlets, however, was discouraged.

The question of freedom of movement is likewise controversial. Refugees were free to leave the camps (Human Rights Watch 2014) and frequently did so for a number of destinations (Wilson 2014b). With their SADR passport or identity card provided by the state-movement, they could travel to other places in Algeria, the pasturelands of Western Sahara, Mauritania, and states that recognized SADR. A significant migration destination was Moroccan-controlled Western Sahara. In this case, refugees might arrive as an official "returner," welcomed by the Moroccan government with subsidies and housing. Alternatively, they might acquire Mauritanian identity papers to disguise their identity from the Moroccan authorities in order to make an informal visit that was politically distinct from an official "return."[6] Yet the most coveted destination for migrants was Europe, where SADR papers were not recognized. Refugees with their sights on Europe could request, via the SADR Ministry of Interior, an Algerian passport from the Algerian government. It has been suggested that the majority of the estimated ten thousand Sahrawis in Spain alone (Gómez Martín 2011: 52 n88) have traveled on Algerian passports issued through this route.[7] There are also significant Sahrawi communities in France and Italy and small communities elsewhere; many of these Sahrawis are likely to have traveled on such passports. Nevertheless, there is no transparency as to the procedure and criteria for the issuance of Algerian passports through this route. I frequently met refugees whose requests for such passports had been left unresolved, in some cases for years. Refugees felt that both the state-movement and Algeria shared responsibility for such delays. Martín Gómez (2011: 208 n121) suggests, though, that pressure from the EU to reduce immigration from North Africa may be the driving force squeezing access to Algerian passports.

Looking beyond freedoms of expression and movement, freedom of association in the camps was curtailed and was planned to remain so until independence. As in other North African states prior to the Arab Spring, a state of exception cancelling freedom of association had become the norm in the camps. Consequently, although there were some civil society associations in the camps (Human Rights Watch 2014), there were no political parties among Sahrawi exiles. Even assuming that refugees had freedom of expression orally and freedom of movement in the form of freedom to leave (if not "to arrive" somewhere), given the constraints on freedom of association, could the camps—more broadly, could a space of exception—host democratic relations?

In understandings of democracy dominant in the late twentieth century, the freedom to form political parties for whom candidates vote in multiparty elections has come to be seen as essential. It has been assumed that single-party systems, or the effective disabling of any viable opposition parties, prevent the political subjects of those systems from engaging in democratic relations (Diamond 2002). Yet this very presumption has led multipartyism to become the target of criticism over the extent to which, in and of itself, it can guarantee democratic outcomes.

Harri Englund (2002) has shown for Malawi that the overall agreement there between the different parties on principles such as a liberal constitution leaves scant ground on which to distinguish between parties. The result is that allegiances are formed on regionalist rather than policy-based lines. The fulfillment of a formula for a contested election becomes a façade of democratic "paraphernalia" (Englund 2002: 173) that stifles public deliberation and participation. In the case of multiparty Yemen, Lisa Wedeen (2003) demonstrates how the ruling party used electoral law to disqualify the opposing candidate, replacing him with a candidate who was effectively a stooge of the ruling party grafted on to the opposition party.

Such empirical studies of how it is not multiple parties per se that make an election contested show in practice what has been argued in political theory: that a minimal procedural definition of democracy is not enough to ensure democratic relations. The latter also require elements such as participation and deliberation in decision making that cannot themselves be guaranteed by a contested electoral framework (Whitehead 2002; Wedeen 2003). Electorates can be acutely aware of the shortcomings of a procedural minimum for democracy. For example, popular demand in Botswana in the 1970s for single-party rule has been analyzed as a local critique of the failure of contested elections to achieve a more meaningful democratic government, as defined locally—one that would include ongoing accountability between elections (Comaroff and Comaroff 1997).

If a received idea of democracy as secret ballot multi-party elections has been shown to be wanting, it has also been shown that participation in democratic relations can be accommodated in sociohistorical manifestations that do not fit the current hegemonic procedural norm. Arguing that the public spheres analyzed by Jürgen Habermas as formative of Euro-American democracy are historically specific rather than universalistic precursors to democratic relations, Wedeen (2007) holds that gatherings in Yemen for chewing the mild stimulant *qaṭ* are contemporary public spheres where democratic relations are enjoyed. Lucia Michelutti (2007) has called for recognition of the multiple ways in which democracy can be "vernacularized," that is, socially embedded, as best fits specific contexts. The double thrust of appeals to recognize both the shortcomings of procedural norms for democracy and the potential of alternative procedures underscores that there is no scholarly consensus as to the definition of "democracy," either in anthropology (Paley 2002) or beyond (Whitehead 2002). In this light, the question whether unusual arrangements, even a state of exception, might accommodate democratic relations remains very much open.

Having been granted permission by the organizing committee to observe the 2008 elections in the camps, I was able to explore this very question.

## Pluralizing Elections Without Parties

The organizing committee for the 2008 elections suggested that I attend pre-electoral discussion meetings, polling, and vote counting in the *wilāyah* of Auserd. As one of the constituencies most affected by the electoral modifications, a *wilāyah* was an ideal setting in which to study the reforms.

On February 16, the day before the opening of the pre-electoral meetings, all the candidates in Auserd (and the anthropologist) were invited to gather in the *wilāyah* headquarters for a meeting explaining the schedule for the coming days. Almost all of the candidates were present. We gathered in a long, thin room furnished with mattresses, on which the candidates sat or reclined. As we waited for the meeting to begin, I introduced myself to each of the candidates and asked about his or her candidacy, as well as for thoughts about the SNC and the reforms.

The first cluster of candidates were incumbent MPs. The first, a man, had been an MP since 2003, and he enumerated his considerable administrative experience that would allow him to qualify for candidacy under the new rules. He discussed at some length the role of the SNC in holding governmental institutions to account. Thinking at the time that I was asking an appropriate question for an election, I inquired, "What ideas distinguish you from other candidates?" He responded, "We are special. In other states you have to present ideas. For us the Parliament is a tool for liberation."

The next candidate was a female incumbent. Younger, and also with less administrative experience, she explained that she qualified to stand again thanks to her being an incumbent. She explained that this Parliament would be new because its members would have "culture" (*al-thaqāfah*), whereas former MPs had had experience. When I asked about her goals for the new Parliament, she replied that she hoped a Family Code would be passed and then continued: "We all have ambition for independence. Other Parliaments agree on a budget. But we don't have any resources. The priority is the social sector: health and education."

The third candidate was the male incumbent from another *dairah*. He talked at length about the history of the SNC and its origins in the *ait arbaʿīn* (see Chapter 1), not missing the opportunity to weave into his account of the history of Western Sahara that the first people to colonize the region had been "the English."

The next group were first-time candidates, young men who had studied and held degrees. They talked more briefly about their own experience, not at all about the role or future of the SNC. I eventually found myself near two young women, also first-time candidates. Both were graduates and teachers in local primary schools. They seemed nervous and shy of the meeting. Leaning forward, one of them asked me, "Do you know the [names of] tribes?" and giggled as I named a few. They each then leaned forward and told me from which tribe they hailed.

When the meeting began, the overseer of the elections explained that each candidate would, in the various media broadcasts, have several minutes to say what ideas he or she wanted to implement. I was intrigued; I had learned relatively little so far from my conversations with the candidates about their "ideas" for "implementation."

The first stage in the dissemination of candidates' ideas was the radio broadcasts. As some of the candidates waited in line outside Auserd's radio studio after the group meeting on February 16, I used the opportunity to interview more candidates. I was later told that the radio interviews were broadcast live and that there were no recordings. So I was unable to hear the broadcasts themselves.

February 17 was the first of two days of pre-electoral discussion meetings (*nadawāt*). On the morning of February 17, all the candidates were invited to address the *nadwah* for employees in the *wilāyah* central administration, giving me the opportunity to hear the speeches of the seventeen (of nineteen) candidates who attended. The *nadwah* took place in a large hall. As was typical for meetings in the *wilāyāt*, those in attendance sat cross-legged on the carpet, with men and women tending to cluster together in same-sex groups. There was a table with chairs at the head of the hall to accommodate the presiding committee. The audience was limited, initially numbering some twenty people but growing as the morning progressed. The reception for the candidates was vibrant all the same, with each candidate's opening and conclusion being met with applause. I wondered if now I would hear more about the "ideas" of some of the more reticent candidates. Yet, as each candidate spoke, my doubts increased that I was raising the right question. The two shy teachers' speeches were the shortest and, while noticeably delivered with greater nervousness, they were not unusual in tenor. The first teacher thanked "the state" for the opportunity to stand and for its encouragement for "young people with culture" and wished all the candidates success. The second teacher opened by saying, "We should not think that we are better than the army," burst into tears, and sat down—to intense ululation and applause. I reflected that I had never heard election speeches like this, yet this was also true for the candidates and voters, this being the first time that election speeches had ever been held in the camps.

The candidates' speeches had been a strong pull for those who attended the *nadwah*, for, at the conclusion of the presentations, many in the audience stood up to leave. This prompted the *nadwah* president to call people back, sometimes by name. The remaining work of the morning had still to be done, namely, reading out the documents prepared by the state-movement. These explained the history of the SNC, dating back, in this account, to the *ait arbaʿīn*, and the role and scope of the reforms, about which *nadwah* attendees could ask questions.

Parallel meetings took place in each *dairah* over February 17 and 18, with similar discussions and slots for candidates' speeches. I attended *dairah* meetings on both days, hearing candidates deliver live speeches to full rooms. On the evenings of February 17and 18, I watched the television broadcasts over evening tea with Māghalāha's family. Fourteen of nineteen candidates gave speeches. One older female candidate discussed specific ideas for how public services in the *wilāyāt* could be improved. She was the exception, however. After the elections, when I worked on my recordings of the television broadcasts with two different people helping me to translate difficult passages, both of them eventually told me they were struggling to do so because "[the candidates] aren't saying anything." Listening to and watching the candidates prior to the elections, I found myself irresistibly drawn into forming some of my own opinions about their candidacy (which I kept to myself and my notebook). Yet I was curious to assess both the extent to which voters availed themselves of the opportunity to gather information about candidates through the new media channels and the extent to which the media channels might have influenced voters' choices.

After the close of the second day of *nadawāt*, in the late afternoon Māghalāha's ever-patient daughter Khanātha accompanied me to the homes of our neighbors, so that I could ask them whether they had gathered information about candidates from the radio, television, or *nadawāt*. As was often the case in my attempts to question interlocutors formally, they had more questions for me than I did for them. It took some time to acquire answers to my questions, and, when I came to write up my notes from this excursion, I found that I had responses from twenty-one people. Somewhat discouraged by the difficulties I had encountered in gathering responses, I repeated the formal exercise with only two men who ran stalls in the market. I pursued further interest in the electoral media through informal conversations with interlocutors. Although the number of responses to the formal exercise was small, the responses gave some informative indications of voters' reactions with regard to the new media channels.

The formal responses revealed that five people reported hearing some radio broadcasts, ten reported hearing television broadcasts, and nine reported attending a *nadwah* on the morning of February 17.[8] For the six who had not heard the radio, television, or the *nadwah*, the reasons given included the following: one woman of advanced age was recently bereaved at the time; one was a man in the market who had been at his stall all the time; four were young women, a time of life at which there are heavy domestic labor responsibilities. Two young women voiced this constraint explicitly, one saying that her mother was away (the implication being that she herself, therefore, had greater domestic responsibilities), and another telling me, "Don't ask me about the candidates; ask me what I've been doing in the kitchen." Of the nine who reported attending the *nadwah*, six were women of the age when they were likely to have daughters who could take on domestic work and when they themselves might well have responsibilities in the *ḥayy* or *dairah*, as some indeed did. Of the eleven young women I questioned, only three had attended the *nadwah*. This confirmed what I could see for myself when I would attend *nadawāt*—it was more likely to be middle-aged or older women who would attend, younger women bearing greater responsibilities for performing domestic labor for their own or their mothers' households.

The exercise also indicated that the television broadcasts had reached a greater audience. This made sense in that the radio broadcasts took place in the morning, a time when many were busy with administrative and domestic responsibilities. The television broadcasts took place at night, when families usually gathered to make tea and might run their television sets from the solar panels that had been charged that day. Yet what interested me the most was that four people, when I asked them if they had gathered information about candidates from the new media channels, responded, "We know them." One of these respondents added that he knew them "by their three names," meaning the name given to the person and the name of the father and grandfather. This statement must be understood in the context of interlocutors often telling me that, if they knew someone's three names, they would be able to know from which *qabīlah* that person hailed.

The assertion "We know the candidates" suggests that (at least some) voters were not looking to the election media to find out about candidates' "ideas." It seemed that most of the candidates understood this well and had not used their electoral speeches to discuss "ideas." In fact, in informal discussion about the elections, several interlocutors explained to me their view that candidates refrained from discussing "ideas" not merely because, as some candidates had been telling me, the SNC and the situation of the Sahrawi refugees was "different" but also because it was considered improper among Sahrawis in general to talk about programs for the future as if it were in the power of one person to achieve these things. As one young woman explained, "When people hear someone say that they will do this or that or the other, they think that they are lying and won't vote for them."

What work were the electoral speeches doing, then, at least in the context of the 2008 elections? The response "We know [the candidates]" offers a prompt. This response voiced (some) voters' feeling that, as a community ("*We* know them"), voters already had access to information about the candidates, independent of the new media opportunities offered in these elections. This prior knowledge might even include knowledge about a candidate's *qabīlah* (that is, knowing the "three names").

These claims, made on behalf of a community, to possess existing knowledge about the candidates, invite reflection on what, if anything, was new about the forms of knowledge that the election media put into circulation. Common ways for refugees to "know" others included residence, administrative affiliation, family, education (for younger generations), and sometimes *qabīlah* relations. The new media opportunities focused on candidates' professional and political experience, but it is conceivable that some voters might already know this kind of information about candidates. If anything, the election media needed to be supplemented (as implied by the more expansive reply about knowing the candidates by their three names) to fill the lacunae about candidates' *qabīlah* membership. The fact that some candidates in Auserd, who did not take up *any* of the opportunities to address voters in person or on the radio or television, went on to win suggests that plenty of voters were satisfied with the way they knew candidates, without having recourse to the election media. Were the electoral media redundant, then? Did they add nothing new, or were they merely novel in unimportant ways?

Consideration of the different ways of knowing candidates—and persons more generally—in the camps clarifies an important novel element of the elections media. Conversations that I heard among voters suggested that voters' claims to "know" candidates rested on varying grounds. If some voters would state that they knew a candidate, following up by naming his or her *qabīlah*, others would refer to knowing the candidate through his or her work in the state-movement's administration (even if, as a later conversation once revealed, a voter also knew a certain candidate as a fellow *qabīlah* member). While it is by no means surprising that for the refugees there was not one way of "knowing" somebody, all those different ways have in common that someone is known through the sphere of the extent of his or her reputation. The importance of personal reputation has been much emphasized in studies of Bedouin elsewhere (Abu-Lughod 1986; Leinhardt 2001). It has been claimed that no man can have influence outside the sphere of his reputation and that personal reputation is an important means through which the authority of a *shaykh* is legitimized (Lancaster 1981: 43, 73—but see Peters 1990: 120). All the ways of "knowing" others that Saharawi refugees habitually mentioned involved knowing a person within the sphere of his or her reputation. The novelty of the electoral media was that they offered information that was *beyond* the sphere of that person's reputation. This mode of knowing candidates was probably new for the vast majority of the voters. Some of the candidates did not entrust their electoral chances to these new ways of knowing: in Auserd some of the winners did not disseminate information via any of the new media channels (other than having their résumé read out in their absence).

That employing the new electoral media was not *necessary* to win does not preclude the possibility that their uptake may have been decisive, or helpful, in other cases, although, unfortunately, I do not have data about the reception of the media on a scale sufficient to address this question. I did learn that the official media were shadowed by parallel practices which, while not prohibited, fell outside the scope of the state-movement's approved electoral initiatives. Some candidates "sent people round" to seek electoral support, sometimes to a candidate's fellow tribespersons. In the wake of the elections, this was cited to me by some losing candidates as a decisive factor in the overall outcome—a claim that is hard to investigate. What can be asserted is that the introduction of the new modes of dissemination about candidates presented voters, and candidates, with the challenge of an appeal to their votes via a new form of knowledge unlinked from reputation. This was in addition to the already multiple ways of knowing current in the camps. The aggrandized plurality of ways of knowing at stake in these elections was important not only for unseating the potential influence of *qabīlah* membership on the casting of votes but also in and of itself. For these elections, fought between candidates from the same liberation movement and without multiple political parties, now begin to look intriguingly pluralizing.

In these elections, voters were being asked to choose between competing claims of qualification for office. The new conditions for candidacy had an effect that voters and election organizers recognized explicitly: voters were faced with candidates who had on the one hand experience (*al-khibrah*), and on the other hand "culture" (*al-thaqāfah*), that is, those who had attained a certificate of higher education. Although the criteria imposed a minimum of

Figure 12. Polling station prepares to receive voters, Auserd, 2008 (photo by Alice Wilson).

work experience on all candidates, those younger candidates who had degrees and work experience, but not senior administrative experience, were seen as representing culture, while the other candidates, including incumbent MPs, were seen as representing experience. I heard various friends discussing their chosen candidates, mentioning that they had chosen such and such a person because he or she had culture. In interviews with candidates after the elections, the theme of the electorate's respective preference for experience or "culture" was prominent. Electoral organizers also commented on the results in terms of the balance between *al-thaqāfah* and *al-khibrah*. At the same time, in the state-movement's messages in the pre-election discussion meetings, voters were being urged to vote for candidates with competence (*al-kafā'*). This was contrasted, sometimes implicitly, sometimes explicitly, with voting for someone because he or she was from a particular *qabīlah*.

In their local context, then, these elections were arguably hotly contested—not between political parties or different policy platforms but

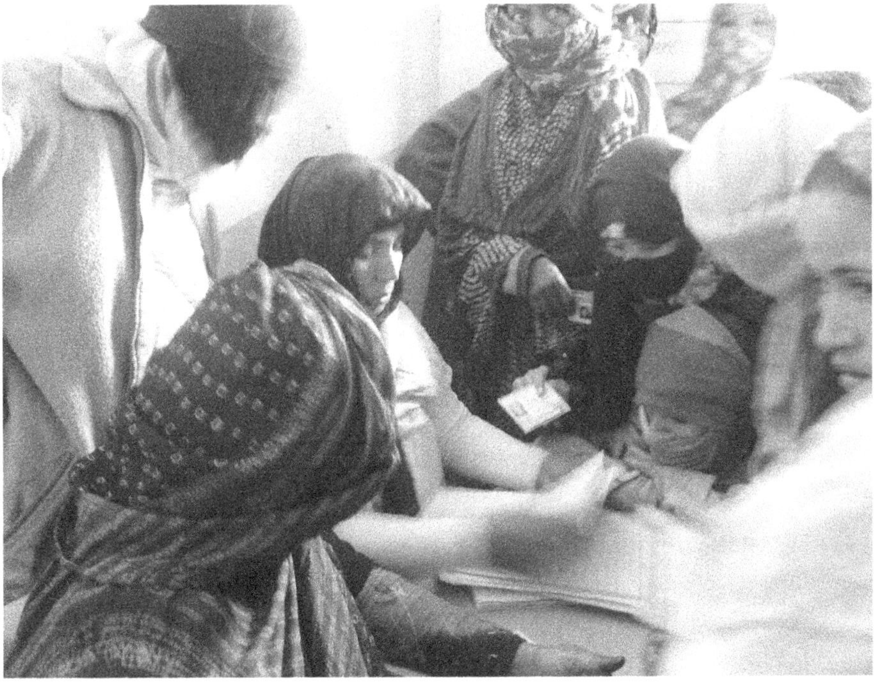

Figure 13. Voters seek to have their names ticked off against the list of voters, Auserd, 2008 (photo by Alice Wilson).

between different modes of thinking. Established and familiar modes of knowing, related to personal reputation that might be expressed across a number of fields, were competing with new, alternative ways of knowing not necessarily linked at all to personal reputation. Different ideas of what qualified a candidate for office were in competition: experience, educational level, competence, family, and *qabīlah* relations were at least some of them, while the state-movement had already defined a minimal level of experience and/or education that candidates had to possess to stand for election. These forms of plurality were only magnified by the fact that, in the *wilāyāt*, voters could choose between more candidates than ever before, since they voted for a list of candidates for the whole *wilāyah* rather than simply for one *dairah*. In certain electoral circles such as Rabouni, some voters described to me that voters also made choices about whether to vote for a candidate who was informally known to give preference to perceived interests of SADR as a state authority, or those of Polisario as a liberation movement. This is described by one Sahrawi commentator as an area of internal debate in refugee politics (Es-Sweyih 2001: 86–7), although I myself did not hear this debate voiced in reference to the *wilāyāt*. Close scrutiny of these elections without multiple parties shows them to be arguably more pluralizing than some multiparty elections.

## Winners and Losers

In large part because of the elements of competition in these elections, the atmosphere felt highly charged as I sat with women in a *nadwah* in a *dairah* of Auserd on the eve of voting, listening to candidates who had come to make their five-minute speech. The atmosphere was heavy with anticipation and celebration. The *dairah* musical group had composed songs in preparation for the gathering, and one of the singers had brought in a plastic tub on which to beat out a drum rhythm as they sang. Women attending the *nadwah* extemporized poetry, calling out to each other and responding. It was sometimes a struggle to hear the candidate who had come to give his or her five-minute address to the *nadwah*. One of these candidates was Fatma. She opened with a short line of poetry, captivating the audience and eliciting intense applause from the floor. When the *nadwah* ended as sunset fell (there being no electricity in the building), women of all ages, and by then a few men, gathered at the back, went their way to pray, feed goats, and discuss with their friends their candidates of choice. If a mark of democratic elections is uncertainty as to the outcome and the real possibility that incumbents might lose (Schmitter and Karl 1991: 82), then the outcome of these elections, for the voters and candidates concerned, felt uncertain indeed.

On election day in Auserd, I visited four polling booths during voting. The stations were run on similar lines, with varying levels of noise and the control of people moving in and out. Typically, in the main room of the administrative building, organizers had put up handwritten signs indicating the voting station (a table with a sealed ballot box) for each neighborhood. Voters queued up outside and then again inside. Voters first handed in (for collection after polling was complete) their ID card to have their names ticked off the voter list. Once given a ballot, voters sometimes went out of the polling station to discuss with companions before filling the paper in. While visiting polling stations, I met a few observers sent by candidates, as was each candidate's right. (Most candidates had not availed themselves of the opportunity—as one female candidate remarked, "How could people stay all day to observe when they have the housework and everything?") I approached two observers and asked how they had found the electoral process. They were in high spirits: "We have no observations," they replied. "The operation is a success." Some voters, such as an old woman whom I saw walking painfully on crutches, had made great efforts to make it to the polling station. In a few cases, voters met with disappointment, such as one woman who discovered that she was registered to vote in Rabouni, and not her *dairah*, and so would be unable to vote at that station.

After polls closed, I stayed on at one booth throughout vote counting. Five of the six *dawāir* polling stations and the central polling station at the *wilāyah* for those who worked in the central administration had their votes counted and returned that evening, and, indeed, the winning candidates for the other three *wilāyāt* were announced that evening on the radio. But one *dairah* in Auserd remained at vote counting until 23.00 (11p.m.). So the results for Auserd, like those of February 27 camp, were announced the next day on February 20.

Of the nineteen candidates in Auserd, only two of the incumbent MPs retained their seats. Despite the quota, Auserd was also the only *wilāyah* to return only two female MPs, the same number as had been elected in the previous elections without the quota. The two successful women candidates were one of the returned incumbents and the shy teacher who had thanked "the state" for the opportunity to stand for election. Smara and Dakhla elected four women MPs of seven, and Elayoune elected three of six. February 27, the women's school, surprised everyone when the incumbent female MP, a veteran of Polisario, was defeated by a male candidate with an army background. As for the representation of young people, in Auserd all the winning candidates were under forty-five and half of them under thirty. The new MPs for the *wilāyah* reflected the expectations of increased competence, according to the state-movement's own definition. Three of those elected in Auserd had certificates of higher education—in one case, a Master's and in the other cases a BA. Of the other three, one had an army background (considered of great prestige in the camps), and the other two were previous MPs. The incumbent candidate who had told me that the Parliament was a tool for liberation lost his seat; he reflected to me on the day he lost that he felt that the voters had chosen a balance of experience and educational level. The incumbent who had extolled the history of Sahrawi democratic institutions also lost his seat; he complained to me that not enough credit had been given to those with experience.

Twenty-six candidates emerged as winners in the *wilāyāt*. Yet what gains, and what losses, were made in terms of the stated aims of the reforms—to broaden representation, to increase the competence of MPs, to discourage voting along *qabīlah* lines, and, ultimately, to deepen a democratic mandate in the camps? There are only limited results from the elections available in the public domain through which to address such questions. The total number of votes cast for each candidate was not published beyond the reading aloud, once and unrecorded for media broadcast, of results for a particular polling station (in the case of a *dairah*, the results for that *dairah* and that *wilāyah* as a whole were read aloud). In an interview after the elections, a senior electoral figure shared selected electoral statistics with me. The average voter turnout across all constituencies was 45.83 percent, with the highest (81 percent) and lowest (16.11 percent) turnouts falling in two military regions. The results for winning candidates in Auserd as a percentage of votes, matched with the results that I had heard read out on results day, suggested that some 2,770 valid ballots were cast in Auserd. But in the absence in the public domain of a more complete overview of electoral outcomes, we must turn elsewhere to assess the reforms in the light of their own goals.

On the question of whether the SNC became more representative, the reforms ushered in a changing of the guard to a considerable degree. The senior electoral official whom I interviewed proudly shared the official calculations that, of the elected MPs, 18.86 percent were graduates, 34.61 percent were women, 57.67 percent were young people, and 61.53 percent were new to the role. As regards the representation of women, the reform of electoral constituencies and the quota have been seen as successful (Rossetti 2008). Indeed, of the total fifty-three members of the SNC elected in 2008, eighteen were female. As a proportion, this is all the more impressive when it is recalled that fifteen of the seats were open only for male candidates (the army and the Consultative Council) and that the nominated candidate for Head of the SNC was male. Of the remaining thirty-seven seats, four were reserved for women (the Women's Union), so, of the thirty-three seats that either female or male candidates could in practice compete to gain, women won fourteen—without even fielding candidates for at least four of those thirty-three seats (there were no female candidates in Rabouni).

These figures notwithstanding, the high proportion of female MPs overall, and in those seats potentially open to competition between female and male candidates, should not be equated with electoral success in other criteria such as actual gains in the number of seats previously held by men and now held by women and even increases in the number of voters willing to prefer a female candidate to a male candidate. The design of the electoral constituencies meant that, in practice, most electoral constituencies were polarized along gendered lines. The *wilāyāt* and February 27 camp were predominantly female constituencies. For instance, the head of the electoral committee in one *dairah* in Auserd estimated there were about thirty men registered to vote there. The quota system was, therefore, introduced in constituencies where there was a clear majority of female voters in the first place. It did little, then, to put to the test whether men were more willing to choose female candidates over male candidates.

The hike in 2008 from twelve to eighteen women MPs was not necessarily due to more voters choosing female candidates where previously they had chosen male colleagues. Extra seats became available to women thanks to reform to the constituencies. The Women's Union's representation rose from one to four seats, granting three more seats for women. Two further seats were allotted to the *wilāyāt*, one each to Smara and Dakhla, respectively. Thus, when these constituencies returned four female MPs each, an advance on the two each had returned in 2006, in fact, arguably only one seat in each *wilāyah* had moved from male to female occupancy. The fourth seat was the extra seat that had been created for the 2008 elections, so technically was not a shift from male to female occupancy. One further seat moved from male to female occupancy in Elayoune (which returned three female members). But a seat moved from female to male occupancy in the women's school, February 27. The overall number of female MPs was completed by the incumbent member for the Young People's Union, who achieved 100 percent of the available votes, even gaining the vote(s) of her opponent(s). The electoral constituencies of the mass unions were formed of the executive members of the Union in question. Thus, these elections may have been fought in constituencies where the number of voters did not surpass double figures. These were hardly the most contested of constituencies, then, and exceptional results such as obtaining 100 percent of the vote plausibly arise from that circumstance.

Overall, then, although the gain in seats for female candidates between the two Parliaments may have been six seats, the electoral design introduced three new women-only seats and two new seats in female-dominated constituencies. Much was gained for women through the manipulation of electoral constituencies. The extent to which changes in voting patterns increased the number of women elected remains largely unknown in the public domain. That no women even stood as candidates in Rabouni is a sign that there was still far to go in women taking themselves and each other, and being taken by men, as serious candidates for political office in some contexts. Indeed, it should be noted that the quota system never achieved a popular mandate in the 2007 PGC, where it was rejected. It only came into effect by presidential decree in the absence of a sitting SNC between the PGC and the SNC's reelection. The quota remained highly contested throughout its application, including among certain women who rejected the idea of a "gift" from "the state."

Skepticism notwithstanding, the increased representation of women, the impression given by the 2008 results of women's electoral success, and the 2008 quota design that obliged female-dominated electorates to vote for at least two women may have helped normalize the idea of women serving in high political office, and thereby contributed to a long-term change in voting patterns and greater support for future female candidates. Indeed, where the 2007 PGC rejected the use of a quota to boost female representation, the 2011 PGC went on to approve the use of quotas to support women's representation in political office.[9] In 2014, a female candidate, standing without a quota, was elected to represent the previously male-dominated Rabouni.

There was a noticeable rise in the number of candidates and elected MPs who were "young." But the rise in the representation of women and young people must be problematized as evidence that the SNC had become more "representative." Thanks to the representation of the Women's and the Young People's Union, women and young people were already social categories defined as deserving guaranteed representation. The design of the electoral constituencies and the introduction of the qualifications for candidacy may have made the SNC more inclusive of the social categories that the state-movement was already prepared to recognize as deserving of guaranteed political representation. But they did little to promote the candidacy of social groups still taboo to name as potentially needing greater political representation, such as artisans, former slaves, and freedmen. The candidacy of members of these groups was legitimized to the extent that, if they met the criteria, they bore the stamp of the state-movement's approval. But potential continuing stigma against them was not addressed specifically.

In another respect, even though the reforms made political office more inclusive of selected groups, at the same time they made political representation more exclusive, as those who could not meet the criteria were now disqualified from candidacy. The opportunity to undertake higher education or a high-ranking administrative/political career is restricted in any society. In the state-movement, students had the chance to study without fees and with support toward accommodation and, sometimes, living costs, in Algeria and other countries with "friendly" relations with the state-movement. Each student of wage-earning age was, nevertheless, one fewer wage earner for a family back in the camps who might sorely need that person's wage-earning capacity. The late revolutionary period, in which many families relied for survival on members engaging in fields of economic activity that precluded the completion of higher education or full-time professional and/or political careers in the camps, exacerbated the gap between those who could afford to undertake education and work for the state-movement and those who could not. The 2008 electoral reforms were disenfranchizing for the latter. The reforms therefore made political representation in the state-movement more inclusive *and* more exclusive at the same time.

What of the reforms' attempts to diminish the influence of *qabīlah* relations on the casting of votes? In an interview after the elections, one official was confident that "Most winning candidates do not have a local tribal base. We can see this." In the absence of detailed information in the public domain about voters and votes cast, such claims are hard to evaluate independently. Some refugees still felt that tribalism led to discrimination: I came to know of one (unsuccessful) candidate in the *wilāyāt* from an artisan background, who said with despondency after the election, "The problem is tribalism." While I had heard some voters discuss their chosen candidates in terms of profession and qualification, I heard others reel off lists of preferred candidates to each other by tribe. Perhaps what can be said is that, given the different forms of knowledge and grounds for qualification voters faced, the reforms undermined the potential influence of *qabīlah* relations on votes and gave voters viable options for choosing candidates on other grounds.

## Democratic Casualties

I have suggested that the 2008 electoral reforms belong to a trajectory of attempts to accommodate a democratic mandate in the camps. This trajectory is a complex instance in the palimpsest of the state-movement's engagement with *qabīlah* relations. In a limited arena (the alleged *jamāʿah* legacy), *qabīlah* relations were courted for explicit visibility in the palimpsest on the grounds that they showed how Sahrawis were "democratic before democracy" (see Chapter 2). Otherwise, the broad thrust of the state-movement's position was to seek to displace *qabīlah* relations on the grounds that they were (mostly) incompatible with democratic political relations. In such a context, the possibility that candidates might come to be elected on the grounds of *qabīlah* loyalties was an unwelcome irruption in the palimpsest. One strategy for dealing with this possibility was to seek to minimize any effect through the use of multiple-member constituencies and ballots, as we have seen was the case in the 2008 elections.

This was one of a number of strategies of implicit recognition of and tolerance for managed "reappearances" of *qabīlah* relations. Arguably, one such strategy entailed covert arrangements intended to ensure that ministerial positions represented a broad range of *qabā'il*. For instance, in 2007–2008, the positions of president, prime minister, and head of the SNC were distributed between the three broad, and traditionally rival groupings of *qabā'il* across Western Sahara and adjacent territories, namely, the Tekna, Rgaybāt, and Awlād Delīm (see Chapter 1). Some refugees at the time interpreted this as a means of representing the three main groupings of *qabā'il* in the highest levels of the state-movement. Likewise, some refugees assumed that the president and prime minister sought to represent a range of *qabā'il* among ministers. "It is like Lebanon," one Sahrawi student (of political science) told me, seeing in Lebanon's prescribed allotment of some public offices on a confessional basis a parallel to an alleged implicit distribution of office in the state-movement on the basis of *qabīlah* membership.

This covert policy was believed by some to operate widely in civil service appointments. One siesta in the summer of 2008, I was among a group of young women taking refuge from the heat in a room with an air conditioning unit run from a generator. One of the young women was too chatty to sleep and recounted to her friend the story of how she believed she had been passed over for a desirable public sector post so that the post could go to a member of a small *qabīlah*. She herself was from the largest unit referred to, in the camps, as a *qabīlah*. "It is better," she added, apparently with nonchalance, "that they mess things up for one person rather than for a whole *qabīlah*." The existence of such a policy, of course, does not feature in official state-movement discourses. But there seem few grounds on which to expect that the camps might be exempt from the "political tribalism" affecting the distribution of political offices that has been noted elsewhere in MENA (Ayubi 1995: 242).

The palimpsest effect, through which *qabīlah* relations were construed as both a threat *and*, at the other extreme (the alleged *jamā'ah* legacy), a support to democratic political relations, invites reconsideration of the question of the relationship between tribes and democracy. The simultaneous rejection and embracing of *qabīlah* relations in the state-movement's attempted construction of democratic relations destabilizes skepticism that "tribes are bad for democracy." There is far more creativity at play from politicized actors in the making, and breaking, of relationships through which tribes come to be experienced as antithetical to *or* supportive of democratic projects. The character of political relations beyond the presence of tribes per se affects any particular manifestation of the relationship between tribes and democracy.

Just as the case of the state-movement destabilizes the notion that tribes are bad for democracy, so it revisits the question of whether there can be democratic relations in a state of exception such as the camps and in particular whether multiple parties are necessary for meaningful elections. In the camps, pluralization was introduced to elections through a number of means other than via multiple parties, confronting voters with choice and competition and leading to uncertainty of outcome. If it has already been shown that multiparty paraphernalia is not in and of itself sufficient to guarantee democratic participation (Englund 2002), then elections in the camps suggest how it is possible to have pluralized elections without multiple parties. It emerges that, even in a space of exception such as the camps, possibilities for democratic political relations can be created. There can be a polis in exile.

While this may be the case, the experience of democratic relations in a state of exception is necessarily constrained by those circumstances. Yet perhaps an experience of constraint, if extreme in a state of exception, is not a distinguishing feature of democratic projects in such circumstances. Rather, the project of democracy itself might be inherently prone to "democratic casualties"—imperfect accommodations that see regrettable fallouts of a mandate that aims to deepen democratic relations but whose priorities in selected areas entail the neglect of others. The 2008 reforms generated such democratic casualties. Trying to legitimize candidates whose age, gender, or background might otherwise have given them little chance of being taken seriously, the reforms excluded those whose circumstances did not lend themselves toward a career in the administration or public services of the state-movement. They made political representation in the camps *both* more inclusive *and* more exclusive at the same time.

Rather than being specific to a state of exception, democratic casualties are surely familiar to citizens of democratic projects elsewhere. Each society engaging in a project of democracy makes compromises, sets priorities, and lives with its own democratic casualties. Debate among the citizens of any democratic project, whether it takes place in the media, *qaṭ* chews, tea ceremonies, cafés, or pubs, will at any time offer a snapshot of the democratic casualties with which those citizens wrestle. The casualties may become all the more obvious in a time of the redrawing of the rule book, such as was the case for the electoral reforms in the camps in 2008.

What may characterize experiences of democratic relations in a state of exception, at least in the Sahrawi refugee case, is that the scale of democratic casualties is taken to an extreme, resulting in the constraints of which Sahrawi refugees, and many of their observers, are so critical. If Sahrawi refugees, by not abandoning the state-movement and its support for self-determination, tolerated these constraints, this was, in a way, their consent to bear a democratic casualty on an unusual scale. Committed to pursuing self-determination through the democratic means of a referendum, the refugee community lived without immediate freedoms of other kinds, in the hope that—thereby avoiding the potential schisms of multiple parties that, they feared, might weaken the liberation movement—they might still enjoy an overarching democratic freedom that, once attained, might lead to greater freedoms across the board. From this perspective, a great obstacle to the advancement of democratic relations in the camps is the lack of international political support for a referendum on self-determination—a "democratic deficit" that cannot be laid on Sahrawis' shoulders. The international political community's sense of accountability to the Sahrawi people and their acknowledged right to self-determination has been poor. The lack of political freedoms in the camps must be recognized, but a concern with exposing democratic deficits in the Sahrawi refugee case should surely not remain silent about the unaccountable forms of power in the international community that proclaim rights, without addressing the question of the responsibility to see that the enjoyment of those rights is not impeded.

In the 2008 SNC elections, the democratic casualties were not only those persons whose position within the political, economic, and social realities of that historical moment excluded them in the new rules of the game. Some of those who also became casualties were the pioneers of advances under the old rules of the game. Fatma, with whose story I opened my discussion of democratic relations in the camps, was not reelected to office in 2008. She narrowly missed making it, coming seventh in the list for six seats. When I returned to visit her in her home to inquire about her views of the recently completed elections, I asked her if she would stand again. She paused, reflectively, before answering: "If circumstances permit."

In February 2012, I returned to the camps, allowing me to observe the SNC elections as they played out in the again updated rules of the game. Having heard that Fatma was going to stand again for elections, I returned to her home to interview her. I remembered well her lively reception from the floor during the *nadwah* in 2008, when her opening poem had met with intense applause and ululation. I found her home as calm and tidy as I remembered it. Fatma herself was seated and breastfeeding her child of a few months. We discussed what each of us had done in the time since the last elections. She had been appointed to a senior administrative position in Rabouni but had chosen to stand for election in her *dairah*, rather than in her place of work. When the results came in, Fatma was not elected.

# Conclusion: Revolution as Moral Contract

This book has approached state power and sovereignty as a set of social relations, and in doing so has explored how the social relations of one project of sovereignty can be remade into those of another. In Sahrawi refugees' state-movement, a fusion of liberation movement and partially recognized state, the social relations of one project of sovereignty—tribes in specific historical circumstances in what became Western Sahara—were remade into the social relations of an alternative project of sovereignty, state power.

This remaking of sovereignty was complex, acquiring the characteristics of a palimpsest. Initially, as explored in Part I, the state-movement pursued aspirations to overwrite and obscure the social relations of tribes. It created new administrative units as alternative forms of segmentation; it moved activities out of tents, where *qabīlah* relations had been nurtured, into a tangible public domain, where the social relations of state power were fostered. The exception to this overwriting of tribes was an instance of "trompe-l'oeil." A particular aspect of *qabīlah* relations, the *jamā'ah* or tribal council, was deliberately configured as an alleged preexisting democratic heritage, on which the state-movement could draw to legitimize its own claims to democratic practice.

Despite these aspirations to overwrite tribes, close attention to three arenas of the social relations of sovereignty—deciding on the state of exception, a monopoly over legitimate coercion deployed to appropriate resources, and the management of (in)equalities—suggested that in each of these arenas the state-movement undertook compromises. Part II thus explored how, rather than merely rejecting the social relations of tribes, the state-movement reworked these social relations to pursue its own goals of governance. In the process, popular justice rose and fell, the state-movement innovated its own form of taxation, and marriage practices were reinvented.

In contrast to these aspirations and compromises, there were also dilemmas of unruly irruptions of *qabīlah* relations. These dilemmas were perceived as disturbing both by officers of the state-movement and by lay refugees. Part III examined how the refugee community was perturbed by the possibility that a marketizing economy and voting in elections created new opportunities for putting tribal loyalties before revolutionary and nationalist goals.

My depiction of the aspirations, compromises, and dilemmas in Sahrawi refugees' remaking of sovereignty highlights broader theoretical implications: for sovereignty and state power, for exile, and for revolution.

When sovereignty is approached as a set of social relations, state power appears as a particular, but not exclusive, ethnographic form of the social relations of sovereignty. Familiar notions can be problematized, specifically that certain *forms* of sovereign power, such as claimed monopolies on the state of exception and on legitimate coercion to appropriate resources, might be specific to state power (Weber 1965; Schmitt 1985). Instead, the state-movement's recycling of the social relations of tribes as it sought to claim monopolies on the state of exception and on legitimate coercion to appropriate resources suggests how claimed monopolies in these areas may pertain to other projects of sovereignty—such as tribes at specific historical moments in Western Sahara.

The state-movement's pursuit of a monopoly on legitimate coercion through the conscription of refugees' labor and the redistribution of rations suggests the broader role of both appropriation and redistribution in Euro-American and North African notions of the tax-extracting state. The state-movement's innovation on classic taxation via labor conscription and rations distribution also invites us to revisit the relationship between sovereignty, people and territory. Territory, so important in Weberian conceptions of the sovereignty of state power, is claimed by the state-movement, but is only partially available (in the form of the Polisario-controlled areas of Western Sahara). In practical terms, this territory is too distant to be accessible on a daily basis to the refugees. Consequently, the social relations of sovereignty in the Sahrawi refugee camps play out between persons, that is, between governing authorities and governed constituencies (Sneath 2007). But, like the social relations of property, the social relations of sovereignty play out *between* persons *in relation* to things, or resources. If these resources may often take the ethnographic form of territory—the presence of which has been taken for granted in Weberian approaches to state power—in Sahrawis' case of state power in exile, other resources, such as refugees' labor and rations, became the resources around which the social relations of sovereignty operated.

On the question of governing authorities working in exile, the Sahrawi refugee camps suggest how displacement is not necessarily an obstacle to the operation of the social relations of sovereignty. Political relations in the camps go beyond the scenario of a government-in-exile—an exiled government that is displaced from territory and population. The case of the camps calls for a more expansive term for the (displaced) practice of state power and governance: what I call "governance-in-exile." As refugees' electoral experiences show, governance-in-exile is not restricted to "bare life," persons whose rights can be violated with impunity, but can host a polis, albeit with democratic casualties.

With Sahrawi refugees having consistently and explicitly conceptualized their remaking of sovereignty as a revolution (*thawrah*), their experiences also invite reflection on the notion of revolution itself. To conclude, I look back at the preceding chapters in the light of wider reflection on revolution and suggest how Sahrawis' and other revolutions can be understood as a moral contract.

## Revolution as Moral Contract

Revolution is once again becoming the subject of scholarly debate in the wake of the Arab Spring. As Bjorn Thomassen (2012) points out, the study of revolution has generally been dominated by political scientists and historians who focus on how and why revolutions happen. Anthropological insights from the ethnographic study of revolutions, Thomassen asserts, have not been brought together into a coherent field of knowledge.

Influential discussion of revolution has tended to assume that what defines a revolution is the aim of capturing of state power (for example, Tilly 1993).[1] Yet such state-centrism has also been tempered. As discussed earlier (Chapter 5), for Theda Skocpol (1979), it is useful to distinguish social revolution on the grounds that, unlike a coup d'état, the aim is not merely to establish a new governing authority. The aim is instead more far-reaching: to change the way that the state is structured and the class structure that is legitimized and reproduced by the state. We also saw that Donald Donham (1999), taking further the implications of Skocpol's approach, understands revolution as the remaking of microsocial relations, over and over again.

Historian Abdel Razzaq Takriti (2013) echoes such an anthropological approach when, arguing against state-centrism in accounts of revolution, he sees revolution in terms of a process or set of practices—which can have taken place even when, ultimately, state power is not definitively captured.

If revolution is a process, then anthropologists have examined useful ways of framing this process: as the remaking of microsocial relations (Donham 1999); as a liminal moment for those involved (see Thomassen 2012); as self-sacrifice (Holbraad 2014). Writing of Sahrawis' revolution in particular, Sophie Caratini (2003) interprets their revolution as the formation of a new social contract between governed persons and governing authorities, focused specifically on the elimination and replacement of tribes as a governing authority.

Such processual interpretations of revolution have inspired the framing of revolution explored here. The process of revolution, at least for Sahrawi refugees, entailed in the first instance remaking the social relations of sovereignty—with aspirations to overwrite the social relations of tribes. This is not to suggest that a remaking of the social relations of sovereignty would be the exclusive prerogative of revolutions. But a revolutionary setting, characterized by the attempt to reorganize governing authorities and legitimate forms of social inequalities, might well prove an extreme case for such remaking.

Nevertheless, as this book has explored, tribes were not merely eliminated in the Sahrawi revolution and its remaking of the social relations of sovereignty. There were compromises whereby the social relations of tribes were a resource drawn upon and recycled in the making of the social relations of state power. There were also dilemmas whereby tribes reappeared in locally unwelcome ways. This raises the question whether the re-emergence of tribes in such compromises and dilemmas implies that, ultimately, Sahrawis' revolution—if understood as a new social contract eliminating tribes—had "failed"?

Rather than indicating "failure," perhaps the nuanced re-emergence of tribes illuminates a deeper process underpinning refugees' experience of revolution. This process might be understood in terms of another kind of "contract," not so much a social contract focused on the elimination of a previous governing authority but what I call a "moral contract." According to the terms of this moral contract, both refugees and the state-movement—governed constituencies and governing authorities—expected of each other that the aims of revolution, such as national liberation and the achievement of self-determination, should be given priority, at moments of potentially conflicting interests, over alternative interests such as personal material advancement or the interests of a particular family or tribe.

Revolution as moral contract would not necessarily demand that there be no role for the social relations of tribes, then. Rather, as the palimpsest of the combined overwriting and reappearance of the social relations of tribes suggests, both the social relations of tribes and those of the state movement could coexist. The crucial question would be, in moments of potential conflict, which were given priority.

In their navigation of daily life, refugees seemed to acknowledge the coexistence, rather than the incompatibility, of the social relations of tribes and those of state power. For instance, when I was in the pasturelands, one day a car came to our encampment. The car pulled up close to one of our tents, and the male driver approached my host aunt. Both their greetings were inflected with a sense of anticipation. What did the driver want? After a few rounds of greeting, he broke off to ask, "Whose tents are these?" My host aunt hesitated, before answering "We're the tents of the Sahara," using the common abbreviation for "Western Sahara." The man replied, with a hint of impatience, "Yes, we're all tents of the Sahara, but whose tents are you?" The emphasis of his question was now clear. He wanted to know to which tribe those of us living in the tents belonged. My host aunt replied, naming the tribe to which she and her brother belonged. The visitor immediately followed up, by explaining that he was looking for tents that belonged to another tribe—had we seen them, or did we know in which direction they might be found? In this exchange, my host aunt had replied with impeccable revolutionary sensibility, avoiding the mention of specific tribes. The man's acquiescence that, indeed, all tents were those of the people of Western Sahara and his insistence on needing to know the specific tribe to be able to find the people for whom he was looking showed how, in practical terms, these identities did not have to be mutually exclusive.

The question of prioritization remains, though. Another conversation, back in the refugee camps, suggests how refugees could signal to themselves and to others their awareness that persons belonged both to tribes and to a national community engaged in a liberation movement—and that there was, nevertheless, an expected order of importance between them. On one occasion when Zaynabu's nephew, Salama, was visiting her home in Smara camp, he asked me about my recent trip to another camp. As we talked, he realized that he knew someone whom I had met there. He exclaimed, "Haa! You know so-and-so? He's 'my big tribesman' [*wuld 'ammī al-kabīr*]." *Wuld 'amm*, the preferred turn of phrase in Hassaniya for father's brother's son (FBS), was often used in everyday conversations between refugees. I was familiar with the distinction made between a classificatory FBS or fellow tribesman (*wuld 'amm*), and a direct FBS (*wuld 'amm ẓahran*, literally "through the back"). But I had never heard of *wuld 'ammī al-kabīr*, my "big" *wuld 'amm*.

In Hassaniya, *al-kabīr* is used as a qualifier signifying, literally, greater age or size, and metaphorically greater importance. For example, a person's natal tent will be referred to as *al-khaymah*. The tent of one's grandparents—which is both older, by definition, but also the site for a greater range of relatives (grandchildren, uncles, aunts) to meet and, therefore, socially more important—is referred to as *al-khaymah al-kabīrah*. *Wuld 'ammī al-kabīr* employed the second nuance of *al-kabīr*, meaning of greater importance. It turned out that the two young men in question were not *awlād 'amm* at all in the sense of being fellow tribesmen. But having studied together abroad for long years in Cuba, they referred to each other and to other Sahrawis who had studied in Cuba in this way as a joke.

This joke worked in a number of ways. On one level, the young men were criticizing people who felt a connection on the basis of common *qabīlah* membership and simultaneously saying that their connection based on friendship was stronger and more important than that: it was *al-kabīr*. As Salama went on to explain to me, "We say it because we don't like tribalism." The way these young Sahrawis used the phrase, then, was intended as a means of undermining the predominance of regular tribalism. But the phrase also worked to recognize simultaneously both the relationships of common membership in a *qabīlah* and the relationships of shared membership in something being valued as more important, the social relations of the state-movement and its nation-state building project. This phrase made sense to an audience in the camps in a context where everyone was aware of these spheres of membership. The phrase signaled that tribalism might well exist there but was still less important than the encompassing project of common membership in the state-movement. Finally, this joke was especially nuanced because it reclaimed some of the very vocabulary that had been prohibited in the initial phases of the ban on tribalism. The phrase both brought the vocabulary of *wuld 'amm* back into use—as a means of resisting the state-movement's most extreme projects of social control—at the same time as it conceded acquiescence with the ultimate goals of the state-movement to make nationalism more important than *qabīlah* membership. Like the incident in the pasturelands, the phrase *wuld 'ammī al-kabīr* suggests that there is room for the coexistence of the social relations of the state-movement and those of the *qabīlah*. But *wuld ʿammī al-kabīr* clarifies an expected hierarchy between them—the state-movement was *al-kabīr*, that is, more important than *qabīlah* relations.

The notion that a moral contract underpinned Sahrawis' revolution helps explain some of the points of controversy that arose in the refugee camps, explored in the preceding chapters. When the state-movement distributed extra rations along what I called a "parallel" system of redistribution, to help refugees who faced exceptional costs for events such as a wedding or a naming ceremony, refugees did not criticize such practice as a form of corruption (Chapter 4). Rather, I argued, such parallel redistribution appeared to refugees, in the context of local historical practices of redistribution, as the legitimate responsibility of governing authorities. Such parallel distribution only became problematic in the camps once the state-movement suspected that external auditing authorities from the international aid sector would find evidence of "corruption" in such practices. Yet, if officials of the state-movement were perceived by refugees to be using resources made available to them by virtue of their official position to advance their own personal interests—for instance, reserving coveted places to study or travel abroad for relatives—this was indeed criticized by refugees as a form of corruption. The meaningful form of corruption for refugees, it would seem, was an instance when the moral contract to put national interests above other interests, such as those of personal gain or the *qabīlah*, was contravened. "Parallel" aid distribution did not contravene that moral contract and was not subject to local criticism. Nepotism, however, did contravene that moral contract and, where perceived, was the target of widespread criticism.

The state-movement, too, can be seen as expecting refugees to keep their own side of the moral contract. In asking refugees to hold back from sumptuous wedding celebrations (Chapter 5), it expected refugees to put national interests before the desire to stage a wedding that would honor guests—and perhaps incite their envy. The moments of greatest mutual disappointment between refugees and the state-movement occurred when each perceived of the other that the moral contract of putting revolutionary priorities first had been contravened. Which issues and goals should be made into priorities could of course be under debate. As the old joke from the 1980s had expressed (Chapter 2), the perceived interests of political service might be construed at given moments to be in competition with administrative service. At such moments of tension between the apparent interests of a liberation movement and a state power, when refugees faced competing pressures in their bid to be revolutionaries and citizens, the moral contract was painfully exposed.

Discontent at the contravention of an underlying moral contract was ultimately a sign that expectations of that moral contract persisted. The moral contract proved more enduring over time, then, than the notion of a new social contract to eradicate the importance of tribes. Indeed, the terms of the new social contract modified over time, with tribes making an at least partial comeback. If revolutionary efforts continued, after (at the time of writing) some forty years in which the ultimate goal of self-determination had not been achieved, then the enduring moral contract seems to have proved an effective means, at least here, of keeping revolution going. In a situation of what we might call "revolution fatigue," where, after years caught in the dual liminality of exile and revolution, would-be revolutionaries tired of living in exceptional conditions and pined after grander weddings and more comfortable homes, the moral contract—and through it the revolution—persisted.

A moral contract requiring that the broadest level of collective interests be placed above rival, more specific interests may not be exclusive to situations of revolution. Indeed, the terms explored here as a moral contract might also be helpful for understanding other programs for social change, of various political hues. If potentially relevant beyond the context of revolution, perhaps a moral contract putting collective interests above more specific interests is as constitutive of revolution as are the remaking of social relations (Donham 1999) and the reorganization of state power and its attendant inequalities (Skocpol 1979).

Even when the eyes of the world turned to observe revolutions across the Arab world, the Sahrawis' revolution, for all its nearly forty years, remained probably the least known of the region's revolutionary movements. Yet this seemingly invisible revolution can project visibility: it throws into relief the intersection of revolution, a moral contract, and the remaking of sovereignty.

# APPENDIX 1. NOTES ON TRANSLITERATION AND TRANSCRIPTION

For modern standard Arabic words, I follow the American Library Association-Library of Congress system, except where I have adapted a common English spelling, for example, *dairah*, *dawāir* for the districts in Sahrawi refugee camps.

For words with meanings specific to the Hassaniya dialect of Arabic, or words that are used in Hassaniya but not in modern standard Arabic, I use the American Library Association-Library of Congress system to transliterate the pronunciation of words.

For place names such as Smara, Tifariti, and so forth and for names of interlocutors, I have opted for the most readable form in English.

# APPENDIX 2. TRIBES IN WESTERN SAHARA (FROM HODGES 1982)

Hodges's spelling and terminology have been retained.

| *Tribe* | *Sub-tribe* | *Fraction* |
|---|---|---|
| Reguibat ech-Charg or Lgouacem | Ahel Brahim Ou Daoud | Ahel Sidi Allal |
| | | Ahel Belqacem Ou Brahim |
| | | Sellam |
| | | Selalka |
| | | Ahel Lahsen Ou Hmad |
| | | Lehmeidenet |
| | | Oulad Sidi Hamad |
| | | Jenha |
| | Lebouihat | Ahel Daddah |
| | | Ahel Qadi |
| | | Ahel Haioun |
| | | Ahel Sidi Ahmed Ben Yahya |
| | | Lemrasguia |
| | | Ahel Sidi Abdellah Ben Moussa |
| | Laiaicha | Ahel Belal |
| | | Ahel Beilal |
| | Foqra | Ahel Ahmen Ben Lahsen |
| | | Ahel Lemjed |
| | | Ahel Taleb Hamad |
| | | Rema |
| | | Lemnasra |
| | | Seddadgha |
| | | Oulad Sidi M'hamed |

(continued)

| *Tribe* | *Sub-tribe* | *Fraction* |
|---|---|---|
| Reguibat es-Sahel | Oulad Moussa | Oulad el-Qadi |
| | | Ahel Bellao |
| | | Oulad Moueya |
| | | Oulad Lahsen |
| | | Oulad Hossein |
| | Souaad | Ahel Brahim Ben Abdallah |
| | | Ahel Ba Brahim |
| | | El-Gherraba |
| | | Oulad Bou Said |
| | | Ahel Khali Yahya |
| | Lemouedenin | Ahel Ahmadi |
| | | Sereirat |
| | Oulad Daoud | Ahel Salem |
| | | Ahel Tenakha |
| | | Ahel Baba Ammi |
| | Oulad Borhim | |
| | Oulad Cheikh | Ahel Delimi |
| | | Ahel Baba Ali |
| | | Lemouissat |
| | | Lahouareth |
| | | Lahseinat |
| | | Ahel el-Hadj |
| | Thaalat | Ahel Dekhil |
| | | Ahel Meiara |
| | | Ahel Rachid |
| | Oulad Taleb | Oulad Ben Hossein |
| | | Oulad Ba Brahim |
| | | Oulad Ba Aaissa |
| | | Oulad Ba Moussa |
| | | Ahel Dera |
| Arosien | Oulad Khalifa | |
| | Oulad Sidi Bou Mehdi | |
| | Ahel Sidi Brahim | |
| Oulad Tidrarin | Ahel Taleb Ali | |
| | Oulad Moussa | |
| | Oulad Ali | |
| | Labourat | |
| | El-Faaris | |
| | Lahseinat | |
| | Oulad Souleiman | |

| Tribe | Sub-tribe | Fraction |
|---|---|---|
| | Ahel Esteila | |
| | Ahel Hadj | |
| | Lidadsa | |
| Filala | Oulad Sidi Ahmed Filali | |
| | Ahel Ben Mehdi | |
| | Ahel Faki Ben Salah | |
| Fouikat | Ahel Cheheb | |
| | Ahel Lagoueyed | |
| | Ahel Abdahou | |
| | Aila Ould Said | |
| Ait Lahsen (Tekna) | Id Daoud Ou Abdallah | |
| | Injouren | |
| | Ait Bou Meghout | |
| | Ait Yahya | |
| | Rouimiat | |
| | Ait Bou Guezzaten | |
| | Ait Hassein | |
| | Ait Saad | |
| Izarguien (Tekna) | Echtouka | |
| | El-Guerah | |
| | Ait Said | |
| Oulad Delim | Oulad Tegueddi | |
| | Loudeikat | |
| | Oulad Khaliga | |
| | Serahenna | |
| | Oulad Ba Amar | |
| Oulad Bou Sbaa | Oulad el-Hadj Ben Demouiss | |
| | Oulad Sidi Mohammed Ben | |
| | Demouiss | |
| | Oulad Brahim | |
| Skarna | Ahel Bakar | |
| | Adhahla | |
| | Oulad Moumen | |
| Taoubalt | Oulad Sidi Djemaa | |
| | Oulad Khelaif | |
| Lemiar | Ahel Sidi Amar | |
| | Ahel Brahim | |
| | Ahel Ahmed | |

(continued)

| *Tribe* | *Sub-tribe* | *Fraction* |
|---|---|---|
| Mejat | El-Grona | |
| | El-Beyed | |
| | Ahel Mohammed Ben Brahim | |
| | Ahel Ali Salem | |
| Imeraguen | | |
| Menasir | Oulad Ali Serg | |
| | Oulad Mohammed Aidi | |
| Chenagla | | |
| Ahel Cheikh Ma el-Ainin | | |
| Ahel Berikallah | | |

# NOTES

## Introduction: The Social Relations of Sovereignty

1. The classical Arabic for pasturelands would be *bādiyah*, but in Hassaniya it is pronounced *badīah*.

2. In this book, I follow UN usage and refer to the territory over which the Polisario Front and Morocco are in conflict as Western Sahara.

3. For example, tribes were banned in Mauritania in the 1960s and 1970s (Villasante 2006), in Sudan from independence to the 1990s (Casciarri 2006), Somalia in the 1970s (Lewis 1979), the liberation movement in Dhufar, Oman, in the 1960s and 1970s (Takriti 2013), socialist Mozambique (West 2009), and the People's Democratic Republic of Yemen (Lackner 1985).

4. Territory has also been seen as essential to the sovereignty of tribes in some settings in the Middle East, e.g., Weir 2007.

5. Refugees with sufficient resources (in terms of funds and the availability of household members) can visit the pasturelands in Polisario-controlled Western Sahara. Some Sahrawis raise animals there year-round. As of 2007, the state-movement has also encouraged the development of civilian populations in new urban developments in the Polisario-controlled areas of Western Sahara (see Wilson 2014b). Families who move to live in these towns are no longer eligible to receive refugee rations, since they will no longer have crossed an international border and therefore can no longer be classified as refugees according to current definitions.

6. For a discussion of anthropological approaches to property relations, see, e.g., Pottage and Mundy 2004.

7. I retain the transliteration in common use for the Djemaa.

8. For a detailed account of Sahrawi nationalism and the early history of Polisario, see Hodges 1983. Sahrawi nationalism has received considerable scholarly attention (e.g., San Martín 2010; Zunes and Mundy 2010). Recognizing the importance of Sahrawi nationalism as a driving force for Sahrawis' pursuit of self-determination, I focus the attention of my ethnographic inquiry on questions of governance in the Sahrawi refugee camps, which incorporate and transcend a nationalist agenda.

9. On the proceedings and findings of the International Court of Justice, see Hodges 1983: 368–72; Joffé 1986.

10. For a discussion of UN attempts to find a political solution to the Western Sahara conflict, see Zunes and Mundy 2010.

11. The report on Western Sahara of the UN High Commissioner for Human Rights, officially released only to Morocco, Algeria, and Polisario, was unofficially made available on a pro-self-determination website, http://www.arso.org/OHCHRrep2006en.pdf, accessed January 14, 2014.

12. On the politics of Morocco's position on Western Sahara, and the interests of Morocco's and Polisario's allies, see Hodges 1983; Shelley 2004; Zunes and Mundy 2010; Willis 2012; Roussellier and Boukhars 2014.

13. Algeria's assertions that the refugees, though located in Algerian territory, fall under the jurisdiction of SADR for the protection of their rights do not conform with international law (Human Rights Watch 2014: 19).

14. On the politics of refugee movements to and from Moroccan-controlled Western Sahara, see Wilson 2014b.

15. For an account of some refugees' involvement in smuggling, including drug smuggling, see Scheele 2012: 105, 209. On SADR's prosecution of refugees accused of smuggling drugs, see Human Rights Watch 2014.

16. In some cases, I have also changed biographical details to maintain a refugee's anonymity.

## Chapter 1. Hindsight Visions: Tribe and State Power as Projects of Sovereignty

1. On the career of Shaykh Mal'ainīn, see Hodges 1983: 55–60.

2. I am grateful to David Sneath for discussions on this point.

3. As Jacques Berque (1954) noted, the names of tribes in North Africa have proved remarkably long-standing across the centuries.

4. On the relationship between a *qabīlah* and the control of land and water resources, see Caratini 1989b.

5. The lack of a named common ancestor has been noted of other entities referred to as "tribes" in the Middle East (Tapper 1990: 53).

6. A distinction has been observed between religious elites who paid tribute to warrior elites and those who did not but collected their own tribute from protégés (Caro Baroja 1955: 30).

7. For a discussion of the historical presence up to the mid-twentieth century of *igawen* in what would become Western Sahara, see Deubel 2012.

8. Sahrawis serving in the Tropas Nómadas of the Spanish colonial armed forces were permitted to bear arms (Caro Baroja 1955: 33).

9. On different forms of tribute in Mauritania, see Boulay 2003: 70–71 and Bonte 2008: 415–50.

10. This account was given by a member of the Awlād Mousa tribe of the Sahel (west) section of the Rgaybāt.

11. This account was told to me by a member of a Tekna tribe, the Ait Ousa.

12. This account was told by a member of the ʻAyaishi tribe of the Sharg (east) section of the Rgaybāt.

13. See Joseph Chelhod's (1996) essay on *qabīlah* for an alternative interpretation of the relevance of the root *q-b-l*.

## Chapter 2. Revolutionary Foundations: Unmaking Tribes and Making State Power

1. For my description of *firgān*, I draw on Caro Baroja (1955) and Caratini (1989b).

2. See examples of the makeup of *firgān* in Caro Baroja 1955: 195–228.

3. The Popular Revolution disappointed Gaddafi on several counts. People did not take enough interest in the committees and congresses; absenteeism was high among leaders and members; tribal authorities were using congresses to pursue their own interests; and committees prioritized local issues over national concerns (Mattes 1995: 90).

4. Lippert (1985: 8–9) describes how a larger number of committees was reduced to the five mentioned above, with the Justice Committee being the new addition at the time of that reform.

5. Few refugees arrived in exile with their own animals (Hodges 1983: 233).

6. Due to the political sensitivity of support for Polisario in Moroccan-controlled Western Sahara, representatives from the latter could not always attend a PGC in person. At the thirteenth PGC in 2011, representatives from Moroccan-controlled Western Sahara attended the PGC for the first time since 1991 (UN Security Council 2012: 2).

7. Other cases of diasporas being included in the political community of the (perceived) home state power include Eritreans in exile, the Tamil diaspora, and France's parliamentary constituency for its northern European expatriates, established in 2012.

8. Accounts of the 1988 events are rare and usually brief (Zunes 1999; Shelley 2004). Hernández (2001) offers testimonies from former residents of the camps who have gone to Moroccan-controlled areas of Western Sahara.

9. I address the reconfiguration of the *jamāʻah* in judicial spheres in Chapter 3.

10. Es-Sweyih (2001: 78), however, disagrees that there is any resemblance between the *ait arbaʻīn* and the SNC.

11. Such nonrecognition has not necessarily impeded local councils' functioning (Venema and Mguild 2002).

12. See also Joffé's (1995: 150) analysis that Gaddafi's direct democracy can be traced back to his "tribal" upbringing.

## Chapter 3.Unpopular Law: Tribal, Islamic, and State Law and the Fall of Popular Justice

Epigraph: Foucault 1980: 1.

1. There are no publicly available figures produced by the state-movement on the incidence of crime in the refugee camps. In 2008, refugee judges told me there had been five cases of murder in exile. In 2007, rape became a subject of controversy when two men were tried, convicted, and imprisoned for the rape of a woman during a car journey across the open desert between two refugee camps.

2. For an account of conditions in the male prison, see Human Rights Watch 2014.

3. For a wider discussion of techniques whereby the state-movement seeks to claim legitimacy as a governing authority, even in the absence of full legal recognition in international forums, see Wilson and McConnell 2015.

4. For Caro Baroja 1955: 44, the Ait Lahsan (Tekna), Izargiyen (Tekna), Awlād Delīm, Arosien, and Rgaybāt have *'urf.* Nevertheless, the subjection of the Awlād Tidrarīn to the protection of the Awlād Delīm is considered by his interlocutors to have invalidated their *'urf.*

5. For a list of crimes addressed by *'urf*, see Caro Baroja 1955: 43.

6. Elsewhere, Caro Baroja (1955: 24) recognizes a distinction between "civil" and "religious" *shuyūkh* but does not give details of their respective roles.

7. Comparably, elsewhere in MENA, an angry wife becomes "*za'alana*" (Peters 1978: 326) or "*hardane*" (Ginat 1982: 176) or must receive material gifts from her husband if he has offended her (Lhote 1944: 294).

8. In refugees' memories of the early revolutionary period, polygamy was rare. Yaḥḍi also mentioned that the Justice Committee dealt with unpaid debts, with the committee tending to favor "the weakest person."

9. Discussion of popular justice in Libya (Mason 1978; Mayer 1978; Vandewalle 2006), the People's Democratic Republic of Yemen (Lackner 1985), the PLO (Botiveau 1999), and Dhufar's liberation movement (Takriti 2013: 118) leaves questions regarding the relationship between prerevolutionary and revolutionary legal officers and the operation of new legal institutions.

10. On punishments for prohibited sexual relations, see verses 24: 2, 3 of the Qur'an: "The woman and the man guilty of adultery or fornication flog each of them with 100 strips."

11. In the other schools of Islamic law, proof of adulterous sexual relations is either a confession given freely four times or the witnessing of four persons to the sexual act occurring (Schacht 1964: 177).

12. Zuhur (2005: 33) notes, "under applications of Islamic law, rape involved compensation, particularly to a virgin, for the action, and also for the corresponding reduction in her bride price."

13. I do not suggest that SADR sought to apply "Islamic law," however defined. While categories of crime in Islamic law, such as the criminalization of adultery, are

respected in the SADR penal code, the notion of corporal punishments for this and other crimes has not been adopted.

14. Elena Fiddian-Qasmiyeh (2014) has argued that, in its discourse targeting Spanish civil society, the state-movement even seeks to distance itself from Islam.

15. The building of mosques in the refugee camps had been opposed by those refugees who had interpreted their erection as a sign that exile had acquired permanence (see Wilson 2014a). Outside the context of exile, mobile pastoralist Sahrawis pray in the open air, sometimes at places marked for prayer by a row of stones. In Auserd camp, Māghalāha's husband had set up a suitable row of stones beside their tent where he prayed.

16. Nevertheless, an amount is fixed for *diyah* in Malikite jurisprudence (Ben Hounet 2012).

## Chapter 4. Tax Evasion: Appropriation and Redistribution Without Tax or Rent

Epigraph: Schumpeter 1954 [1918]: 7.

1. While conventional routes for tax and rent were inaccessible for the state-movement, these possibilities were not wholly foreclosed. The state-movement raises revenue from contracts sold to petroleum exploitation companies for the prospective right to explore for petroleum in a postconflict Western Sahara (Randi Irwin, personal communication). The state-movement also has camel herds in Polisario-controlled areas of Western Sahara, which were mentioned to me by one Sahrawi diplomat as a potential source of revenue. As internal trade developed in the refugee camps (see Chapter 6), the state-movement began to operate customs houses charging a percentage on goods brought over land from Mauritania to be sold in the camps.

2. I thank Abderahmane Moussaoui for pointing out the nuances of *makhzan*.

3. As the UN does not recognize SADR, it works as a partner not with the SRC but with the Algerian Red Crescent (ARC). The ARC, nevertheless, hands over resources to the SRC.

4. Nicola Cozza (2004, 2010) has discussed the clandestine resale of food aid from the Sahrawi refugee camps in Mauritania.

5. For a critique of the idea that the accurate counting of refugees is necessary for the more effective distribution of aid, see Harrell-Bond, Voutira, and Leopold 1992.

6. Refugees' accounts did not clarify when the practice emerged, but it is likely to have emerged with celebrations on a grander scale in the late revolutionary period.

7. While Algeria had claimed in 1976 that there were 165,000 refugees, from 1982 the UNHCR undertook to provide aid to the 80,000 most "vulnerable" refugees (Zunes and Mundy 2010: 127). Following reports of malnutrition, rations increased in 2000 and 2004, then were reduced again in 2005 (Zunes and Mundy 2010: 128). Malnutrition was reported in the camps for data collected in 2010 (Grijalva-Eternod et al. 2012).

8. I thank Abdel Wedoud ould Cheikh for helpful discussion of shame and requests for hospitality.

9. On the conditions of *mnīḥah*, see Caro Baroja 1955: 103–4; Caratini 1989b: 56–57.

10. On tribute in other hassanophone areas, see Boulay 2003: 70–71; Bonte 2008: 415–50. On tribute among other Bedouin groups, for example, *khūwah*, see Patai 1962; Peters 1990; Al Rasheed 1997.

11. Long-term Tibetan exiles in India have, nevertheless, introduced voluntary taxes, also applied to Tibetans in the diaspora. See McConnell 2016.

12. For critical accounts of life in the camps in the early revolutionary period, see testimonies of those who left to go to live in Moroccan-controlled areas (Hernández 2001).

## Chapter 5. Managing Inequalities: Organizing Social Stratification, or Marriage Reinvented

Epigraph: Giddens 1985: 17.

1. While sumptuary marriage laws and national consternation at expensive weddings are not specific to revolutionary contexts, sumptuary marriage laws have been prominent in several revolutions and liberation movements e.g., China (Yan 2003); Dhufar, Oman (Halliday 1974: 380–81); Eritrea (Wrong 2005); Ethiopia (Donham 1999: 151); Palestine (Jean-Klein 2001); the People's Democratic Republic of Yemen (Lackner 1985: 108, 116).

2. For reviews of the debates on "close" marriage, see Holy 1989 and Tapper and Tapper 1992/1993.

3. The incidence of marriage with first cousins (not exclusively between FBD and FBS) in societies with a preference for close marriage is reported to range between 11 and 64 percent (Bonte 2008: 81).

4. On the role of the required groom-to-bride prestation in the marriage contract in Islam, see Mir-Hosseini 1993: 32–33.

5. For Caro Baroja (1955: 268), a wedding lasted seven days if both spouses were virgins, and three days if both spouses had been married previously. Wedding celebrations in Mauritania vary in length from one to three or seven days (Fortier 2001: 52).

6. On modesty (*ḥishmah*, *saḥwah*) among Hassanophones, see de Chassey 1976 and Mitatre 2009.

7. Some refugees also recalled that the state-movement had arranged some marriages directly, especially between soldiers from the SPLA and women in the camps. I thank Andrea Aasgaard (personal communication) for pointing out that a group of Sahrawis conducted research on this.

8. Refugee interlocutors held that a cash prestation from groom to bride's kin was not acceptable in the camps, although it was practiced in Tindouf.

9. In the four (of five) refugee camps that did not have mains electricity, televisions were run on car batteries charged by imported solar panels.

10. Groom-to-bride prestations may be prohibitively expensive elsewhere; for example, in the 1960s, the marriage prestation for a Bedouin young man in the Naqab was the equivalent or two to three years of family income (Marx 1967: 102–3).

11. Guests and relatives worked for free at weddings. Some more affluent families hired paid workers—in my observations these workers were women from Tindouf—to cook for a wedding feast. In interlocutors' explanations, these women were Algerian, not Sahrawi, and interlocutors also placed these women within a racialized category of dark skinned persons.

12. For a discussion of a wife making a divorce compensation to a husband unwilling to grant a divorce, see Mir-Hosseini 1993: 38–39.

13. Although younger refugees apparently knew little of older marriage prestation practices, in other (selected) contexts, young people were encouraged to identity with past practices as a means of preserving "Sahrawi identity."

14. The speech, which I heard live, was delivered in Arabic. I have translated from the Spanish transcript.

15. I withhold the names of the *qabā'il* named to me, since refugees spoke of this as an internal matter. The shift in the relationship between the state-movement and the *qabīlah* is clear without specific *qabā'il* being named.

16. I never heard that *qabā'il* imposed any punishment for the infringement of their suggested prohibitions.

## Chapter 6. Troubling Markets: Tribes, Gender, and Ambivalent Commodification

1. As Dilley (1992) and others (Mandel and Humphrey 2002; Elyachar 2005) have stressed, there can be no such thing as "the market" but rather historically specific markets in particular settings and cultures.

2. Full discussion of Sahrawi refugees' international migration and how migrants' remittances and physical returns to the camps reshaped social relations there falls beyond the scope of the present study. On Sahrawis' migration to Spain from the 1970s to the 2000s, see Gómez Martín 2011.

3. Refugees also bought and sold at a large weekend market in Tindouf. As a foreigner without access to Tindouf, I did not visit this market myself.

4. The rise of markets in the camps has been studied by Pablo San Martín (2010: 126–69).

5. On the portrayed and actual role of women in the administration of the state-movement, see Allan 2010; Rossetti 2012; Fiddian-Qasmiyeh 2014.

6. The remittance-reliant construction industry in the Sahrawi refugee camps was booming in 2007 and 2008. But in the wake of the global financial crisis in late 2008, remittances from Europe dropped off and construction in the camps suffered.

## Chapter 7. Party-less Democrats: Electing the Best Candidate or the Biggest Tribe

1. In 2012, the constituencies were again revised. February 27 camp, renamed Boujdour, became a *wilāyah* of three seats, the Students' Union was granted a seat, and the Women's Union went back to having one seat.

2. A similar principle of each voter putting forward multiple names is followed in other state-movement elections, such as for the National Secretariat.

3. Debates about the prevalence of authoritarianism, and obstacles to democratization, in MENA are too wideranging to be reviewed here. For a discussion of arguments in the light of the Arab Spring, see Bellin 2012.

4. The Human Rights Watch delegation of 2007 visited both the refugee camps and the Moroccan-controlled areas of Western Sahara. See Human Rights Watch 2008.

5. After 2006, when a leader associated with *khaṭṭ al-shahīd* was perceived to move away from support for self-determination to a more pro-Moroccan position, this group lost credibility in the camps. See Bennani 2006.

6. On the complex circumstances of "returners" from the camps to Moroccan-controlled Western Sahara, see Wilson 2013, 2014b.

7. Refugees whose ancestors had been registered with the French authorities in Algeria, for instance in Tindouf, were able to apply for Algerian passports on those grounds, rather than through the SADR Ministry of Interior.

8. Three people told me that they had taken up all three opportunities to hear from the candidates. All three were women with local administrative responsibilities and so were perhaps giving me the answer that they believed was the ideal answer, especially for a person of their local standing in the state-movement.

9. The 2012 elections altered the quota design, revised constituencies, and saw thirteen female MPs elected.

## Conclusion. Revolution as Moral Contract

1. For other examples of state-centric approaches, see Dunn 1989.

# REFERENCES


Ababsa, Myriam. 2009. "La recomposition des allégeances tribales dans le Moyen-Euphrate syrien (1958–2007)." *Études Rurales* 184 (2): 65–78.

Abdoul, Mohamadou. 2004. "Démocratisation, ethnicité et tribalisme: Jeux identitaires et enjeux politiques en Mauritanie." In *Regards sur la Mauritanie*, ed. Mohamadou Abdoul et al., 15–79. L'Ouest saharien: Cahiers d'études pluridisciplinaires 4. Paris: Harmattan.

Abu-Lughod, Lila. 1986. *Veiled Sentiments: Honour and Poetry in a Bedouin Society.* Berkeley: University of California Press.

———. 1993. *Writing Women's Worlds: Bedouin Stories.* Berkeley: University of California Press.

———. 1999. *Veiled Sentiments: Honor and Poetry in a Bedouin Society.* 2nd ed. Berkeley: University of California Press.

Abu-Mershid, Osama, and Adam Farrar. 2014. "A History of the Conflict in Western Sahara: Myths, Nationalisms, and Geopolitics." In *Perspectives on Western Sahara*, ed. Anouar Boukhars and Jacques Roussellier, 3–27. Lanham, Md.: Rowman & Littlefield.

Agamben, Giorgio. 1998. *Homo Sacer: Sovereign Power and Bare Life.* Trans. Daniel Heller-Roazen. Stanford, Calif.: Stanford University Press.

Agier, Michel. 2002. "Between War and City: Towards an Urban Anthropology of Refugee Camps." *Ethnography* 3 (3): 318–41.

———. 2011. *Managing the Undesirables: Refugee Camps and Humanitarian Government.* Cambridge: Polity.

Allan, Joanna. 2010. "Imagining Sahrawi Women: The Question of Gender in POLISARIO Discourse." *Journal of North African Studies* 15 (2): 189–202.

Al Rasheed, Madawi. 1997. *Politics in an Arabian Oasis: The Rashidis of Saudi Arabia* London: Tauris.

Albergoni, Gianni. 2000. "Écrire la coutume: Une tribu bédouine de Cyrénaïque face à la modernité." *Études Rurales* (155/156): 25–49.

Amnesty International. 2011. *Annual Report 2011: The State of the World's Human Rights.* London: Amnesty International.

Antil, Alain. 2004. "Gérer des élections pluralistes dans le cadre d'une démocratie "imposée": L'exemple des élections d'octobre 2001 en Mauritanie." In *Regards sur la*

*Mauritanie*, ed. Mohamadou Abdoul et al., 91–115. L'Ouest saharien: Cahiers d'études pluridisciplinaires 4. Paris: Harmattan.

Arieff, Alexis. 2012. "Western Sahara." Congressional Research Service. http://www.fas.org/sgp/crs/row/RS20962.pdf, accessed February 17, 2013.

Asad, Talal. 1970. *The Kababish Arabs: Power, Authority and Consent in a Nomadic Tribe*. London: C. Hurst.

Ayoub, Mahmoud M. 1991. *Islam and the Third Universal Theory: The Religious Thought of Mu'ammar al-Qadhdhafi*. London: Kegan Paul International.

Ayubi, Nazih N. 1995. *Over-Stating the Arab State: Politics and Society in the Middle East*. London: Tauris.

Bailey, Clinton. 2009. *Bedouin Law from Sinai and the Negev: Justice Without Government*. New Haven, Conn.: Yale University Press.

Bäschlin, Elisabeth. 2004. "Democratic Institution Building in the Context of a Liberation War: The Example of Western Sahara and Polisario Front." In *New Challenges in Local and Regional Administration*, ed. Max Barlow and Doris Wastl-Walter, 137–53. Aldershot: Ashgate.

Bayart, Jean-François. 1993. *The State in Africa: The Politics of the Belly*. London: Longman.

BBC. 2009. "Turkish PM given hero's welcome." http://www.un.org/ga, accessed February 17, 2009.

Bellin, Eva. 2012. "Reconsidering the Robustness of Authoritarianism in the Middle East: Lessons from the Arab Spring." *Comparative Politics* 44 (2): 127–49.

Ben Hounet, Yazid. 2009. *L'Algérie des tribus: Le fait tribal dans le Haut Sud-Ouest contemporain*. Paris: Harmattan.

———. 2010. "La tribu comme champ social semi-autonome." *L'Homme* 194 (2): 57–74.

———. 2012. " 'Cent dromadaires et quelques arrangements': Notes sur la diya (prix du sang) et son application actuelle au Soudan et en Algérie." *Revue des Mondes Musulmans et de la Méditerranée* 131: 203–21.

Bennani, Driss. 2006. "Interview Mahjoub Salek: 'Le Maroc n'a rien compris au Sahara'." *Tel Quel* 243 (October).

Benton, Lauren A. 2009. *A Search for Sovereignty: Law and Geography in European Empires, 1400–1900*. Cambridge: Cambridge University Press.

Berque, Jacques. 1954. "Qu'est-ce qu'une tribu nord-africaine?" In *Éventail de l'histoire vivante: Hommage à Lucien Febvre*, ed. Fernand Braudel, 261–71. Paris: Armand Colin.

Bhatia, Michael. 2001. "Western Sahara Under Polisario Control: Summary Report of Field Mission to the Saharawi Refugee." *Review of African Political Economy* 88: 291–98.

Bleuchot, Hervé. 1982. "The Green Book: Its Context and Meaning." In *Libya Since Independence: Economic and Political Development*, ed. J. A. Allan, 137–64. London: Croom Helm.

Bonte, Pierre. 2007. *Essai sur les formations tribales dans le Sahara occidental: Approches comparatives, anthropologiques et historiques*. Bruxelles: Luc Pire.

———. 2008. *L'émirat de l'Adrar mauritanien: Harim, compétition et protection dans une société tribale saharienne*. Paris: Karthala.

Bonte, Pierre, and Yazid Ben Hounet. 2009. "Introduction." *Études Rurales* 184 (2): 33–46.

Botiveau, Bernard. 1999. "Palestinian Law: Social Segmentation Versus Centralization." In *Legal Pluralism in the Arab World*, ed. Baudouin Dupret, Maurits Berger, and Laila al-Zwaini, 73–87. The Hague: Kluwer Law International.

Boulay, Sébastien. 2003. "La tente dans la société maure (Mauritanie), entre passé et présent: Ethnologie d'une culture matérielle bédouine en mutations." Ph.D. Dissertation, Paris: Musée National d'Histoire Naturelle.

Bourdieu, Pierre. 1962. *The Algerians*. Ed. and trans. Alan C. M. Ross. Boston: Beacon.

———. 1977. *Outline of a Theory of Practice*. Trans. Richard Nice. Cambridge: Cambridge University Press.

Brown, Wendy. 2010. *Walled States, Waning Sovereignty*. New York: Zone.

Burke, Edmund. 1972. "The Image of the Moroccan State in French Ethnological Literature: A New Look at the Origins of Lyautey's Berber Policy." In *Arabs and Berbers: From Tribe to Nation in North Africa*, ed. Ernest Gellner and Charles Micaud, 175–99. London: Duckworth.

Cameron, Angus. 2006. "Turning Point? The Volatile Geographies of Taxation." *Antipode* 38 (2): 236–58.

Campbell, Madeline Otis. 2010. "Dissenting Participation: Unoffical Politics in the 2007 Saharawi General Congress." *Journal of North African Studies* 15 (4): 573–80.

Caratini, Sophie. 1989a. *Les Rgaybāt (1610–1934)*. Vol. 1, *Des chameliers à la conquête d'un territoire*. Paris: Harmattan.

———. 1989b. *Les Rgaybāt (1610–1934)*. Vol. 2, *Territoire et société*. Paris: Harmattan.

———. 2000. "Système de parenté sahraoui: l'impact de la révolution." *L'Homme* 154–55: 431–56.

———. 2003. *La république des sables: Anthropologie d'une révolution*. Paris: Harmattan.

Caro Baroja, Julio. 1955. *Estudios saharianos*. Madrid: Consejo Superior de Investigaciones Científicas, Instituto de Estudios Africanos.

———. 1966. "Los nómadas y su porvenir: Conferencia pronunciada en el salon de actos del CSIC el día 19 de febrero de 1965." *Archivos del Instituto de Estudios Africanos* 78: 61–71.

Casciarri, Barbara. 2001. "La gabila est devenue plus grande: Permanences et évolutions du 'modèle tribal' chez les pasteurs Ahamda du Soudan arabe." In *Émirs et présidents: Figures de la parenté et de la politique dans le monde arabe*, ed. Pierre Bonte, Edouard Conte, and Paul Dresch, 273–99. Paris: Harmattan.

———. 2006. "Readapting the Gabila: The Ahmada Pastoralists of Central Sudan and the State 'Tribal Federalism' Politics in the mid-1990s." In *Nomadic Societies in the Middle East and North Africa: Entering the 21st Century*, ed. Dawn Chatty, 204–38. Leiden: Brill.

Caton, Steven C. 1990. "Anthropological Theories of Tribe and State Formation in the Middle East: Ideology and the Semiotics of Power." In *Tribe and State Formation in the Middle East*, ed. Philip Khoury and Joseph Kostiner, 74–108. Berkeley: University of California Press.

Chalfin, Brenda. 2010. *Neoliberal Frontiers: An Ethnography of Sovereignty in West Africa*. Chicago: University of Chicago Press.

Chatty, Dawn. 1980. "The Pastoral Family and the Truck." In *When Nomads Settle: Processes of Sedentarization as Adaptation and Response*, ed. Philip C. Salzman, 80–94. New York: Praeger.

Chelhod, Joseph. 1971. *Le droit dans la société bédouine: Recherches ethnologiques sur le 'orf ou droit coutumier des Bedouins*. Paris: Librairie Marcel Rivière et Cie.

———. 1996. "Kabila." In *The Encyclopedia of Islam*, ed. H. A. R. Gibb and P. J. Bearman, 334–35. Leiden: Brill.

Clark, Phil. 2007. "Hybridity, Holism and 'Traditional Justice': The Case of the *Gacaca* Courts in Post-Genocide Rwanda." *George Washington International Law Review* 39 (4): 765–837.

Comaroff, John L, and Jean Comaroff. 1997. "Postcolonial Politics and Discourses of Democracy in Southern Africa: An Anthropological Reflection on African Political Modernities." *Journal of Anthropological Research* 53 (2): 123–46.

———. 2009. "Reflections on the Anthropology of Law, Governance and Sovereignty." In *Rules of Law and Laws of Ruling: On the Governance of Law*, ed. Franz Von Benda-Beckmann, Kebeet von Benda-Beckmann, and Julia Eckert, 31–59. Farnham: Ashgate.

Cooke, Bill, and Uma Kothari. 2001. *Participation: The New Tyranny?* London: Zed.

Corbet, Alice. 2008. *Nés dans les camps: Changements identitaires de la nouvelle génération de réfugiés sahraouis et transformation des camps*. Ph.D. Dissertation, Paris: École des Hautes Études en Sciences Sociales.

Corsín Jiménez, Alberto. 2013. *An Anthropological Trompe-l'Oeil for a Common World: An Essay on the Economy of Knowledge*. Oxford: Berghahn.

Cozza, Nicola. 2004. "Singing like Wood-Birds: Refugee Camps and Exile in the Construction of the Saharawi Nation." Ph.D. Dissertation, Oxford University, Social Sciences Division.

———. 2010. "Food and Identity Among Sahrawi Refugee Young People." In *Deterritorialized Youth: Sahrawi and Afghan Refugees at the Margins of the Middle East*, ed. Dawn Chatty, 119–42. Oxford: Berghahn.

Crivello, Gina, Elena Fiddian, and Dawn Chatty. 2005. "The Transnationalisation of Care: Sahrawi Refugee Children in a Spanish Host Program." Lessons Learned

Report. Oxford: Refugee Studies Centre, Queen Elizabeth House, University of Oxford.

Dahlerup, Drude. 2006. "Introduction." In *Women, Quotas, and Politics*, ed. Drude Dahlerup, 3–31. New York: Routledge.

Davis, John. 1987. *Libyan Politics: Tribe and Revolution: An Account of the Zuwaya and Their Government*. London: Tauris.

Dawod, Hosham. 2003. "The 'State-ization' of the Tribe and the Tribalization of the State: The Case of Iraq." In *Tribes and Power: Nationalism and Ethnicity in the Middle East*, ed. Faleh Abdul-Jabar and Hosham Dawod, 110–35. London: Saqi.

de Chassey, Francis. 1976. *L'étrier, la houe et le livre*. Paris: Harmattan.

———. 1984. "Les multiples devenirs étatiques d'une 'société sans état' saharienne: Considérations inactuelles sur l'unité des pays maures." In *Enjeux sahariens*, ed. Pierre-Robert Baduel and Maurice Barbier, 199–212. Paris: Centre National de la Recherche Scientifique.

Deubel, Tara. 2012. "Poetics of Diaspora: Sahrawi Poets and Postcolonial Transformations of a Trans-Saharan Genre in Northwest Africa." *Journal of North African Studies* 16 (4): 295–314.

Diamond, Larry. 2002. "Elections Without Democracy: Thinking About Hybrid Regimes." *Journal of Democracy* 13 (2): 21–35.

Dilley, Roy. 1992. "Introduction." In *Contesting Markets: Analyses of Ideology, Discourse and Practice*, ed. Roy Dilley, 1–34. Edinburgh: Edinburgh University Press.

Domenech Lafuente, Ángel. 1953. "Sáhara español: Del vivir nómada de las tribus." *Cuadernos de Estudios Africanos* 21: 31–43.

Donham, Donald L. 1999. *Marxist Modern: An Ethnographic History of the Ethiopian Revolution*. Berkeley: University of California Press.

Dresch, Paul. 1989. *Tribes, Government and History in Yemen*. Oxford: Clarendon.

———. 2006. *The Rules of Barat: Tribal Documents from Yemen*. Sanaa: Centre Français d'Archéologie et des Sciences Sociales.

Du Puigaudeau, Odette. 2009. *Arts et coutumes des maures*. Casablanca: Le Fennec.

Dunn, John. 1989. *Modern Revolutions: An Introduction to the Analysis of a Political Phenomenon*. 2nd ed. Cambridge: Cambridge University Press.

Dupret, Baudouin. 2006. "Legal Traditions and State-Centred Law: Drawing from Tribal and Customary Law Cases of Yemen and Egypt." In *Nomadic Societies in the Middle East and North Africa: Entering the 21st Century*, ed. Dawn Chatty, 280–301. Leiden: Brill.

Elizondo, Luis, Chejna Mohamed Mehdi, and Marisa Sanz. 2008. *Microcréditos en el Sáhara: Manual para la solicitud de crédito en los campamentos saharauis*. Bilbao: Hegoa.

Elyachar, Julia. 2005. *Markets of Dispossession: NGOs, Economic Development, and the State in Cairo*. Durham, N.C.: Duke University Press.

Englund, Harri. 2002. "Winning Elections, Losing Legitimacy: Multi-Partyism and the Neopatrimonial State in Malawi." In *Multi-Party Elections in Africa*, ed. Michael Cowen and Liisa Laakso, 172–86. Oxford: James Currey.

Es-Sweyih, Mohamed-Fadel Ismaïl. 2001. *La République sahraouie*. Paris: Harmattan.

Evans-Pritchard, Edward. 1940. *The Nuer: A Description of the Modes of Livelihood and Political Institutions of a Nilotic People*. Oxford: Clarendon.

Farah, Randa. 2008. "Refugee camps in the Palestinian and Sahrawi National Liberation Movements: A Comparative Perspective." *Journal of Palestinian Studies* 38 (2): 76–93.

———. 2010. "Sovereignty on Borrowed Territory: Sahrawi Identity in Algeria." *Georgetown Journal of International Affairs* 11 (2): 59–66.

Fathaly, Omar, and Monte Palmer. 1980. *Political Development and Social Change in Libya*. Lexington, Mass.: Heath.

Feldman, Ilana. 2008. *Governing Gaza: Bureaucracy, Authority, and the Work of Rule, 1917–1967*. Durham, N.C.: Duke University Press.

Fiddian-Qasmiyeh, Elena. 2014. *The Ideal Refugees: Gender, Islam and the Sahrawi Politics of Survival*. Syracuse, N.Y.: Syracuse University Press.

Firebrace, James, and Jeremy Harding. 1987. *Exiles of the Sahara: The Sahrawi Refugees Shape Their Future*. London: War on Want.

Flores Morales, Ángel. 1946. *El Sahara español: Ensayo de geografía física y económica*. Madrid: Alta Comisaría de España en Marruecos.

———. 1954. *El Sahara español*. Madrid: Publicaciones Españolas.

Fortier, Corinne. 2000. "Corps, différence des sexes et infortune: Transmission de l'identité et des savoirs en islam malékite et dans la société maure de Mauritanie." Ph.D. Dissertation, Paris: L'École des Hautes Études en Sciences Sociales.

———. 2001. "Le rituel de mariage dans la société maure: Mise en scène des rapports sociaux de sexe." *Awal* 23: 51–73.

Foucault, Michel. 1980. "On Popular Justice: A Discussion with Maoists." In *Power/Knowledge: Selected Interviews and Other Writings, 1972–1977*, ed. Colin Gordon, 1–36. New York: Pantheon.

———. 1991. "Governmentality." In *The Foucault Effect*, ed. Graham Burchell, Colin Gordon, and Peter Miller, 87–104. Chicago: University of Chicago Press.

Frésia, Marion. 2009. *Les Mauritaniens réfugiés au Sénégal: Une anthropologie critique de l'asile et de l'aide humanitaire*. Paris: Harmattan.

Fried, Morton H. 1975. *The Notion of Tribe*. Menlo Park, Calif.: Cummings.

Gabiam, Nell. 2012. "When 'Humanitarianism' Becomes 'Development': The Politics of International Aid in Syria's Palestinian Refugee Camps." *American Anthropologist* 114 (1): 95–107.

Gale, Lacey Andrews. 2007. "Bulgur Marriages and 'Big' Women: Navigating Relatedness in Guinean Refugee Camps." *Anthropological Quarterly* 80 (2): 355–78.

Gellner, Ernest. 1990. "Tribalism and the State in the Middle East." In *Tribe and State Formation in the Middle East*, ed. Philip Khoury and Joseph Kostiner, 109–26. Berkeley: University of California Press.

Gellner, Ernest, and Charles Micaud, eds. 1973. *Arabs and Berbers: From Tribe to Nation in North Africa*. London: Duckworth.

Giddens, Anthony. 1985. *The Nation-State and Violence*. Cambridge: Polity Press.

Gimeno, Juan Carlos. 2007. *Transformaciones socioculturales de un proyecto revolucionario: La lucha del pueblo Saharaui por la liberación*. Caracas: Programa Cultura, Comunicación y Transformaciones Sociales, CIPOST, FaCES, Universidad Central de Venezuela.

Gimeno Martín, Juan Carlos, and Mohamed Ali Laman. 2007. "Transformaciones socioculturales en los campamentos de refugiados saharauis al sur de Argelia (1975–2005)." In *Conocimiento, desarrollo y transformaciones sociales: Aproximaciones antropológicas contemporáneas*, ed. Juan Carlos Gimeno Martín, 387–425. Málaga: SEPHA.

Ginat, Joseph. 1982. *Women in Muslim Rural Society*. New Brunswick, N.J.: Transaction.

Gómez Martín, Carmen. 2011. *La migración saharaui en España: Estrategias de visibilidad en el tercer tiempo del exilio*. Saarbrücken: Editorial Académica Española.

Gómez Martín, Carmen, and Cédric Omet. 2009. "Les 'dissidences non dissidentes' du Front Polisario dans les camps de réfugiés et la diaspora sahraouis." *Année du Maghreb* 5: 205–22.

González de la Rocha, Mercedes. 1994. *The Resources of Poverty: Women and Survival in a Mexican City*. Oxford: Blackwell.

Gramsci, Antonio. 1971. *Selections from the Prison Notebooks of Antonio Gramsci*. Ed. and trans. Quintin Hoare and Geoffrey Nowell Smith. London: Lawrence & Wishart.

Griffiths, John. 1986. "What Is Legal Pluralism?" *Journal of Legal Pluralism and Unofficial Law* 24: 1–55.

Grijalva-Eternod, Carlos S., Jonathan C. K. Wells, Mario Cortina-Borja et al. 2012. "The Double Burden of Obesity and Malnutrition in a Protracted Emergency Setting: A Cross-Sectional Study of Western Sahara Refugees." *PLoS Med* 9 (10): e1001320.

Guyer, Jane. 1992. "Representation Without Taxation: An Essay on Democracy in Rural Nigeria, 1952–1990." *African Studies Review* 35 (1): 41–79.

———. 2004. *Marginal Gains: Monetary Transactions in Atlantic Africa*. Lewis Henry Morgan Lecture Series. Chicago: University of Chicago Press.

Guyer, Jane, and Pauline Peters. 1987. "Conceptualising the Household: Issues of Theory and Policy in Africa." *Development and Change* 18 (2): 197–214.

Halliday, Fred. 1974. *Arabia Without Sultans*. Harmondsworth: Penguin.

Hanoteau, Adolphe, and Aristide Letourneux. 1872. *La Kabylie et les coutumes kabyles*. Vol. 2. Paris: A. Challamel.

Hansen, Thomas Blom, and Finn Stepputat. 2005. "Introduction." In *Sovereign Bodies: Citizens, Migrants, and States in the Postcolonial World*, ed. Thomas Blom Hansen, and Finn Stepputat, 1–36. Princeton, N.J.: Princeton University Press.

Harper, Richard. 2000. "The Social Organisation of the IMF's Mission Work: An Examination of International Auditing." In *Audit Cultures: Anthropological Studies in Accountability Ethics and the Academy*, ed. Marilyn Strathern, 21–53. London: Routledge.

Harrell-Bond, Barbara. 1986. *Imposing Aid: Emergency Assistance to Refugees*. Oxford: Oxford University Press.

Harrell-Bond, Barbara, Eftihia Voutira, and Mark Leopold. 1992. "Counting the Refugees: Gifts, Givers, Patrons and Clients." *Journal of Refugee Studies* 5 (3/4): 205–25.

Harris, Olivia. 1981. "Households as Natural Units." In *Of Marriage and the Market: Women's Subordination Internationally and Its Lessons*, ed. Kate Young, Carol Wolkowitz, and Roslyn McCullagh, 136–55. London: CSE Books.

Hart, David M. 1998. "The Rgaybat: Camel Nomads of the Western Sahara." *Journal of North African Studies* 3 (4): 28–54.

Hatt, Doyle G. 1996. "Establishing Tradition: The Development of Chiefly Authority in the Western High Atlas Mountains of Morocco, 1980–1990." *Journal of Legal Pluralism and Unofficial Law* 37–38: 123–54.

Hayden, Robert M. 1984. "A Note on Caste Panchayats and Government Courts in India: Different Kinds of Stages for Different Kinds of Performances." *Journal of Legal Pluralism and Unofficial Law* 16 (22): 43–52.

Hegland, Mary. 2013. *Days of revolution: political unrest in an Iranian village*. Stanford, Calif.: Stanford University Press.

Hernández, Angela. 2001. *Sáhara: Otras voces*. Málaga: Algarazara.

Hobsbawm, Eric. 1983. "Introduction: Inventing Tradition." In *The Invention of Tradition*, ed. Eric Hobsbawm and Terence Ranger, 1–14. Cambridge: Cambridge University Press.

Hodges, Tony. 1982. *Historical Dictionary of Western Sahara*. African Historical Dictionaries 35. London: Scarecrow.

———. 1983. *Western Sahara: Roots of a Desert War*. Beckenham: Croom Helm.

Holbraad, Martin. 2014. "Revolución o muerte: Self-Sacrifice and the Ontology of Cuban Revolution." *Ethnos* 79 (3): 365–87.

Holley, Robert. 2008. *Basic Findings from Interviews with Recent Returnees from Tindouf*. Morocco: Moroccan American Center for Policy.

Holy, Ladislav. 1989. *Kinship, Honour and Solidarity: Cousin Marriage in the Middle East*. Manchester: Manchester University Press.

Human Rights Watch. 2008. *Human rights in Western Sahara and in the Tindouf Refugee Camps*. New York: Human Rights Watch.

———. 2012. *Morocco and Western Sahara*. New York: Human Rights Watch.

———. 2014. *Off the Radar: Human Rights in the Tindouf Refugee Camps*. New York: Human Rights Watch.

Humphrey, Caroline. 2002. *The Unmaking of Soviet Life: Everyday Economies After Socialism*. Ithaca, N.Y.: Cornell University Press.

Hylland Eriksen, Thomas. 1995. *Small Places, Large Issues*. London: Pluto.

Ibn Khaldūn. 1958. *The Muqaddimah: An Introduction to History*. Trans. Franz Rosenthal. London: Routledge and Kegan Paul.

International Court of Justice (ICJ). 1975. *Western Sahara Advisory Opinion*. The Hague: International Court of Justice.

Irwin, Randi L. Forthcoming. "Derivative States: Property Rights and Claims-Making in a Contested Territory." Department of Anthropology, New School, New York.

Isidoros, Konstantina. 2015. "The Silencing of Unifying Tribes: The Colonial Construction of Tribe and its 'Extraordinary Leap' to Nascent Nation-State Formation in Western Sahara." *Journal of the Anthropological Society of Oxford* 7 (2): 168–90.

Jean-Klein, Iris. 2001. "Nationalism and Resistance: The Two Faces of Everyday Activism in Palestine During the Intifada." *Cultural Anthropology* 16 (1): 83–126.

———. 2003. "Into Committees, Out of the House? Familiar Forms in the Organization of Palestinian Committee Activism During the First Intifada." *American Ethnologist* 30 (4): 556–77.

Jensen, Erik. 2005. *Western Sahara: Anatomy of a Stalemate*. Boulder, Colo.: Lynne Rienner.

Joffé, George. 1986. "The International Court of Justice and the Western Sahara Dispute." In *War and Refugees: The Western Sahara Conflict*, ed. Richard Lawless and Laila Monahan, 16–30. London: Pinter.

———. 1995. "Qadhafi's Islam in Local Historical Perspective." In *Qadhafi's Libya, 1969–1994*, ed. Dirk J. Vandewalle, 139–56. Basingstoke: Macmillan.

Juliano, Dolores. 1998. *La causa Saharaui y las mujeres: Siempre hemos sido muy libres*. Barcelona: Icaria.

Kalmo, Hent, and Quentin Skinner. 2010a. "Introduction: A Concept in Fragments." In *Sovereignty in Fragments: The Past, Present and Future of a Contested Concept*, ed. Hent Kalmo and Quentin Skinner, 1–25. Cambridge: Cambridge University Press.

———. 2010b. *Sovereignty in Fragments: The Past, Present and Future of a Contested Concept*. Cambridge: Cambridge University Press.

Khoury, Philip, and Joseph Kostiner. 1990. *Tribes and State Formation in the Middle East*. Berkeley: University of California Press.

Krasner, Stephen D. 1999. *Sovereignty: Organized Hypocrisy*. Princeton, N.J.: Princeton University Press.

Kuper, Adam. 1988. *The Invention of Primitive Society: Transformations of an Illusion*. London: Routledge.

Lackner, Helen. 1985. *P. D. R. Yemen: Outpost of Socialist Development in Arabia*. London: Ithaca Press.

Lan, David. 1985. *Guns and Rain: Guerrillas and Spirit Mediums in Zimbabwe*. London: James Currey.

Lancaster, William. 1981. *The Rwala Bedouin Today*. Cambridge: Cambridge University Press.

Lecocq, Jean Sebastian. 2010. *Disputed Desert: Decolonisation, Competing Nationalisms and Tuareg Rebellions in Northern Mali*. Leiden: Brill.

Leinhardt, Peter. 2001. *Shaikhdoms of Eastern Arabia*. Basingstoke: Palgrave.

Lévi-Strauss, Claude. 1959. "Le problème des relations de parenté." In *Systèmes de parenté*, ed. Jacques Berque, 13–20. Paris: École Pratique des Hautes Études.

Lewis, Ioan M. 1979. "Kim Il-Sung in Somalia: The End of Tribalism?" In *Politics in Leadership: A Comparative Perspective*, ed. William A. Schak and Percy S. Cohen, 13–44. Oxford: Clarendon.

Lhote, Jean. 1944. *Les touaregs du Hoggar (Ahaggar)*. Paris: Payot.

Li, Tania. 2010. "Indigeneity, Capitalism, and the Management of Dispossession." *Current Anthropology* 51 (3): 385–414.

Lippert, Anne. 1985. *The Saharawi Refugees: Origins and Organization, 1975–1985*. Ada, Ohio: SPSC Letter.

———. 1992. "Sahrawi Women in the Liberation Struggle of the Sahrawi People." *Signs* 17 (3): 636–50.

López Bargados, Alberto. 2003. *Arenas Coloniales: Los awlad Dalím ante la colonización franco-española del Sáhara*. Barcelona: Bellaterra.

Lovejoy, Paul E. 1983. *Transformations in Slavery: A History of Slavery in Africa*. Cambridge: Cambridge University Press.

Lydon, Ghislaine. 2009. *On Trans-Saharan Trails: Islamic Law, Trade Networks, and Cross-Cultural Exchange in Nineteenth-Century Western Africa*. Cambridge: Cambridge University Press.

Mahé, Alain. 2000. "Les assemblées villageoises dans la Kabylie contemporaine." *Études Rurales* 155–56: 179–212.

Malkki, Liisa H. 1995a. *Purity and Exile: Violence, Memory and National Cosmology Among Hutu Refugees in Tanzania*. Chicago: University of Chicago Press.

———. 1995b. "Refugees and Exile: From 'Refugee Studies' to the National Order of Things." *Annual Review of Anthropology* 24: 495–523.

Mandel, Ruth Ellen, and Caroline Humphrey, eds. 2002. *Markets and Moralities: Ethnographies of Postsocialism*. Oxford: Berg.

Marx, Emmanuel. 1967. *Bedouin of the Negev*. Manchester: Manchester University Press.

Mason, John P. 1978. "Petroleum Development and the Reactivation of Traditional Structure in a Libyan Oasis Community." *Economic Development and Cultural Change* 26 (4): 763–76.

Masquelier, Adeline. 2005. "The Scorpion's Sting: Youth, Marriage and the Struggle for Social Maturity in Niger." *Journal of the Royal Anthropological Institute* 11 (1): 59–83.

Mattes, Hanspeter. 1995. "The Rise and Fall of the Revolutionary Committees." In *Qadhafi's Libya, 1969–1994*, ed. Dirk J Vandewalle, 89–112. Basingstoke: Macmillan.

Maurer, Bill. 2009. "From the Revenue Rule to Soft Law and Back Again: The Consequences for 'Society' of the Social Governance of International Tax Competition." In *Rules of Law and Laws of Ruling: On the Governance of Law*, ed. Franz von Benda-Beckmann, Kebeet Von Benda-Beckmann, and Julia Eckert, 217–35. Farnham: Ashgate.

Mayer, Ann Elizabeth. 1978. "Developments in the Law of Marriage and Divorce in Libya Since the 1969 Revolution." *Journal of African Law* 22 (1): 30–49.

———. 1995. "In Search of Sacred Law: The Meandering Course of Qadhafi's Legal Policy." In *Qadhafi's Libya, 1969–1994*, ed. Dirk J Vandewalle, 113–38. Basingstoke: Macmillan.

McConnell, Fiona. 2009. "Governments-in-Exile: Statehood, Statelessness and the Reconfiguration of Territory and Sovereignty." *Geography Compass* 3 (5): 1902–19.

———. Forthcoming 2016. *Rehearsing the State: The Governance Practices of the Exile Tibetan Government*. Oxford: Wiley.

Mercer, John. 1976. *Spanish Sahara*. London: Allen and Unwin.

Merry, Sally Engle. 1988. "Legal Pluralism." *Law and Society Review* 22 (5): 869–96.

Michelutti, Lucia. 2007. "The Vernacularization of Democracy: Political Participation and Popular Politics in North India." *Journal of the Royal Anthropological Institute* 13 (3): 639–56.

Miller, Ruth Austin. 2007. *The Limits of Bodily Integrity: Abortion, Adultery, and Rape Legislation in Comparative Perspective*. Aldershot: Ashgate.

Mir-Hosseini, Ziba. 1993. *Marriage on Trial: A Study of Islamic Family Law. Iran and Morocco Compared*. London: Tauris.

Mitatre, Claire Cecile. 2009. "Par-delà l'interdit (haram): Une ethnographie du mariage et de la sexualité chez les Sahraouis du Sud marocain." *Ateliers d'Anthropologie* 33. http://ateliers.revues.org/8207, accessed March 21, 2012.

Molina Campuzano, Miguel. 1954. *Contribución al estudio del censo de población del Sáhara Español*. Madrid: Consejo Superior de Investigaciones Científicas.

Molutsi, Patrick, and John D. Holm. 1990. "Developing Democracy when Civil Society is Weak: The Case of Botswana." *African Affairs* 89 (356): 323–40.

Moore, Henrietta. 1994. *A Passion for Difference: Essays in Anthropology and Gender*. Cambridge: Polity.

Moors, Annelies. 1995. *Women, Property and Islam: Palestinian Experiences, 1920–1990*. Cambridge Middle East Studies 3. Cambridge: Cambridge University Press.

Mundy, Jacob. 2006a. "Autonomy and Intifadah: New Horizons in Western Saharan Nationalism." *Review of African Political Economy* 33 (108): 255–67.

———. 2006b. "Neutrality or Complicity? The United States and the 1975 Moroccan Takeover of the Spanish Sahara." *Journal of North African Studies* 11 (3): 275–306.

———. 2007. "Performing the Nation, Pre-Figuring the State: The Western Saharan Refugees Thirty Years Later." *Journal of Modern African Studies* 45 (2): 275–97.

Navaro-Yashin, Yael. 2012. *The Make-Believe Space: Affective Geography in a Postwar Polity*. Durham, N.C.: Duke University Press.

Norris, Harry T. 1986. *The Arab Conquest of the Western Sahara*. Harlow: Longman.

Ong, Aihwa. 2006. *Neoliberalism as Exception: Mutations in Citizenship and Sovereignty*. Durham, N.C.: Duke University Press.

Paley, Julia. 2002. "Toward an Anthropology of Democracy." *Annual Review of Anthropology* 31: 469–96.

Parizot, Cédric. 2006. "Counting Votes That Do Not Count: Negev Bedouin and the Knesset Elections of 17th May 1999, Rahat, Israel." In *Nomadic Societies in the Middle East and North Africa: Entering the 21st Century*, ed. Dawn Chatty, 176–203. Leiden: Brill.

Patai, Raphael. 1962. *Golden River to Golden Road: Society, Culture and Change in the Middle East*. Philadelphia: University of Pennsylvania Press.

Pazzanita, Anthony. 2006. *The Historical Dictionary of Western Sahara*. Lanham, Md.: Scarecrow.

Perregaux, Christine. 1990. *Femmes sahraouies: Femmes du désert*. Paris: Harmattan.

Peteet, Julie Marie. 2005. *Landscape of Hope and Despair: Palestinian Refugee Camps*. Philadelphia: University of Pennsylvania Press.

Peters, Emrys L. 1967. "Some Structural Aspects of the Feud Among the Camel-Herding Bedouin of Cyrenaica." *Africa: Journal of the International African Institute* 37 (3): 261–82.

———. 1978. "The Status of Women in Four Middle East Communities." In *Women in the Muslim World*, ed. Lois Beck and Nikkie Keddie, 311–50. Cambridge, Mass.: Harvard University Press.

———. 1980. "Aspects of Bedouin Bridewealth in Cyrenaica." In *The Meaning of Marriage Payments*, ed. John L Comaroff, 125–60. London: Academic Press.

———. 1990. *Bedouin of Cyrenaica: Studies in Personal and Corporate Power*. Cambridge: Cambridge University Press.

Pine, Frances. 2002. "Retreat to the Household? Gendered Domains in Postsocialist Poland." In *Postsocialism: Ideals, Ideologies and Practices in Eurasia*, ed. Chris M. Hann, 95–113. London: Routledge.

Polanyi, Karl. 1944. *The Great Transformation*. Boston: Beacon.

Polisario Front. 1988. "15 aniversario del frente Polisario." *Sáhara Libre*. Año XIII, Special Edition, May.

Popenoe, Rebecca. 2004. *Feeding Desire: Fatness, Beauty and Sexuality Among a Saharan People*. London: Routledge.

Pottage, Alain, and Martha Mundy, eds. 2004. *Law, Anthropology, and the Constitution of the Social: Making Persons and Things*. Cambridge Studies in Law and Society. Cambridge: Cambridge University Press.

Roitman, Janet L. 2005. *Fiscal Disobedience: An Anthropology of Economic Regulation in Central Africa*. Princeton, N.J.: Princeton University Press.

Rossetti, Sonia. 2008. "Formal and Informal Gender Quotas in State-Building: The Case of the Sahara Arab Democratic Republic." Paper presented at 2008 Australian Political Studies Association (APSA) Conference, University of Queensland, Brisbane, July 6–9.

———. 2012. "Saharawi Women and Their Voices as Political Representatives Abroad." *Journal of North African Studies* 17 (2): 337–53.

Roussellier, Jacques, and Anouar Boukhars. 2014. *Perspectives on Western Sahara: Myths, Nationalisms, and Geopolitics*. Lanham, Md.: Rowman & Littlefield.

Sahara Español Gobierno General de la Provincia. 1975. *Censo 1974*. Aauin: Editorial Gráficas Saharianas.

Sahlins, Marshall. 1972. *Stone-Age Economics*. Chicago: Aldine-Atherton.

Salas, Luis. 1983. "The Emergence and Decline of Cuban Popular Tribunals." *Law and Society Review* 17 (4): 587–612.

Salzman, Philip. 2016. "Tribes and States: Some Theoretical Issues." In *Tribes and States in a Changing Middle East*, ed. Uzi Rabi. London: Hurst.

San Martín, Pablo. 2010. *Western Sahara: The Refugee Nation*. Cardiff: University of Wales Press.

Sāyigh, Yazīd Yūsuf. 1997. *Armed Struggle and the Search for State: The Palestinian National Movement, 1949–1993*. Oxford: Oxford University Press.

Schacht, Joseph. 1964. *An Introduction to Islamic Law*. Oxford: Clarendon.

Scheele, Judith. 2008. "A Taste for Law: Rule-Making in Kabylia (Algeria)." *Comparative Studies in Society and History* 50 (4): 895–919.

———. 2009. *Village Matters: Knowledge, Politics and Community in Kabylia, Algeria*. Woodbridge: James Currey.

———. 2012. *Smugglers and Saints of the Sahara: Regional Connectivity in the Twentieth Century*. African Studies Series 120. Cambridge: Cambridge University Press.

Schmitt, Carl. 1985. *Political Theology: Four Chapters on the Concept of Sovereignty*. Cambridge, Mass.: MIT Press.

Schmitter, Philippe C, and Terry Lynn Karl. 1991. "What Democracy Is . . . and Is Not." *Journal of Democracy* 2 (3): 75–88.

Schumpeter, Joseph. 1954 [1918]. "The Crisis of the Tax State." In *International Economic Papers*, ed. Alan T. Peacock, Ralph Turvey, Wolfgang F. Stolper, and Elizabeth Henderson, 5–38. London: Macmillan.

Scott, James C. 1998. *Seeing like a State: How Certain Schemes to Improve the Human Condition Have Failed*. New Haven, Conn.: Yale University Press.

———. 2009. *The Art of Not Being Governed: An Anarchist History of Upland Southeast Asia*. New Haven, Conn.: Yale University Press.

Shelley, Toby. 2004. *Endgame in the Western Sahara: What Future for Africa's Last Colony?* London: Zed.

Shryock, Andrew. 1997. *Nationalism and the Genealogical Imagination: Oral History and Textual Authority in Tribal Jordan*. Berkeley: University of California Press.

———. 2004. "The New Jordanian Hospitality: House, Host, and Guest in the Culture of Public Display." *Comparative Studies in Society and History* 46 (1): 35–62.

Skocpol, Theda. 1979. *States and Social Revolutions: A Comparative Analysis of France, Russia and China*. Cambridge: Cambridge University Press.

Sneath, David. 2007. *The Headless State: Aristocratic Orders, Kinship Society, and Misrepresentations of Nomadic Inner Asia*. New York: Columbia University Press.

Solà-Martín, Andreu. 2007. *The United Nations Mission for the Referendum in Western Sahara*. Lewiston, N.Y.: Edwin Mellen.

Solana, Vivian. Forthcoming. "Regenerating Revolution: Gender and Generation in the Saharawi Arab Democratic Republic." Department of Anthropology, University of Toronto, Toronto.

Stewart, Frank H. 1987. "Tribal Law in the Arab World: A Review of the Literature." *International Journal of Middle East Studies* 19 (4): 473–90.

———. 2006. "Customary Law Among the Bedouin of the Middle East and North Africa." In *Nomadic Societies in the Middle East and North Africa: Entering the 21st Century*, ed. Dawn Chatty, 239–79. Leiden: Brill.

Taine-Cheikh, Catherine. 1989. "La Mauritanie en noir et blanc: Petite promenade linguistique en *hassaniyya*." *Revue du Mondes Musulmans et de la Méditerranée* 54 (4): 90–105.

Takriti, Abdel Razzaq. 2013. *Monsoon Revolution: Republicans, Sultans and Empires in Oman, 1965–1976*. Oxford: Oxford University Press.

Tamanaha, Brian. 1993. "The Folly of the 'Social Scientific' Concept of Legal Pluralism." *Journal of Law and Society* 20 (2): 192–236.

———. 2008. "Understanding Legal Pluralism: Past to Present, Local to Global." *Sydney Law Review* 30 (3): 375–411.

Tapper, Richard. 1983. *The Conflict of Tribe and State in Iran and Afghanistan*. London: Croom Helm.

———. 1990. "Anthropologists, Historians and Tribespeople on Tribe and State Formation in the Middle East." In *Tribe and State Formation in the Middle East*, ed. Philip Khoury and Joseph Kostiner, 48–73. Berkeley: University of California Press.

Tapper, Richard, and Nancy Tapper. 1992/1993. "Marriage, Honour and Responsibility: Islamic and Local Models in the Mediterranean and the Middle East." *Cambridge Anthropology* 16 (2): 3–21.

Tauzin, Aline. 2001. *Figures du féminin dans la société maure, Mauritanie*. Paris: Karthala.

Tavakoli, Judit. 2015. *Zwischen Zelten und Häusern: Die Bedeutung materieller Ressourcen für den Wandel von Identitätskonzepten saharauischer Flüchtlinge in Algerien*. Berlin: Regiospectra.

Thomassen, Bjorn. 2012. "Notes Towards an Anthropology of Political Revolutions." *Comparative Studies in Society and History* 54 (3): 679–706.

Tillion, Germaine. 1966. *Le harem et ses cousins*. Paris: Le Seuil.

Tilly, Charles. 1985. "War Making and State Making as Organized Crime." In *Bringing the State Back in*, ed. Peter B Evans, Dietrich Rueschemeyer, and Theda Skocpol, 169–91. Cambridge: Cambridge University Press.

———. 1993. *European Revolutions, 1492-1992*. Making of Europe Series. Oxford: Blackwell.

United Nations Security Council. 2012. "Report of the Secretary General on the Situation Concerning Western Sahara." http://www.un.org/ga, accessed November 15, 2012.

Vandewalle, Dirk J., ed. 1995. *Qadhafi's Libya, 1969–1994*. Basingstoke: Macmillan.

———. 2006. *A History of Modern Libya*. Cambridge: Cambridge University Press.

Venema, Bernhard, and A. Mguild. 2002. "The Vitality of Local Political Institutions in the Middle Atlas, Morocco." *Ethnology* 41 (2): 103–17.

Verdery, Katherine. 1996. *What Was Socialism, and What Comes Next?* Princeton, N.J.: Princeton University Press.

———. 2003. *Vanishing Hectare: Property and Value in Post-Socialist Transylvania*. Ithaca, N.Y.: Cornell University Press.

Villasante Cervello, Mariella. 2006. "From the Disappearance of 'Tribes' to Reawakening of the Tribal Feeling: Strategies of State Among the formerly Nomadic Bidán (Arabophone) of Mauritania." In *Nomadic Societies in the Middle East and North Africa: Entering the 21st Century*, ed. Dawn Chatty, 144–75. Leiden: Brill.

Villasante de Beauvais, Mariella. 1998. *Parenté et politique en Mauritanie: Essai d'anthropologie historique: Le devenir contemporain des Ahl Sidi Mahmud*. Paris: Harmattan.

Von Hippel, Karin. 1996. "Sunk in the Sahara: The Applicability of the Sunk Cost Effect to Irredentist Disputes." *Journal of North African Studies* 1 (1): 95–116.

Weber, Max. 1965. *Politics as a Vocation*. Philadelphia: Fortress Press.

Wedeen, Lisa. 2003. "Seeing like a Citizen, Acting like a State: Exemplary Events in Unified Yemen." *Society for Comparative Study of Society and History* 45 (4): 680–713.

———. 2007. "The Politics of Deliberation: *Qat* Chews as Public Spheres in Yemen." *Public Culture* 19 (1): 59–84.

Wehr, Hans. 1976. *A Dictionary of Modern Written Arabic*. Beirut: Librairie du Liban.

Weir, Shelagh. 2007. *A Tribal Order: Politics and Law in the Mountains of Yemen*. Austin: University of Texas Press.

West, Harry G. 2009. "From Socialist Chiefs to Postsocialist Cadres: Neotraditional Authority in Neoliberal Mozambique." In *Enduring Socialism: Explorations of Revolution and Transformation, Restoration and Continuation*, ed. Harry G. West and Parvathi Raman, 29–43. Oxford: Berghahn.

West, Harry G. and Parvathi Raman. 2009. *Enduring Socialism: Explorations of Revolution and Transformation, Restoration and Continuation*. Oxford: Berghahn.

What's in Blue. 2012. "Western Sahara Consultations." 27 November. http://whatsinblue.org/2012/04/western-sahara-consultations.php, accessed June 17, 2012.

Whitehead, Laurence. 2002. *Democratization: Theory and Experience*. Oxford: Oxford University Press.

Willis, Michael. 2012. *Power and Politics in the Maghreb: Algeria, Tunisia and Morocco from Independence to the Arab Spring*. London: Hurst.

Wilson, Alice. 2010. "Democratising Elections Without Parties: Reflections on the Case of the Sahrawi Arab Democratic Republic." *Journal of North African Studies* 15 (4): 423–38.

———. 2012. "Households and the Production of Public and Private Domains: Revolutionary Changes in Western Sahara's Liberation Movement." *Paideuma* 58: 19–43.

———. 2013. "On the Margins of the Arab Spring." *Social Analysis* 57 (2): 81–98.

———. 2014a. "Ambiguities of Space and Control: When Refugee Camp and Nomadic Encampment Meet." *Nomadic Peoples* 18 (1): 38–60.

———. 2014b. "Cycles of Crisis, Migration and the Formation of New Political Identities in Western Sahara." In *Crises et migrations dans les pays du sud*, ed. Marc-Antoine Pérouse de Montclos, Véronique Petit, and Nelly Robin, 79–105. Paris: Harmattan.

———. 2015. "Refracting Custom in Western Sahara's Quest for Statehood." *Political and Legal Anthropology Review* 38 (1): 72–90.

Wilson, Alice, and Fiona McConnell. 2015. "Constructing Legitimacy Without Legality in Long-Term Exile: Comparing Western Sahara and Tibet." *Geoforum* 66: 203–14.

Woodman, Gordon. 1999. "The Idea of Legal Pluralism." In *Legal Pluralism in the Arab World*, ed. Baudouin Dupret, Maurits Berger, and Laila al-Zwaini, 3–19. The Hague: Kluwer Law International.

Wrong, Michela. 2005. *"I didn't do it for you": How the World Betrayed a Small African Nation*. London: Harper Perennial.

Yan, Yunxiang. 2003. *Private Life Under Socialism: Love, Intimacy, and Family Change in a Chinese Village, 1949–1999*. Stanford, Calif.: Stanford University Press.

Yanagisako, Sylvia Junko. 1979. "Family and Housheold: The Analysis of Domestic Groups." *Annual Review of Anthropology* 8: 161–205.

Ziai, Fatemeh. 1995. *Keeping It Secret: The United Nations Operations in the Western Sahara*. New York: Human Rights Watch.

Zoubir, Yahia. 2012. "Tipping the Balance Towards Inter-Maghreb Unity in Light of the Arab Spring." *International Spectator: Italian Journal of International Affairs* 47 (3): 83–99.

Zuhur, Sherifa. 2005. *Gender, Sexuality and the Criminal Laws in the Middle East and North Africa: A Comparative Study*. Istanbul: Women for Women's Human Rights.

Zunes, Stephen. 1988. "Participatory Democracy in the Sahara: A Study of Polisario Self-Governance." *Scandinavian Journal of Development Alternatives* 7 (2–3): 141–57.

———. 1999. "Unarmed Resistance in the Middle East and North Africa." In *Nonviolent Social Movements: A Geographical Perspective*, ed. Stephen Zunes, Lester R. Kurtz, and Sarah Beth Asher, 41–51. Malden, Mass.: Blackwell.

Zunes, Stephen, and Jacob Mundy. 2010. *Western Sahara: War, Nationalism and Conflict Irresolution*. Syracuse, N.Y.: Syracuse University Press.

# INDEX

Words beginning with *al-* (the equivalent of "the") are alphabetized under the element following this particle.

# ACKNOWLEDGMENTS

The kindness, patience, and enthusiasm of many Sahrawis, in the refugee camps in Algeria and beyond, opened many doors (of tents and of other kinds) that led to this book. Though it is so little in return for all that they have shared with me, I thank them: *ya wanni bikum*. More Sahrawis helped me than it is possible to thank here: I ask for my hosts' forbearance, once again, in mentioning only a few by name here.

Four families in particular looked after me in the refugee camps, opening homes and hearts. I thank my host mothers here by the names that I have given them in this book: Sumaya, Khadīja, Zaynabu and Māghalāha. In each family, mothers and their daughters cared for me, taught me to wear my *milḥafah* and to eat with my hands, took me to weddings, rations distributions and on administrative quests, explained the finer points of etiquette to me, forgave my idiosyncrasies and many mistakes, and laid out *firāsh* for me to sleep next to them.

While I did not work formally with a research assistant, in each family members informally took it in turns to help me by introducing me to contacts, accompanying me on a mission to find an interlocutor, explaining scenes and conversations to me, answering endless questions, and delivering me safely to new destinations. I especially thank Khadīja's daughter Fatimetou for her friendship, and Zaynabu's daughters Minetou and Kaltoum for always being there with a smile. Māghalāha's daughters Suelma, Khanātha and Almaʿlūma were formidable teachers and companions, her son Malʿainīn introduced me to colleagues at the Ministry of Information, and his brother ʿAbdi accompanied me to many interviews. Their father, Tawwālu, brightened each day with his good humor. Thanks to Māghalāha's family, I was able to make the unforgettable trip to stay with camel herders in the pasturelands near Bir Lehlu, Western Sahara. The many friendships I was privileged to enjoy with Sahrawis are all indebted to my wonderful teacher of Hassaniya, Mahmoud.

I learned much from my "pseudo-families" where I was happily adopted: at the Ministry of Information, where I taught English, and among the Sahrawi students in Damascus, Syria, in the summer of 2007. Back in the camps, many candidates in the 2008 legislative elections, judges in Auserd camp and in Rabouni, shopkeepers and countless guests at weddings helped me to learn about Sahrawis' lives in exile and beyond.

I am grateful for the help of Polisario officers who helped me carry out this research: Bashir Mustafa Sayed, then head of Polisario's Political Organization, Mohamad wuld Tamik, then minister of information, Yusif wuld Tamik, secretary general of the Sahrawi National Council, Fatma Mehdi, then president of the Women's Union, Khira Abulahi, then minister of Personnel and Training, Sidia, then secretary general of the Ministry of Trade, Jamal wuld Bundir, former member of Parliament and later member of the African Parliament, Khadijetu Tahir at the Ministry of Information, Zrug Lalla at the Ministry of Culture, ElKouri at the Ministry of Culture, and Habib Walla and Brahim Mokhtar when each was serving as head of Protocol. In London, representatives of the Polisario Front Sidi Omar, Limam Ali, Lamine Bouhali and Sidi Breiki supported me in applying for visas for my research in the camps from 2006 to 2014. At the Ministry of Information, Mal'ainīn Lakhal, secretary general of the Union of Sahrawi Writers and Journalists, and Mbarka Mehdi helped me make contacts and gave good advice. As an honorary Sahrawi, Danielle Smith helped introduce me to life in the camps.

Many of those working for aid agencies to provide services for Sahrawi refugees helped me learn about their work, in particular: Simona at the Italian NGO CRIC, Hughes Burrows at the European Union Humanitarian Aid and Civil Protection department, Luis Elizondo at the Basque NGO HEGOA, Annabelle Vasseur and Talia Thisse at Oxfam Belgium, Armen Yadgaryau at the UNHCR, and Richard Dalrymple Jr and Jonathan Campbell in the Algiers office of the World Food Program. I thank Marcia, Marite, Jessica and their colleagues who support the teaching of English in the camps for their friendship and kindness. I am also grateful to Père Thierry and the residents and staff of the Glycines Centre d'Études Diocésain in Algiers for their warm welcome each time I stayed there.

Fieldwork in the refugee camps was made possible thanks to generous funding: in 2006 from Trinity College, Cambridge; in 2007–2009 from a doctoral grant from the UK's Economic and Social Research Council; and in 2011, 2012 and 2014 thanks to the Prométée research project, funded by France's Agence Nationale de la Recherche, and thanks to Homerton

College, Cambridge (2011 and 2012) and Durham University's Addison Wheeler research funds (2014). Writing and further research was supported by a Junior Research Fellowship at Homerton College, University of Cambridge, and an Addison Wheeler Research Fellowship at Durham University. Homerton College also kindly supported research at the National Library in Madrid, Spain, in 2012.

Discussion with colleagues nurtured this project during its many stages. In Cambridge, I am grateful for enlightening discussion with, and constant encouragement from, Marilyn Strathern. Conversations with Paul Anderson, Harri Englund, Caroline Humphrey, George Joffé, Yael Navaro-Yashin and David Sneath helped develop ideas for the book. Naor Ben Yehoyada and Jon Mair were much appreciated and invaluable writing companions. Molly Warrington gave helpful feedback on several chapters. Many thanks to David Watson in the Cartographic Unit of the Department of Geography, Cambridge, for making the two maps. In Durham, Catherine Alexander, Stephen Lyon, Elisabeth Kirtsoglou and Yulia Egorova have been sources of encouragement in the final stages of writing. My thanks go also to Ilana Feldman, Magnus Marsden, Bill Maurer and Philip Salzman for stimulating discussion and feedback. I am grateful to Sidi Omar for his comments on the manuscript, and his encouragement throughout the project. In taking up research on Western Sahara, I moved away from my earlier research interests in Latin America; happily Jorge Domínguez was undeterred, and has been of invaluable counsel at crucial stages in this research.

Opportunities to present and discuss this research at various forums in Europe, North Africa, North America and the Middle East have been enriching. Pierre Bonte was a generous commentator whilst I was visiting the Collège de France in Paris. He is dearly missed. In Paris, Yazid Ben Hounet kindly commented on several chapters. Abdel Wedoud ould Cheikh helped me understand intricacies of Hassaniya, and Abderrahman Almoussaoui discussed Arabic expressions with me. Sébastien Boulay, John Bowen, Baudouin Dupret and others at seminars in Paris and Rabat gave helpful feedback on earlier presentations. At the Harris Manchester Summer Research Institute at the University of Oxford (2012 and 2013), I was able to enjoy helpful conversations with Dawn Chatty, Katherine Hoffman, Wendy James, James McDougall, Judith Scheele and Michael Willis. Each provided helpful feedback at various stages of this project.

During fieldwork and writing, the support of friends and colleagues has been invaluable. In particular, I thank Amy Blakeway, Madeline Campbell,

Tara Deubel, Mark Green, Jessica Johnson, Louise Joy, Daniel Joyce, Melanie Keene, Nayanika Mathur, Fiona McConnell, Jacob Mundy, Natalie Ramm, Amy Rowe, Sally Painter, Bettina Scholz and John Thorne.

At the University of Pennsylvania Press, it has been a pleasure in every way to work with Peter Agree as editor, and Amanda Ruffner the editorial assistant. I owe many thanks to the Press reviewers for their stimulating insights and comments, from which the book greatly benefited. I am grateful to the copy editing team, Alison Anderson and Mary Lou Bertucci, who took great care over the manuscript. Noreen O'Connor-Abel provided helpful pointers for preparing transliterations. The final transliterations were prepared with the help of my colleagues Amira Bennison and Matthew Steele, to whom I am extremely grateful.

The support of my family has been constant throughout fieldwork and writing. It is thanks to my mother, Hélène, who recorded a television program on Sahrawis when I was a teenager, that I first came to hear of Sahrawis in their refugee camps. I first learned to be a researcher from my father, Allan. I dedicate this book to my parents. My sisters, and their growing families, have been a source of good cheer and comfort. It has been my special joy to complete this book with the unfailing support of my husband, Raphaël, my very own oasis.

Material from the following articles has been reproduced with permission: "Households and the Production of Public and Private Domains: Revolutionary Changes in Western Sahara's Liberation Movement," *Paideuma* 58 (2012): 43–65; and "Democratising Elections Without Parties: Reflections on the Case of the Sahrawi Arab Democratic Republic," *Journal of North African Studies* 15, 4 (2010): 423–38.

www.ingramcontent.com/pod-product-compliance
Lightning Source LLC
Chambersburg PA
CBHW032344280326
41935CB00008B/446
*9781512828627*